THE COMPLETE
IDIOT'S
GUIDE® TO

Sewing

by Missy Shepler and Rebecca Kemp Brent

ALPHA

A member of Penguin Group (USA) Inc.

ALPHA BOOKS

Published by the Penguin Group

Penguin Group (USA) Inc., 375 Hudson Street, New York, New York 10014, USA

Penguin Group (Canada), 90 Eglinton Avenue East, Suite 700, Toronto, Ontario M4P 2Y3, Canada (a division of Pearson Penguin Canada Inc.)

Penguin Books Ltd., 80 Strand, London WC2R 0RL, England

Penguin Ireland, 25 St. Stephen's Green, Dublin 2, Ireland (a division of Penguin Books Ltd.)

Penguin Group (Australia), 250 Camberwell Road, Camberwell, Victoria 3124, Australia (a division of Pearson Australia Group Pty. Ltd.)

Penguin Books India Pvt. Ltd., 11 Community Centre, Panchsheel Park, New Delhi—110 017, India

Penguin Group (NZ), 67 Apollo Drive, Rosedale, North Shore, Auckland 1311, New Zealand (a division of Pearson New Zealand Ltd.)

Penguin Books (South Africa) (Pty.) Ltd., 24 Sturdee Avenue, Rosebank, Johannesburg 2196, South Africa

Penguin Books Ltd., Registered Offices: 80 Strand, London WC2R 0RL, England

Copyright © 2011 by Missy Shepler and Rebecca Kemp Brent

International Standard Book Number: 978-1-61564-079-9
Library of Congress Catalog Card Number: 2010913771

13   12   11   8   7   6   5   4   3   2   1

Interpretation of the printing code: The rightmost number of the first series of numbers is the year of the book's printing; the rightmost number of the second series of numbers is the number of the book's printing. For example, a printing code of 11-1 shows that the first printing occurred in 2011.

Printed in the United States of America

Note: This publication contains the opinions and ideas of its authors. It is intended to provide helpful and informative material on the subject matter covered. It is sold with the understanding that the authors and publisher are not engaged in rendering professional services in the book. If the reader requires personal assistance or advice, a competent professional should be consulted.

The authors and publisher specifically disclaim any responsibility for any liability, loss, or risk, personal or otherwise, which is incurred as a consequence, directly or indirectly, of the use and application of any of the contents of this book.

Most Alpha books are available at special quantity discounts for bulk purchases for sales promotions, premiums, fund-raising, or educational use. Special books, or book excerpts, can also be created to fit specific needs.

For details, write: Special Markets, Alpha Books, 375 Hudson Street, New York, NY 10014.

Publisher: *Marie Butler-Knight*

Associate Publisher: *Mike Sanders*

Senior Managing Editor: *Billy Fields*

Executive Editor: *Randy Ladenheim-Gil*

Production Editor: *Kayla Dugger*

Copy Editor: *Amy Lepore*

Cover Designer: *Kurt Owens*

Book Designers: *William Thomas, Rebecca Batchelor*

Indexer: *Celia McCoy*

Layout: *Ayanna Lacey*

Proofreader: *Laura Caddell*

Contents

Appendixes

Introduction

We're always amazed when people say they've been sewing for a certain number of years. We've always been stitching, in one form or another, and simply can't pinpoint a time when we started ... or stopped. Early sewing memories include fumbling oversize yarn needles through printed sewing cards and whip-stitching wardrobes for Barbie dolls. Each of us survived our own personal sewing disasters when we were starting out, and thankfully, we've improved a bit since then.

Through the years, we just kept stitching, even when handmade items weren't "hip." That's a big part of why we're so excited about the renewed interest in sewing. Crafty is cool again, and we couldn't be more thrilled!

Today's sewists seem fearless, with a relaxed style of sewing that's truly "stitch-and-go"! We see them rediscovering sewing skills in classes and online, yet struggling with some of the same techniques that troubled us, too. That's why we put together these sewing instructions, tips, and resources—information we wish we'd had way back when!

Whether you've never picked up a needle and thread or are returning to the stitching life after an extended absence, you'll find essential sewing information here. This book explains the basics of both hand and machine sewing and steps you through specific techniques with fast, fun projects to make. Plus, we've unpuzzled patterns, made sense of measurements, and outlined easy garment constructions.

Ready to get sewing? Read on!

What You'll Find in This Book

Like any other art or craft, sewing is a skill. Once you've mastered the basics, you can build on that foundation. We've structured this book with that idea in mind, starting with simple hand-sewing skills you'll use again and again, teaching you how to make the most of your sewing machine, and introducing and explaining the tools and materials you'll need. We cover common terms and techniques you'll need to know about and simplify the steps for making cute clothes that fit. And because experience is the best teacher, we've included numerous projects throughout so you can practice your newly learned skills. Finally, we point you toward more information, supplies, and local connections within your own community.

Here's how it all breaks down:

Part 1, Let's Start Sewing!, introduces you to simple hand stitches and guides you through getting to know your sewing machine. We get down to details about machine needles and thread and set you straight on squaring up fabric, the importance of pressing, and other essential skills you'll use in every project you make. We also explore standard, utility, and decorative stitches available on most machines.

Part 2, Great Seams, covers a few of the many ways to sew two or more pieces of fabric together. We show you how to sew standard and specialty seams, give common options for finishing seam edges, and offer ideas for alternative endings. We also present super-easy solutions for sewing curved shapes.

Indulge your taste for texture in **Part 3, Sweet Shapes.** In addition to learning how to use darts to add shape to and contour garments, you learn how to transform flat fabric with pleats, tucks, gathering, and ruffles; simple shirring; and different methods of appliqué.

Part 4, Textiles and Trims, takes a closer look at fabric, fasteners, and trims. Learn what fabrics work best for specific tasks and get the inside story on linings and stabilizers. Explore trim types, make your own bias binding and piping, and try out fun trim techniques. Expand your notions knowledge with our overview of simple fasteners and learn to attach buttons, elastic, and zippers.

In **Part 5, Getting into Garments,** we play with patterns, taking the mystery out of body measurements and learning simple fitting techniques. You also learn to pin, mark, and cut like a pro and expand your wardrobe with basic garment construction skills.

Check the appendixes at the back of the book for a glossary of common sewing terms, resources for sewing supplies, additional sewing instruction and inspiration, and tips for finding sewing-related items in your area. Appendix C contains hints for heading off machine mayhem, plus information on standard pattern sizes and instruction on figuring fabric yardage and conversion.

Extras

We've added extra nuggets of sewing knowledge throughout the book. Watch for these tips, definitions, and cautions:

SEWING SENSE

Make sense of sewing terms with these definitions and explanations.

SNIP IT

These tidbits are full of helpful information.

PINPRICK

We've added these cautions to help you avoid possible problems.

SEW SURPRISING

These newsy little nuggets alert you to interesting and useful information.

Acknowledgments and Special Thanks

Many people have contributed to this book. First of all, we want to thank our friends and families for excusing our extended absences (mental and otherwise) while we were working on this project. Thanks go to Marilyn Allen of Allen O'Shea Literary Agency for making the connections; to the publishers and editors at Alpha Books for persevering with this project, especially at such a tumultuous time for the publishing industry; and to Scott Shepler for adding his considerable illustration and photography expertise to the book.

We'd also like to thank Linda Turner Griepentrog, the best sewing resource in the world and our constant cheerleader. She has made such a difference in so many lives!

Special thanks go to the companies that contributed supplies and materials for the projects in this book, especially Westminster Fibers for providing such wonderful Free Spirit Fabrics and Coats & Clark for providing threads and zippers. Please use these products whenever you can (see Appendix B).

And as always, thanks to our mothers, grandmothers, and great-grandmothers for sharing their needle skills with future generations, stitch by stitch.

Trademarks

All terms mentioned in this book that are known to be or are suspected of being trademarks or service marks have been appropriately capitalized. Alpha Books and Penguin Group (USA) Inc. cannot attest to the accuracy of this information. Use of a term in this book should not be regarded as affecting the validity of any trademark or service mark.

Let's Start Sewing!

In the first part of this book, you learn the basics of hand and machine sewing. Beginning in Chapter 1, you start building stitch skills and practicing techniques on quick-to-stitch, practical projects that are also fun to make! In addition, you start assembling a treasury of sewing tools and notions you'll use again and again—even far beyond these pages.

Also in these chapters, we demystify the sewing machine, identify common machine parts, and explain simple skills every successful sewist must know, such as how to change a machine needle, wind a bobbin, sew a straight line, and tame tension troubles. You learn how to choose the right needle and thread for your fabric, how to prepare for your first project, and which machine stitches to use where. Easy-to-follow, step-by-step project instructions include extra information and ideas to advance your skills.

You're going to love sewing and saying, "Thanks! I made it myself!" Let's get stitching!

Hand Stitching

In This Chapter

- Simple hand-sewing tools
- Easy but essential hand-sewing skills
- An introduction to needle and thread
- Sewing stitches to get you started
- Creating a needle case sewing kit

Some people prefer to sew by machine; others love stitching by hand. Often there's a need for both techniques in a project, and having a few simple hand-stitching skills in your sewing arsenal is, well, *handy* for anyone—even the most die-hard, machine-only sewist! Hand stitching is perfectly portable, and it's so easy to get started. Just gather a few simple sewing tools, thread, and fabric, and you're ready to sew!

Hand-Sewing Essentials

You can start to sew with an amazingly small number of tools and materials. The bare essentials you need are pins and needles, scissors, fabric, and thread. It's also helpful to have a needle threader, thimble, tape measure, pincushion, and emery on hand. Let's take a look at each of these basics.

Needles

Needles vary by thickness, length, eye shape and size, and point shape. Needle size is indicated by number. A low number indicates a longer, thicker needle, while a higher number denotes a shorter, finer needle. Choose a needle for the fabric weight and thread thickness you're using. It should be thin enough to pass through the fabric without leaving large holes but strong enough not to break or bend. Be sure the eye's large enough to accommodate the thread you're using and protect it from undue friction that causes fraying.

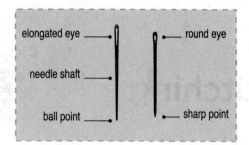

Needles are sized and shaped according to their intended use.

Most needles are inexpensive and are available in packages containing several sizes of one type of needle or an assortment of different types. If you're just starting out, get a variety pack that contains the most commonly used needle types:

Sharps are fine, medium-length, pointed needles with small, round eyes. Choose them for general sewing.

Betweens or *quilting needles* are short needles with small, round eyes. The short needle length facilitates fine, quick, accurate stitches, making betweens a favorite for hand quilting and detailed sewing.

Embroidery or *crewel needles* look similar to sharps but have an elongated eye to accommodate multiple strands of embroidery floss. They're used for general sewing, crewel work, smocking, and embroidery.

Milliners or *straw needles* are fine and similar to sharps but longer. They're the same diameter from tip to eye, so they glide through narrow spaces easily. Milliners were designed to use in making women's hats, but they're also used for basting, pleating, beading, and decorative stitching.

Tapestry needles are large, blunt-tipped needles that feature extra-large eyes to accommodate yarn, floss, and decorative threads used in needlepoint, embroidery, and counted cross-stitch. Their blunt tips pass through the loosely woven or open-mesh materials without splitting the fabric's threads. Tapestry needles can also be used to thread narrow elastic, ribbon, or draw-strings through casings.

Pins

Straight pins are used to hold layers of fabric together for both hand and machine sewing. Like needles, pins come in a variety of forms for specific sewing needs. Pins may have metal, plastic, or glass heads, and the length and thickness of the shaft varies with the intended fabric use. The metal in a pin can make it rust-resistant or rustproof and determines whether or not you can sweep them up with a magnet—a huge help if you happen to drop one … or one hundred!

It's not necessary to have every pin type in your sewing stash, but it is helpful to have a few different kinds. Here are some of our favorites:

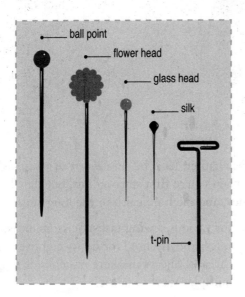

Choose your pins according to the type and thickness of fabric you're using.

Ball point pins have rounded points that slide into knit and delicate fabrics without piercing fabric threads. Available in medium and long lengths, these pins have round, easy-grasp heads.

Flower head pins are extra long, fine, and sharp, perfect for pinning together thick quilt layers or loosely woven lace. The thin diameter allows the pin to slide easily through most fabrics. The flat flower head is easy to grasp and lies out of the way, close to the fabric.

Glass head pins are available in short, medium, and long lengths and can be used with all fabric types and weights. Medium-length pins ($1\frac{1}{16}$ to $1\frac{5}{16}$ inches) are used for most sewing projects. Glass heads make pins easy to spot and grasp, and they hold up to the heat of pressing.

Silk pins are fine, sharp pins used on silks, sheers, and other delicate fabrics. Their thin shafts prevent pinholes in the fabric, while their round glass heads are easy to see and stand up to pressing.

T-pins are strong, heavyweight pins for use with thick, tough, upholstery-weight fabrics and canvas. The pin shaft is bent to form a capital letter T at the head, providing extra leverage when you're pinning heavy layers.

PINPRICK

Never press plastic pinheads. They can melt, leaving permanent colored spots on your project.

To pin fabrics together, insert the pin straight down through the fabric, pivot the pin back up toward the fabric, and push the point back through both layers of fabric. The pin and fabric should lie flat with the pin perpendicular to the raw fabric edge.

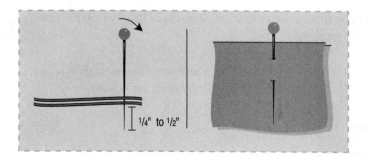

Place pins perpendicular to the fabric edge.

Scissors and Shears

If you remember nothing else after reading this chapter, let it be this: *invest in good-quality sewing shears*. Quality shears may seem pricey when you're first starting out, but they'll cut accurately; last longer; and save you time, money, and mental health in the long run.

Many different scissors and shears are available for various sewing tasks. Scissors measure less than 6 inches in length, have equal size ring handles, and are used for lightweight sewing tasks such as trimming seams and clipping curves or threads. Shears measure 6 inches or longer, have different size handle rings, and are used to cut multiple layers of fabric.

scissors   shears

Use scissors for simple trimming tasks, and save your shears for cutting fabric.

PINPRICK

Using sewing scissors for anything other than cutting fabric can dull or damage the blades. Take care of your sewing scissors by keeping the cutting blades clean and sharp.

Fabric and Thread

If you haven't already noticed, there's a huge selection of fabric and thread out there just waiting for you! Don't be overwhelmed by the number of choices available. Most patterns or projects offer fabric and thread suggestions in the materials list; use those suggestions as a guide for your fabric shopping.

Most sewists fall in love with textiles and collect a stash of favorite fabric and thread. You must be prepared when the sewing bug strikes!

Threader and Thimble

At some point in everyone's life, eyesight gives way to age, and what used to be a simple, seconds-only task—threading a needle—becomes tension-filled turmoil. Save yourself the stress. Use a needle threader. Hand-needle threaders consist of a thin, folded wire loop attached to a handle. The wire loop is flexible, but it's fine and stiff enough to slip easily through the eye of a needle.

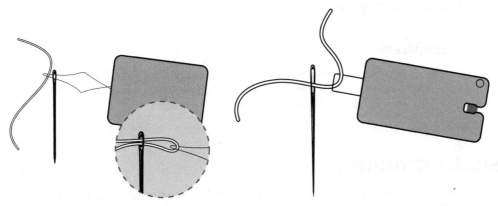

To use a threader (left), place the thread through the threader's wire loop and pull it back through the needle eye. Tapestry needle threaders (right) have rigid, heavier-weight wire loops to accommodate larger yarns, ribbons, and decorative threads.

A thimble is a small covering worn over your fingertip or thumb to protect against painful needle pokes and help you push needles through thick fabrics. Thimbles come in many different shapes and sizes and are commonly made from metal, leather, and rubber. Most people prefer to wear a thimble on the middle finger of their needle hand; others find their index finger more fitting. Experiment to find what works best for your sewing style.

Use the thimble end to push the needle's eye end through the fabric, grasp the point between your thumb and thimble, and pull to complete a stitch.

Tape Measure, Pincushion, and Emery

Tape measures are usually made from plastic or fiberglass that's firm but flexible enough to bend around curves without stretching. Look for a tape measure 60 inches long with inch markings on one side and centimeters on the other.

Pincushions come in many, many shapes and sizes, from tiny, ring-size wonders that fit on a finger to wristwatch-size wraps or pretty little pillows. While traditional pincushions are cloth-covered shapes filled with sawdust and stuffing, more modern magnetic pincushions "capture" metal pins on a brightly colored plastic base. All pincushions have the same purpose—to provide a safe, handy place for storing needles and pins.

The standard segmented tomato pincushion comes with a smaller strawberry shape attached. That strawberry is filled with fine sand or *emery*. Poke pins and needles in and out of an emery-filled strawberry to keep them clean and sharp.

SEWING SENSE

Emery is an abrasive mineral that, when ground into a powder, resembles fine metal shavings. Emery is often used to polish, smooth, or grind away rust or rough spots from metal. In sewing, emery is used to sharpen the tips of pins and needles.

Basic Beginnings

Once you've collected your sewing essentials, it's time to start sewing. Where to begin? With needle and thread, of course!

How to Thread a Needle

First, cut a length of thread about 18 inches long if you're sewing with a single thread and want your stitching to blend in or be less noticeable. Cut the thread twice as long if you're sewing with a doubled thread for strong or boldly visible stitches.

SEW SURPRISING

No ruler? No problem! Eighteen inches is about the length from the tip of your middle finger to your elbow. And why 18 inches? Quite simply, it's a good length for most single-strand sewing jobs. Some techniques will require a longer thread, but threads much longer than 18 inches are more likely to tangle and fray.

Snip the thread end at an angle and slip the angled thread end through the needle eye. Pull ⅓ of the thread length through the needle for single-strand or match the thread ends for double-strand sewing. Don't be surprised if it takes you several tries to thread the needle. If the thread end becomes fuzzy or frayed, snip off the worn part and try again.

Here are some more tips that might help:

- Hold the needle in front of something white to make the needle eye easier to see.

- Moisten the needle eye by licking a finger and then wetting the needle with your finger to help attract the thread to the needle. (Never put a needle in your mouth!)

- Use a needle threader or self-threading needle.

- Moistening the thread end may help smooth errant fibers together, but it can also cause the thread to swell, making it harder to thread the needle.

Self-threading needles have an open eye slot for easy threading.

Two Ways to Tie a Knot

At times, a few tiny quick stitches will adequately anchor your sewing thread in place, but for most utility sewing, you'll need to knot the thread end to keep your stitching secure. There are two ways to tie a knot:

Basic overhand knot: An overhand knot is one of the easiest knots to learn. Just make a loop at the thread end opposite the needle, tuck the thread end back through the loop, and pull the thread ends to tighten the knot. This simple knot works well with thick or less-flexible cords and threads.

Tuck the thread tail through the loop to tie a simple overhand knot.

Pinch, pinch, pull knot: Hold a threaded needle in your right hand, pinching the needle eye to keep the thread in place. Catch the thread end in your left hand and bring it up to the needle, forming a big loop with the thread. Pinch the thread end against the eye of the needle with your right hand and wrap the thread around the needle three times, keeping the wraps close together. Pinch the thread wraps against the needle with your right hand. Release the thread in your left hand, and pull the needle and thread through the wraps until the thread end is all that's left in your right hand. The wraps become a knot!

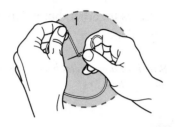

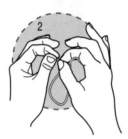

Wrap thread around the needle (1) and then pinch and pull the needle through the wraps (2).

Hiding the Knot

In most instances, you won't want the knot to show on the outside (right side) of your work, so hide it under a fold or at the edge of the fabric.

When possible, hide the knot within a seam.

Basic Sewing Stitches

Certain stitches lend themselves to specific sewing construction needs. Start building your stitch library with this list of basic hand stitches. Not only will you gain the knowledge and skill to make the stitches, you'll also learn which stitch to use when!

SNIP IT

Lefties may want to reverse the instructions throughout and view the illustrations upside down or in a mirror.

Straight and Running Stitches

A *straight stitch* is one of the simplest stitches to make. Working from right to left, bring the needle up through the fabric at A, pulling the thread to the fabric right side. Insert the needle back into the fabric at B, $1/8$ to $1/4$ inch away from A, and pull the thread firmly in place. You've sewn a stitch!

When you sew straight stitches evenly one after another, with stitches and spaces a uniform ⅛ to ¼ inch apart, that's called a *running stitch*. A running stitch is used to join pieces, especially in quilting. To take several stitches at once, "weave" the needle in and out of the fabric, accumulating several stitches on the needle before pulling it completely through.

Basting Stitch

Basting is a series of long running stitches. For the *basting stitch*, follow the instructions for a running stitch but make the stitches and spaces longer than ¼ inch.

Basting is used to hold two pieces of fabric together temporarily when fitting garments or marking hems, before the seams are permanently sewn. Basting stitches are later removed when the seam or project is complete.

Backstitch

As the name might suggest, a *backstitch* starts at the end of the first stitch and moves *backward* to go *forward!* Working from right to left, bring the needle up through the fabric at A, the point where you want your first stitch to end. Reinsert the needle at B, the beginning of the seam or the end of the previous stitch, and bring the point of the needle back up through the fabric ⅛ to ¼ inch beyond A at C. Pull the thread firmly but not so tightly that you cause the fabric to pucker.

To make the next stitch, reinsert your needle at A and bring the needle back up ⅛ to ¼ inch beyond C. Keep the stitches small and even so the front side of your backstitching creates a strong line that resembles machine stitching.

Use backstitching wherever you need a strong seam, or work a few close backstitches at the beginning and end of a hand-stitched seam to secure it.

Blanket or Buttonhole Stitch

The names *blanket stitch* and *buttonhole stitch* are often used interchangeably for this stitch. Buttonhole stitches are placed side by side to create a solid line of thread with a knotlike edge. Blanket stitches are worked ⅛ to ¼ inch apart. Traditionally, the horizontal and vertical portions of the stitch are of equal length, but they can be varied for effect.

Work a blanket stitch from left to right, bringing the needle to the fabric's right side at A. Holding the thread below the line of stitching, insert the needle to the right and above A at B. Rock the needle and bring it back through the fabric at C. The point of the needle must overlap the thread held below the line of stitching. Pull firmly, securing the thread at a right angle.

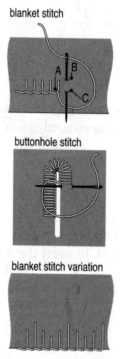

blanket stitch

buttonhole stitch

blanket stitch variation

Use buttonhole stitches to strengthen buttonhole edges or create bar tacks. Use a blanket stitch to attach appliqués and finish raw edges.

Overcast Stitch

The *overcast stitch* is a quick stitch used for finishing fabric edges that might *fray* or unravel. Working from either left or right, bring the needle through the fabric at A, about ⅛ to ³⁄₁₆ inch away from the fabric's edge. Take the needle over the edge of the fabric and bring it back up through to the front of the fabric about ⅛ inch away from the first stitch. Pull the thread snugly against the fabric without puckering or curling the fabric edge.

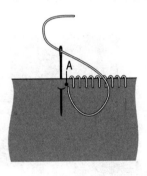

SEWING SENSE

Fray means to unravel or tatter. Woven fabric can become worn, especially at the crosswise edges, creating a rough, uneven fringe.

Blind or Hemming Stitch

A *blind hem stitch* is used primarily for hemming garments when you don't want the hem stitch to show. Use a lightweight thread that closely matches the fabric color to make stitching less noticeable. Finish the hem raw edge before hemming (see Chapter 7 for edge finishes).

Working from right to left, bring the needle to the hem right side less than ⅛ inch from its edge. Pick up just one or two threads of the garment with the needle, slip the needle under the hem edge about ¼ inch farther along the hem, and bring it back to the hem right side. Pull the thread tightly enough to secure the hem but with enough slack to hide the thread on the garment right side. Pulling too tightly creates a dimple.

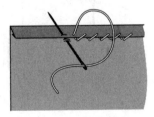

You can also work this stitch between two layers of a fabric, catching one or two threads of the fabric on one layer and taking a small stitch on the opposite fabric layer. Pull the thread to snug the two layers together.

Slip Stitch

The almost-invisible *slip stitch* is used to finish binding edges on a quilt or garment, or to mend seams from the outer (right side) of a garment. To join two folded edges, position the fabrics close to each other with folded edges facing. Bring the needle through the fold on the first edge at A and insert the needle into the second folded edge at B, directly across from A. Take a tiny stitch through the second fold and reinsert the needle next to A. Slip the needle within the fold of edge 1 and bring it to the right side at C. Pull the thread tight to snug the folded edges together.

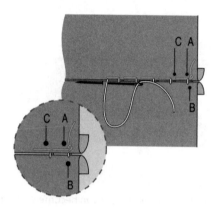

Slip stitches are also used to join a folded fabric edge to a flat fabric piece, lapping the folded fabric edge over the flat fabric.

Whip Stitch

A *whip stitch* is used to join two folded fabric edges when a strong seam is needed. Align the folded fabric edges, and work from right to left. Begin by bringing the needle and thread through the fold of the front fabric at A, hiding the knot inside the fold. Keeping the thread to the right of the needle, bring the needle around the folded edges and insert it through both folded edges at B, taking a tiny stitch through both folds. Pull the thread taut to bring the fabric edges together. Space the stitches evenly, about $\frac{1}{8}$ inch apart.

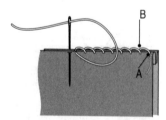

PINPRICK

Be sure to keep the correct tension while you sew. Pulling the thread too tight causes the fabric to pucker and not lie flat. Loose stitching allows fabric layers to pull apart, breaking stitches.

Project: Bare Necessities Needle Case

This pocketed needle case made from felted wool is perfect for carrying your sewing essentials.

This needle case is a lovely way to showcase your hand-sewing skills.

Finished size:

> 4¼×3 inches (closed); 6³⁄₈×4¼ inches (open)

Tools and materials:

> 8½×11-inch sheet of paper
>
> 2 pieces of felted wool, at least 5×12 inches, for the lining and outside of the needle case
>
> Embroidery floss or pearl cotton (size 3 or 5)
>
> ½- to ¹¹⁄₁₆-inch button for case closure
>
> Buttons, beads, felted wool scraps, and other embellishments (optional)
>
> Scissors
>
> Large embroidery or crewel needle to accommodate multiple strands of floss or a heavier thread
>
> Needle threader
>
> Medium-length or longer straight pins
>
> Thimble
>
> Tape measure or ruler

Cutting:

1. Fold the paper in half lengthwise to make a 4¼×11-inch pattern piece. Pin the paper pattern to one piece of wool and trim away the fabric extending beyond the pattern, being careful not to cut into the paper. Remove the pins and pattern from the fabric. Repeat for the second piece of felted wool.

2. Choose one of the fabric pieces for the outside of the needle case. With the tape measure or ruler, measure and use a pencil or other tool to mark a line 1 inch from one short end. Cut along the line to shorten the piece.

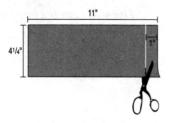

Trim 1 inch from one short end of the outer fabric.

SNIP IT

Most felted wool fabrics look the same on both sides. Check for visual differences before cutting and choose one side of the fabric as the outer or right side, which will be visible in the finished project. The wrong side will be hidden between fabric layers.

Construction:

3. Embellish the right side of the outer fabric as desired with buttons, beads, or appliqués. Cut fun flower shapes from felted wool scraps, varying flower color, size, and shape. Layer flower shapes on the outer fabric and anchor in place with a few quick stitches through the center of the flowers. Highlight the centers with a button, if desired. Don't worry about the wrong side of your work—it will be hidden inside the finished needle case.

4. Finish the short edges of the lining and outer fabric with your choice of stitches, if desired.

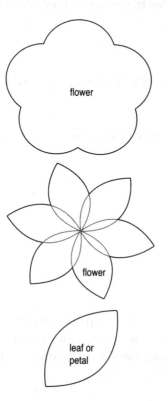

Assemble flowers from individual petals or large single shapes. Vary flower sizes, and stitch along the gray interior lines, if desired.

5. Fold the outer fabric in half with the short ends together. Use straight pins to mark the center fold on each long edge. Pin-mark the lining fabric in the same way.

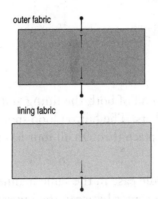

Pin-mark centers of each long edge.

6. Place the outer and lining fabrics wrong sides together, matching the pin-marked center points and aligning the long edges. Pin the layered fabrics together along each long edge.

7. Measure 3 inches from the pin-marked center point toward the right edge of the layered fabrics. Place a pin at this 3-inch mark, 2⅛ inches below the top edge of the fabric.

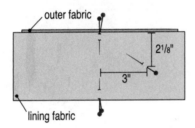

Pin-mark the loop location.

8. Thread a large embroidery needle with a single 18- to 24-inch strand of pearl cotton. Knot the thread end, and stitch through the layered fabrics from the lining side, pulling the knot tight against the lining.

9. On the outer fabric side, insert the needle back through the fabrics about ⅛ inch from the first stitch. Pull the thread to the lining side, leaving a 1- to 1½-inch thread loop on the outer fabric side. Take a small, tight stitch on the lining side to secure the loop in place. Repeat to make a second loop, bringing the needle through the fabric as close to the original stitches as possible and keeping both loops the same length.

10. Bring the needle and thread to the outer fabric side of the needle case, close to the thread loops. Holding the two loops together, work buttonhole stitches around both loops to create one strong loop.

11. Bring the needle and thread back to the lining side at the opposite end of the thread loop, take several small backstitches to secure, and trim the thread ends.

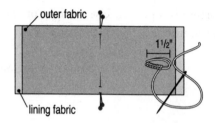

Buttonhole stitch around the thread loops to make a button loop.

12. With the lining side facing up, fold the short end of both the lining and outer fabrics at the 3-inch mark to form the right-side pockets. The button loop should be on the outside of the needle case. Pin the pockets in place through all four layers of fabric, aligning the long edges.

13. Measure, fold, and pin the left side of the needle case in the same manner to form the left-side pockets, leaving a 1½-inch gap at the center between the inner pockets.

14. Using a large embroidery needle and pearl cotton, blanket stitch across the long edges of the needle case to sew the layered fabrics together and secure the folded pocket ends.

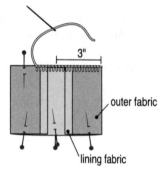

Stitch along the long edges of the needle case to secure the pockets.

15. Close the needle case, and use the thread loop as a placement guide for the button closure. Stitch the button in place on the needle case front (see Chapter 14 for sewing buttons).

Wrap thread around old business cards and tuck them inside the pockets. Add a needle threader, pins, needles, and tiny scissors, and you have a take-along sewing kit!

The Least You Need to Know

- You can start hand sewing with just a few simple tools and materials: needles, pins, scissors, fabric, and thread.
- Threading a needle and tying a knot are quick and easy once you learn how.
- Build a stitch library, starting with basic hand-sewing stitches, and you'll always know what stitch to use when.
- It's easy to make unique and useful hand-sewn items, even with just a few simple skills!

Machine Sewing

In This Chapter

- Common sewing machine parts
- Setting up your machine to sew
- Must-have machine-sewing skills
- Tools, notions, and accessories to get you started

As essential and satisfying as hand sewing can be, there's no substitute for the speed and security of machine-sewn stitches. Before you start machine stitching wildly away, though, take some time to learn a little about your sewing machine first. A few minutes spent mastering the basics now can save you time and frustration later on.

The Anatomy of a Sewing Machine

A marvelous array of sewing machines are available, from simple straight-stitch models to computerized "sewing systems" with decorative stitches, digitized embroideries, and more! Despite their differences, most machines consist of common parts that work together to create a stitch. Your sewing machine manual has specific information about your machine, but most machines are made from common parts.

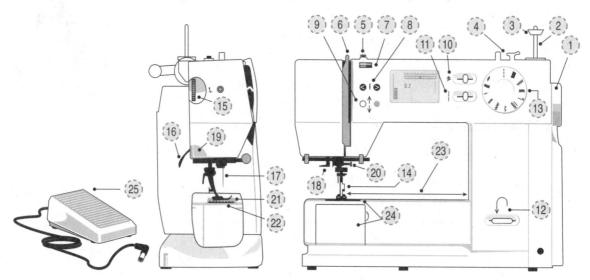

Get to know your sewing machine! Identify these common features on your machine.

1   *Hand wheel:* Turn this wheel to adjust needle height. Always turn the hand wheel *toward* you.

2   *Spool pin:* The spool pin keeps the spool in place while the thread feeds through the machine. Some machines have both horizontal and vertical spool pins.

3   *Spool cap:* The spool cap slips onto the end of the spool pin and holds the spool in place.

4   *Bobbin pin/winder:* Built-in bobbin winders may be found on the top, front, or side of a sew-ing machine. Most winders consist of a bobbin pin to hold the bobbin while the thread is being wound, thread guides for maintaining tension, and a start/stop lever. Some bobbin winders have built-in thread cutters.

5   *Thread guide:* Thread guides may be hoops, discs, or flat metal shapes that pinch or direct the thread to feed it through the machine without tangling and at the correct tension.

6   *Take-up lever:* The take-up lever is a metal finger with a thread guide that moves up and down, pulling thread from the spool and feeding it through the machine.

7   *Tension regulator:* Tension discs pinch the thread as it moves through the machine, and the tension regulator controls the amount of "pinch pressure" the discs exert. Tension discs on the outside of older machines are controlled with a knob or adjustable screw. Newer machines house discs inside the machine casing, and tension is adjusted by a dial or control on the machine front.

8   *Needle position:* Machines may have multiple needle positions, allowing the needle to be moved left or right of the center position. Changing the stitch line in this way is handy for creating multiple lines of stitching.

9   *Needle stop or up/down:* Some machines allow the needle to be set to stop in either an up or a down position. This saves time when pivoting around curves and corners.

10   *Stitch width adjustment:* If your machine has zigzag stitching capabilities, it has a stitch width adjustment. This allows you to alter stitch widths to create a number of different stitch patterns.

11   *Stitch length adjustment:* This control adjusts the length of each stitch by changing the amount of fabric the feed dog pulls through the machine.

12   *Reverse:* Almost all machines have the ability to sew in reverse. Older machines may have a lever controlling which direction the feed dog pushes fabric through the machine. Newer machines have a quick reverse button used to sew a few stitches or stitch continuously in reverse.

13   *Stitch selector:* Use the stitch selector to choose which stitch you'd like to use. Many machines feature a number of built-in stitches: straight stitch, zigzag, buttonhole, blind hem, etc.

14   *Presser foot:* The presser foot works with the feed dog to move fabric evenly through the machine. When the presser foot is lowered, it engages the tension discs and presses the fabric beneath the foot against the feed dog. The upper part of the foot, called the ankle, is usually screwed onto the machine securely; the lower part may include a quick-release mechanism for changing presser feet.

15   *Presser foot pressure control:* This control adjusts the amount of pressure the presser foot applies to fabric as it feeds beneath the needle. Increase pressure when sewing heavy fabric and decrease pressure when sewing lightweight or thin fabric.

16   *Presser foot lifter:* This lever, located above the presser foot at the back or side of the machine, raises and lowers the presser foot. When the presser foot is lifted, the tension discs are disengaged, and the fabric will not feed through the machine.

PINPRICK

If you have an older machine, or have picked up a used one, take it to a reputable sewing machine dealer for an evaluation and cleaning before you begin sewing with it. The dealer can alert you to any needed repairs and save you from the frustration of working with a worn-out machine.

17   *Needle:* The needle carries the upper thread through the fabric to create a stitch. Specialty needles are available for specific stitching needs.

18   *Needle threader:* Some machines have built-in needle threaders. Threaders have a tiny hook that swings through the needle eye, catches the thread, and pulls it back through the eye when the threader is released.

19   *Thread cutter:* Some machines have a built-in thread cutter near the needle area. To use the cutter, raise the presser foot and remove the stitched piece from the machine. Pull both the threads over the cutter's shielded blade to cut them.

20   *Needle clamp screw:* Tighten and loosen this screw to release or secure the needle in place.

21   *Stitch plate:* The stitch plate, also called a needle or throat plate, is a flat metal piece below the presser foot. Slots in the plate allow the feed dog to push the fabric along. A hole or slot admits the needle carrying the top thread through the fabric. Straight stitch plates have a single small hole to guide the needle and create uniform stitches. Zigzag stitch plates have a wide needle slot to accommodate decorative stitches. Guidelines marked on the plate help you align the fabric beneath the needle. Most stitch plates are removable for cleaning.

22   *Feed dog:* The feed dog is a toothed metal piece below the stitch plate that moves up and down to push the fabric along beneath the needle. Stitch length is controlled by how much fabric the feed dog moves.

23   *Throat:* The throat of a machine refers to the open space between the needle and the machine housing. A large throat is helpful when sewing bulky fabrics and large projects like quilts.

24   *Bobbin cover:* The bobbin cover is a plate or hinged door that protects the bobbin mechanism. Open the bobbin cover to replace the bobbin and clean the bobbin area or case.

25   *Foot control:* Like the gas pedal in a car, the foot control regulates the machine speed.

Threading the Machine

Home sewing machines create stitches by interlocking the needle thread with a second thread coming from the bobbin. Proper threading of both is essential for attractive, secure stitches. Your sewing machine manual provides instructions for threading your specific machine, but if you're missing your manual, follow these general steps:

1. Raise the needle to its highest position by turning the hand wheel or pressing the needle-up button. This also raises the take-up lever.

2. Raise the presser foot to disengage the tension discs, allowing the thread to move freely.

3. Place a spool of thread on the spool pin. Add the spool cap to hold the spool in place on a horizontal pin.

4. Pull the thread across the top of the machine and through the first thread guide. The thread should unwind easily from the spool.

5. Bring the thread to the front of the machine, down through the tension discs (if the discs are external on your machine), and around the next thread guide.

6. Pull the thread up and through the hole or slot in the take-up lever.

7. Pull the thread down through any remaining thread guides and place the thread through the needle eye. Some machines have built-in needle threaders that make quick work of threading the needle. To thread a machine needle by hand, check your sewing machine manual or follow the groove in the needle shaft to determine from what direction (left to right or front to back) to thread the needle. With the presser foot up, you should feel little resistance when pulling the thread through the machine. Lower the presser foot and gently pull the thread. You'll be able to feel that the tension discs are now engaged.

SEW SURPRISING

A close examination of the needle reveals a cue for threading: a vertical groove along the needle shaft. Use your fingernail to locate the groove and insert the thread from the grooved side.

8. Insert a bobbin (you learn more about bobbins in the following "Bobbin Basics" section), taking care that its rotational direction is correct and that the bobbin tension spring is engaged. Raise the presser foot and hold the needle thread while lowering and raising the needle one time to loop the top thread around the bobbin thread. Gently pull the end of the needle thread to bring the bobbin thread up through the needle hole in the stitch plate. Pull both top and bobbin thread ends under the presser foot and toward the back of the machine.

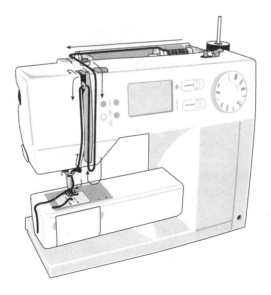

Most sewing machines follow a similar thread path: across, down and around, up, down, and through.

Bobbin Basics

Bobbins look like miniature metal or plastic thread spools. The bobbin holds the bottom thread that makes the wrong-side portion of the machine stitch. Your machine may have a drop-in bobbin that's placed directly into the bobbin assembly, or a bobbin and bobbin case that fit inside the assembly. The bobbin assembly, located beneath the needle and presser foot, is accessed from the side, front, or top of the machine.

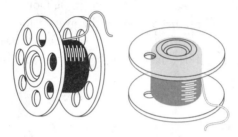

Consult your machine manual and use the correct bobbin to avoid damaging the machine.

Here's how to wind a bobbin:

1. Use a spool cap to secure a spool of thread on the spool pin.

2. Pull the thread around the bobbin-winding tension disc or thread guide and back toward the bobbin pin.

3. Wind the thread around the bobbin several times, or pass the end of the thread through the bobbin, allowing the thread end to extend 2 or 3 inches past the bobbin.

4. Place the bobbin on the bobbin pin and hold the thread end. Run the winder for several seconds to secure the thread on the bobbin. Stop the winder and trim the thread end close to the bobbin.

5. Restart the bobbin winder. Most bobbin winders will automatically stop when the bobbin is full. If necessary, stop the bobbin winder when the bobbin is nearly wound full of thread. Don't overfill the bobbin; it must spin easily inside the bobbin case.

6. Remove the bobbin from the bobbin pin and cut the thread, leaving a thread tail 2 or 3 inches long.

PINPRICK

Always begin with an empty bobbin for a smoothly wound bobbin that can create the best stitches. If necessary, unwind and discard the leftover thread from a previous project.

Most drop-in bobbin machines have a small diagram on the machine indicating the correct bobbin orientation. Simply drop the bobbin into place and guide the thread tail under the bobbin tension spring.

To insert a bobbin into a bobbin case, hold the bobbin on the edge so the thread tail winds off the back of the bobbin. Holding the open side of the bobbin case toward the bobbin and the tension spring toward you, slip the bobbin inside the bobbin case. Pull the thread tail through the slit in the bobbin case and into the opening under the bobbin spring. When you pull the thread tail, the bobbin should rotate inside the bobbin case in a clockwise direction. Hold the bobbin case latch to insert the case into the bobbin assembly. Fold the latch against the bobbin case when the case is securely in place.

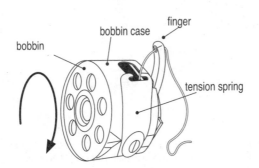

Place the bobbin thread through the finger hole to add extra tension when embroidering or using specialty threads.

To remove the bobbin case, raise the needle to the highest position and grasp the latch to pull the case out of the bobbin assembly.

Basic Presser Feet

Presser feet are designed to hold the fabric against the feed dog while creating a particular stitch or seam. Most sewing machines include a set of basic presser feet for general sewing needs.

A straight-stitch foot has a small needle hole for optimum feed dog contact and to guide the needle in forming perfect straight stitches. A zigzag foot has an elongated needle opening to accommodate the side-to-side stitch pattern of a zigzag or satin stitch and a groove underneath to accommodate the heavier thread buildup of satin and decorative stitches. A narrow zipper foot positions the needle close to bulky piping, trims, and zippers.

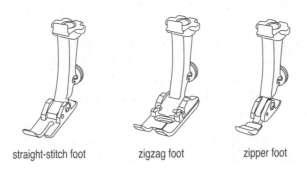

straight-stitch foot   zigzag foot   zipper foot

Straight-stitch, zigzag, and zipper feet are the essentials for most sewing machines.

Basic presser feet may also include an edging or blindstitch foot, an open-toe foot (for extra visibility with decorative stitches), and a buttonhole foot.

Specialty presser feet are used for specific sewing techniques. An overlock foot, for example, works well to finish seams on stretchy knits. A darning foot or an open embroidery foot provides plenty of visibility for freehand embroidery and machine quilting. A walking foot provides a second feed dog above the fabric to keep thick fabric from shifting under the needle.

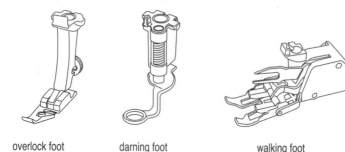

Overlock, darning, and walking feet are great accessories to pick up as you expand your sewing kit.

overlock foot   darning foot   walking foot

Modern sewing machines have quick-change presser feet that are easy to remove and replace. Exact steps vary; in general, raise the presser foot, release the current presser foot, replace it with the foot you want to use, and secure the new foot in place. Older machines may require you to loosen or remove a small screw to change presser feet.

Basic Machine-Sewing Skills

Knowing your sewing machine and how to use it is the difference between hours of irritation and a lifetime of sewing fun. Master these basic machine skills for sewing success!

PINPRICK

Small children and pets are often fascinated by the moving sewing machine parts. Keep little hands clear of the needle while sewing, and avoid unnecessary medical emergencies by declaring your sewing space a small person– and pet-free zone.

Changing the Needle

A sharp new needle can solve a number of sewing problems, from skipped stitches to shredded thread. Change the machine needle to meet a project's particular needs or to replace a dull, damaged, worn, or bent needle. Some sewists start each new sewing project with a fresh needle. We advocate replacing the needle after 8 hours of sewing time. In the long run, needles are much less expensive than sewing machines, so when in doubt, change it out!

To change a needle, raise the needle to its highest position and lower the presser foot. Loosen (but don't remove) the small clamp screw that holds the needle in place. Pull the needle down to remove it from the machine. Be very careful not to drop the needle through the stitch plate.

One side of the needle's upper shaft is flat. Take note of which direction (right, left, or back) the flat side faces, insert the new needle in the same orientation, and tighten the clamp screw to secure the needle in place. The needle should not move if you tug down on it. Check the screw during sewing sessions to be sure the machine's vibrations haven't loosened it.

> **SEW SURPRISING**
>
> Unsure which way to turn? Just remember "righty-tighty, lefty-loosey." Turn a screw to the right (clockwise) to tighten or to the left (counterclockwise) to loosen. Place a slice of foam pencil grip around the clamp screw to make it easier to grip or keep a small screwdriver handy.

Safely dispose of used needles by designating a tiny tin or prescription bottle as a used-needle receptacle. When the tin is full, seal it with strong tape and toss it in the trash. Dispose of individual needles by wrapping the sharp point in layers of tape to avoid poked fingers.

Changing Stitch Settings

Stitch settings refer to three separate attributes: selection (or type), width, and length of stitch. Depending on your machine, you may be able to select from basic stitches, such as straight, zigzag, stretch, and blindstitch, or from hundreds of decorative stitches.

The stitch width determines how wide or narrow a stitch will be, and the available width depends on your machine's capability. You can shorten or elongate stitches by altering stitch length. Depending on the machine, select stitches and set width and length by pushing buttons (on computerized machines) or positioning levers or dials (on older machines).

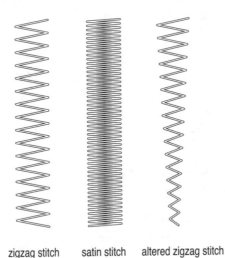

Adjusting the width and length of a single stitch selection creates a number of unique stitches. Shorten a zigzag stitch length, for example, to create a satin stitch.

zigzag stitch   satin stitch   altered zigzag stitch

Stitching a Straight Line

One of the simplest machine-sewing skills is stitching forward and back. Start by raising the presser foot and pulling the top and bobbin threads below the presser foot to the back of the machine. Place two fabric pieces right sides together, aligning raw edges along one side, and slide them under the presser foot.

Align the raw fabric edges along a stitch plate guideline and lower the presser foot. If the fabric shifts, raise the presser foot and readjust it. Hold the top and bobbin thread tails against the bed of the machine to prevent tangling, and gently press the foot pedal. After the machine has made a few stitches, release the thread tails and concentrate on keeping the fabric edges aligned with the guide. You're sewing!

When you reach the edge of the fabric, take your foot off the pedal to stop the machine. If your machine stops with the needle in the fabric, press the needle up button or turn the hand wheel to raise the needle. Raise the presser foot to release the fabric and pull your stitched piece toward the back and side, out from under the presser foot. Snip the thread ends close to your stitching.

Secure seams by stitching in reverse, or *backstitching*, at the start and end of a seam. Some machines have a preprogrammed securing stitch that stitches forward and then back for a set number of stitches or ties a knot before continuing on with the seam.

SEWING SENSE

Sewing in reverse at the start or end of a seam is often called **backstitching** or **backtacking.** To backstitch at the start of a seam, sew forward a few stitches, reverse sew directly over those stitches, and sew forward to complete the seam. To reduce stitch bulk, begin ⅜ inch from the start of the seam with reverse stitches to the fabric edge and then sew forward to complete the seam. The extra stitches made when backstitching can create unwanted bulk in some projects. An alternative to backstitching is to use a very short stitch length for about ¼ inch at the seam beginning and end.

Tension Time

Tension refers to the balance between the needle and bobbin threads. A balanced line of machine stitching looks the same on the top and bottom of the fabric. To test your machine's tension, thread the needle with one thread color and use a different color of the same brand, weight, and type of thread in the bobbin. Set a stitch length of about 2mm or 12 stitches to the inch and straight stitch across two fabric layers.

If thread tensions are balanced, you'll see the needle thread only on one side and the bobbin thread only on the other. The interlocking threads will be hidden between the fabric layers.

If the top thread tension is too tight, the bottom thread will appear on the top fabric. Loosen the top tension by turning the tension dial to a lower number. Move the dial in small increments—a little goes a long way!

If the top thread tension is too loose, the top thread appears on the bottom fabric. Tighten the top tension by turning the tension dial to a higher number. Test stitch and readjust again if needed.

balanced tension

tight top tension

loose top tension

Stitches lock together between fabric layers when tension is balanced.

You can adjust bobbin tension by turning the bobbin case tension screw. Turn the screw clockwise to tighten bobbin tension and pull the top thread farther down into the fabric. Turn it counterclockwise to loosen the bobbin tension. A little goes a long way! Turn the screw only a ⅛ to ¼ turn before test stitching.

To test bobbin case tension, place a fully threaded bobbin in the case. Hold the thread in one hand and gently "bounce" the bobbin case over your opposite hand. If the case drops down in slight steps, the tension is normal. If the case drops quickly, the tension is too loose. Test stitch on scrap fabric after making any adjustments.

PINPRICK

Many manufacturers advise against adjusting bobbin cases, so consider purchasing a second bobbin case for specialty thread settings.

Tension issues can have multiple causes. Check these common culprits before adjusting tension settings:

Misthreaded machine. Missing a single thread guide or threading with the presser foot down and tension discs engaged can cause tension trouble. Raise the presser foot and rethread both needle and bobbin.

Bumpy bobbin. Winding new thread over old, or an inconsistently wound bobbin, can cause bobbin thread to misfeed. Remove thread from an incorrectly wound bobbin and rewind.

Not-so-clean machine. Dust and lint accumulate quickly inside machines. Use a small brush to clear away lint and thread ends between tension discs, under the stitch plate, and inside the bobbin assembly.

Dings and damages. A dropped bobbin may look fine, but even small distortions can cause tension problems. Check the bobbin for signs of wear, such as dents in metal bobbins and stress marks on plastic. When in doubt, use a new bobbin.

A Treasury of Tools and Notions

Having the right tool for a task makes it easy to get great results! Build your treasury of sewing tools gradually, as you learn what works best for you.

Essentials:

- Sewing machine with basic presser feet
- A small pair of scissors for snipping threads
- 8-inch bent handle dressmaker's shears
- Machine-sewing needles in a variety of types and sizes
- Needle threader
- Thimble
- Seam ripper
- Tape measure
- Pincushion
- Pins

- Seam gauge
- Tailor's chalk or marking tools
- Extra bobbins
- Point turner/creaser
- Steam iron
- Ironing board or surface
- Pressing cloth
- Thick towel (for padded pressing surface)
- Cleaning brush
- Sewing machine oil (if approved by your machine's manufacturer)

Notions:

- Thread in various weights, types, and colors
- Embroidery floss
- Buttons
- Hooks and eyes
- Snaps or snap tape
- Hook-and-loop tape
- Zippers

- Elastic in various widths
- Interfacing
- Fusible web
- Liquid seam sealant
- Bias tape
- An assortment of ribbons, rickrack, and trims

Optional items:

- Rotary cutter, ruler, and mat
- Pinking shears or pinking/wavy blade for rotary cutter

- Bodkin or turning tool
- Finger presser/wooden iron

- Teflon pressing sheet or parchment paper
- Pattern tissue or paper
- Seam roll or rolled towel
- Pressing ham

- Magnifying glass
- Specialty presser feet: walking, overlock, open-toe embroidery, piping
- Sewing table

Project: Biscornu Pincushion

Showcase your newfound machine-sewing skills! Here, you'll give two simple squares a twist to create this interestingly shaped pincushion, whose name is French for "weird" or "bizarre." If you want, make the squares bigger and create a pillow instead!

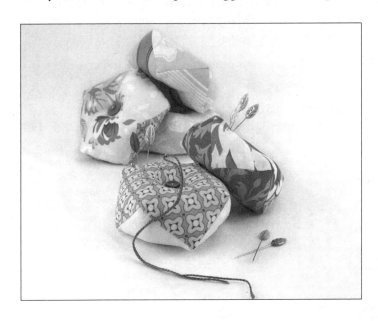

Stitch this sweet pincushion quickly and easily with some simple sewing machine skills.

Finished size:

4¹/₂×4¹/₂×1¹/₂ inches

Tools and materials:

2 (5¹/₂-inch) squares of cotton fabric in contrasting colors

Button

All-purpose thread

Stuffing (see sidebar)

Ruler

Marking pen or pencil (removable)

Scissors

Straight pins

SNIP IT

What to stuff with? Wool—whether fabric, yarn scraps, or unspun roving—contains natural lanolin to protect and lubricate pins. Another choice, polyester fiberfill, is lightweight and easy to find.

Construction:

1. Seam allowance is the space between the seamline and the raw edge of the fabric. The seam allowance for this project is ½ inch. You may find it helpful to measure and mark the seamline ½ inch inside the cut edges of each square on the wrong side of the fabric.

2. Folding a piece of fabric in half is a quick way to find the center along an edge. Fold one square in half to make a 5½×2¾-inch rectangle, and crease the seam allowances. Open the square and clip into the seam allowance only at each crease, making the clips about ⁷⁄₁₆ inch long. Be careful not to cut all the way to the seamline. These quick clips make it easier to sew the two squares together later on.

3. Fold the same square in half the opposite way and repeat step 2. Fold and clip the second square the same way.

4. Lay one square on the other, right sides together, as shown in the following figure. Notice that the squares aren't aligned; instead, the corners of one square correspond to the midpoints of the other square's sides.

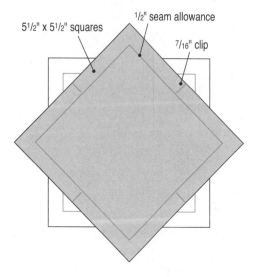

5½" x 5½" squares
½" seam allowance
⁷⁄₁₆" clip

Align the clipped seam allowances of one square to the corners of the other square.

5. Pin the midpoint of one side to its corresponding corner. Notice that the clipped seam allowance opens wide to bend around the corner.

6. Begin stitching about ½ inch before the pinned corner. Backstitch to secure the beginning of the seam, stitch to the corner, pivot with the needle down, and continue to stitch along the first inch of the next side.

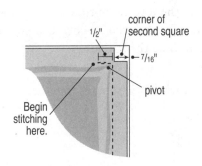

The clipped seam allowance spreads as it turns the corner.

SEW SURPRISING

Use this quick trick for stitching corners: stitch up to the corner (where the seamlines intersect, not the fabric edge), stopping with the needle in the down position. With the needle anchoring the fabric in place on the machine, lift the presser foot and rotate the fabric 90 degrees, aligning the fabric for the seam on the other side of the corner. Lower the presser foot, and continue stitching.

7. Match the next corner of the top square to the corresponding midpoint of the bottom square. Stitch and pivot as before. At each pivot point, check to be sure the seamline pivots just below the clipped edges so no raw edges will be visible in the finished pincushion.

8. Continue stitching around the pincushion, matching corners to midpoints as you go. Stop stitching and backstitch about ½ inch past the last midpoint/corner. This leaves an opening for turning the project right side out and stuffing.

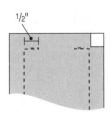

Leave an opening on one side for turning and stuffing.

SNIP IT

Don't be concerned when the project doesn't lie flat. As long as the portion you're sewing is flat and matched correctly as it passes under the needle, all's well.

9. Carefully reach through the open seam and grasp the far side of the pincushion. Pull the pincushion through the opening to turn it right side out and use a chopstick or the eraser end of a pencil to smooth the corners outward.

10. Stuff firmly and slipstitch the opening closed by hand.

11. Pinch the center of the pincushion, pushing the top and bottom fabrics close together. Using a double strand of thread, hand stitch through the pinched center, securing it in place. Sew a button to the pincushion top to hide the stitching.

Experiment! Make a Biscornu pillow by sewing 18-inch fabric squares together.

The Least You Need to Know

- Understanding how your machine works is essential to successful sewing.
- Master basic skills, such as threading, bobbin winding, and changing the needle, to get the most out of your sewing experience.
- Don't be afraid! Most tension issues can be tamed with a few easy adjustments.
- Learning to stitch forward and back puts you on the path to successful sewing adventures!

Machine Needles and Thread

In This Chapter

- Parts and points of machine needles
- Machine needle types and sizes
- Thread fibers and facts
- Quick tips for choosing needles and threads

Two tiny things are at the heart of sewing: needle and thread. Whether you sew by hand or machine, these items are essential for stitching, and choosing the right combination ensures success.

Machine Needle Know-How

Ball point, embroidery, topstitching, sharp—the array of machine needles available can be confusing at first glance. Select a needle based on the fabric and thread you want to use. Different needle types are designed for specific sewing techniques or fabric types, and different needle sizes accommodate certain thread choices and fabric weights.

The Anatomy of a Machine Needle

Both hand and machine needles are designed to carry thread through fabric, but unlike hand-sewing needles, the eye of a machine needle is near the point.

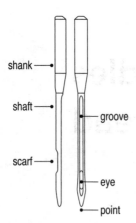

Machine needles share some commonalities with hand-sewing needles, but they are different.

The *shank* is the thickest section of the machine needle, rounded with one flat side. The shank is inserted into the machine's needle bar and held in place with a clamp screw.

The *shaft* is the long, narrow section below the shank. Shaft thickness varies with needle type, and shaft diameter determines needle size.

As with hand-sewing needles, the *eye* is the hole that carries thread through the fabric. Eye size and shape vary among needle types.

The needle *point* pierces the fabric, carrying the top thread down to form a stitch with the bobbin thread. Point shape (sharp, rounded, or punching) varies according to needle type.

The *groove* along the needle shaft cradles and protects the thread as it passes through the fabric. Groove size varies with needle type and size, and heavier threads need deeper grooves.

The small indentation above the eye on the needle back is the *scarf.* It allows the bobbin mechanism to hook the needle thread, forming a stitch.

The Point of It

Look closely and you'll see that not all needle points are the same. Sharp or regular point needles have strong, sharp points for piercing through thick, densely woven fabrics. Ball point needles are rounded to slide through jerseys and knits without snagging or damaging fabric threads. Universal points lie somewhere in between; the slightly rounded shape allows them to stitch through most woven and knit fabrics satisfactorily.

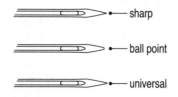

The type of needle you need depends on the fabric you're sewing.

Needle Size, System, and Type

Machine-sewing needles are identified by a series of numbers and letters. One set of numbers indicates the needle size. A second set of numbers is often accompanied by letters and defines the needle system and needle type.

American and European needle manufacturers use different size numbering systems, so needle size is often indicated with two numbers, one for each system, as shown in the following table.

Machine Needle Sizes

	Thinner								Thicker
European	60	65	70	75	80	90	100	110	120
American	8	9	10	11	12	14	16	18	19

In both numbering systems, the number refers to the diameter of the needle's shaft. The higher the number, the thicker the shaft. For example, a 60/8 needle would be very slim and fine, while a 120/19 size is a thick, heavy-duty needle. Use fine needles for lightweight fabrics and thicker, stronger needles for heavyweight fabrics.

SNIP IT

Manufacturers stamp the needle size onto the shank, but the tiny type can be hard to read. To help keep track of which needle you're using, label sections of a pincushion with common needle sizes and use a pin to mark what needle is currently in use. Store used needles in the marked segments. Some sewists write the needle type and size on a sticky note and post it on their machine.

The needle system indicates which type of machine—home sewing, serger, or commercial—a needle is designed for. The 130/705 H system fits most *h*ome sewing machines. (When in doubt, check your machine manual or ask your local machine dealer.) Additional letters indicating needle type may appear after the letter H, such as J for "jeans" or N for "topstitching."

Tiny variations in a needle's shaft thickness, groove depth, eye size, and point shape make a huge difference in stitch quality. For best results, choose a needle type that works with your fabric and thread choices. The following table should help you make your selections.

Machine Needles

Needle Type	Description	Fabric/Use
Universal	Slightly rounded point, standard-size eye	For general-purpose sewing; can be used on both woven and knit fabrics

continues

Machine Needles   (continued)

Needle Type	Description	Fabric/Use
Ball point (S, SES, SUK)	Smooth, medium ball point, standard-size eye	Also includes stretch and jersey needles; designed for elastic knit and stretch woven fabrics such as silk, jersey, Lycra, or faux suede
Jeans or denim (J)	Sharp point and thick, strong shaft	For sewing heavy, tightly woven fabrics such as denim, canvas, duck, or upholstery fabrics, or any time a traditional sharp point is needed
Microtex or sharp	Fine, sharp point with a narrow shaft	Designed to pierce tightly woven fabrics such as silk, lightweight faux suede, microfiber, etc., cleanly
Topstitching (N)	Sharp point with elongated eye, large groove, and deeper scarf	Designed for use with heavy topstitching thread or two strands of all-purpose thread; use the smallest needle size that accommodates your thread to avoid leaving noticeable holes in the fabric
Quilting (Q)	Tapered, slightly rounded point	For machine quilting through multiple fabric layers and intersecting seams
Embroidery (E)	Slight ball point and larger, elongated eye; the scarf protects thread from breaking or shredding	Designed specifically for machine embroidery; reduces friction and damage to delicate decorative threads
Metallic (MET)	Sharp point with large, elongated eye	Designed for use with metallic threads; large groove and scarf protect the thread and prevent skipped stitches

Needle Type	Description	Fabric/Use
Leather (L)	Sharp, wedge-shape cutting point	Point cuts through leather and suede; stitch accurately because the needle leaves large, permanent holes
Twin or double (ZWI)	Two needles attached to a single shaft	Stitch two parallel lines in a single pass; use for decorative and heirloom stitching on machines with zigzag capabilities (Check your machine manual for compatibility.)

Final Notes on Needles

Before we finish the machine needle section, we'd like to leave you with a few last thoughts on machine needles:

- When choosing a needle, first pick the thread for your fabric and project. Next, narrow the needle choices to types compatible with the fabric. Finally, select a needle size to work with the thread. The needle groove should comfortably cradle the thread, which should pass through the eye easily.

- Shredded thread can be caused by too-small needles or by a rough spot (or burr) in the needle eye. Change to a new or larger needle if you encounter this problem.

- Purchase a package of assorted needle sizes so you'll have options when stitching begins.

- Test stitch using the needle, thread, and fabric you've chosen before beginning your project.

Thread Tales

Many types of thread are available, from standard sewing threads in an amazing array of colors to decadent decorative threads as lush as thick yarn. Different sewing tasks require different threads, and your thread selection depends on the final effect you desire. So however do you choose? Read on!

Not All Threads Are Created Equal

Most sewing threads begin as natural or man-made synthetic fibers that are twisted or spun into tiny yarns. Two or three of these tiny yarns are combined into a single strand, giving the thread strength, flexibility, and balance. The number of yarns combined to create a single thread is called the *ply*. A number of finishing techniques can be applied to plied thread to add strength and luster or reduce fuzz:

- A *soft* finish means no further processing is applied.

- *Mercerizing* adds strength and luster, making the thread appear shiny and silky.

- *Gassed* threads are smooth and lint-free, with the fuzz removed, and have a shiny finish.

- *Glazed* threads are lustrous and have a hard, protective finish. Use them with caution because some finishes can leave a gummy residue in your machine.

- *Bonding* adds a tough resin finish to filament polyester and nylon threads.

In addition to spun thread, there are several other methods of thread construction:

- *Continuous filament thread* is made by extruding long fibers of a synthetic material such as rayon or polyester, resulting in a strong, consistent, lint-free thread.

- *Corespun thread* combines a continuous filament core with a cotton or polyester fiber cover.

- *Textured threads* are mechanically treated to be soft and full to the touch. These threads have a certain amount of elasticity.

- *Monofilament thread* is a single synthetic filament extruded to a certain size.

What's in Your Thread?

Thread may be made from a variety of fibers, both natural and man-made:

Cotton thread is a soft, strong, durable, and easy-care natural fiber. It's available in a number of thread weights and is often mercerized, gassed, and glazed. One hundred percent cotton thread is a favorite for quilting and for embroidery when a shiny look is undesirable.

A corespun thread, *cotton-wrapped polyester* blends the superior strength and resiliency of a continuous filament core with natural cotton's ability to withstand the high heat of ironing. Some all-purpose sewing threads are cotton-wrapped polyester.

Polyester is a strong, durable, colorfast, heat-resistant synthetic thread that retains its shape and recovers after stretching. Spun polyester, found in most all-purpose polyester threads, looks like cotton and is made from short fibers that are spun together. Filament polyester threads can be shaped to reflect maximum light for a beautiful shine; trilobal polyester is an example.

Even though it's derived from plant cellulose, *rayon* is considered a manufactured fiber. Less durable and weaker than polyester, rayon takes dye well but is not colorfast. Rayon tends to weaken when wet and is not the best choice for construction seams. Rayon is heat-resistant, soft, and has a high sheen, making it a good choice for embellishment and embroidery.

Synthetic *nylon* thread is sometimes referred to as polyamide and is available in monofilament or textured form. Although nylon thread is strong, it can become brittle and yellow with age. Be careful when ironing because nylon will melt under high heat. Wooly nylon thread is stretchy and often used in lingerie, swimsuits, and sportswear. Heavyweight nylon thread is used in upholstery, drapery, luggage, shoes, and handbags.

> **SEW SURPRISING**
>
> Some nylon threads, sold as "fusible," are made to melt under iron temperature and fuse fabrics together.

Silk is a strong, smooth, high-sheen thread. More elastic than cotton, silk is often used on thin, delicately woven fabrics or sheers. Very fine silk thread is a favorite for hand appliqué and basting.

Metallic thread has a nylon or polyester core wrapped in a metallic foil. Better-quality metallics have an outer coating to protect against needle friction, but metallics may be heat sensitive. When working with metallics, place the spool on a vertical thread stand to reduce loops and kinks, and use a metallic needle or a larger needle size to reduce friction. Use a lightweight thread in the bobbin and stitch slowly, loosening the top tension if necessary.

Weighty Issues

Thread sizing standards vary among manufacturers and are based on how thread is constructed. The Cotton Count System is used to size spun threads and the Denier System is used for sizing filament threads, while the Tex System is an attempt at a universal standard, regardless of construction. With so many systems, it's easier to compare and contrast favorite thread types. That's where our thread comparison guide comes into play.

> **SEW SURPRISING**
>
> Like other textiles, thread ages with time. Older, weaker threads become brittle and break easily and shouldn't be used for sewing. To keep thread from tangling, secure the ends in the angled groove or slot on the end of the spool. Pop tops and snap spools have similar features for securing thread ends. Store thread out of direct sunlight and in airtight containers to keep the fibers dust-free and safe from fading. For eye candy, color-sort thread and store in clear glass jars!

Lightweight Thread		
Thread Type	Needle Size	Use
YLI Silk #100 100% silk	60/8 or 70/10	Fine machine quilting, hand or machine appliqué.
Aurifil™ Mako 50/2 100% cotton	70/10 or 80/12	Strong, smooth lint- and trouble-free thread, for machine quilting and piecing, and general sewing by hand and machine.
Coats & Clark Dual Duty XP® Fine Corespun Polyester	60/8 or 75/11	Strong, smooth thread for pucker- free seams in fine fabrics.

Medium Weight Thread		
Thread Type	Needle Size	Use
Coats & Clark Dual Duty XP® General Purpose Corespun Polyester	70/10 to 100/16	Strong, smooth thread for hand or machine sewing on all fabrics.
Gütermann Natural Cotton 100% cotton CNe 50	70/10 or 80/12	Fine, strong thread with silklike luster, for all types of hand and machine sewing.
Mettler Metrosene® 100% polyester or silk finish 100% mercerized cotton	70/10 or 80/12	All-purpose sewing thread.
YLI Machine Quilting 40/3 100% cotton	70/10 or 80/12	Machine quilting and decorative stitching.

Heavyweight Thread		
Thread Type	Needle Size	Use
Aurifil™ Mako 28/2 100% cotton	80/12 or 90/14	Strong, smooth lint- and trouble-free thread, for hand and machine quilting and decorative sewing.
Sulky® Blendables All-Purpose Mercerized Cotton 100% cotton 12 and 30 wt.	80/12 or 90/14	Strong, matte finish for all-purpose machine and hand sewing and decorative work.
YLI Jeans Stitch 100% spun polyester Size 30	90/14 or 100/16 topstitch	Heavy weight thread for use with denim, canvas, or similar weight fabrics; use for topstitching or hemming jeans.
Coats & Clark Button and Carpet Thread® Polyester/cotton	90/14 or 100/16 or crewel needle for handstitching	A strong, heavy thread for bold topstitching, cording, and buttonholes.

Specialty Thread		
Thread Type	Needle Size	Use
elastic thread	wind on bobbin by hand	High-stretch polyester blend, available in a limited number of colors. Use for smocking and shirring.
bobbin thread 100% cotton 60/2	wind on bobbin	A lightweight thread for use in the bobbin when sewing with specialty threads, or for machine embroidery.
invisible polyester monofilament thread	75/11 or 80/12	Strong, smooth, soft, clear monofilament for invisible appliqué, quilting, and blindstitch- ing. Use smoke color on dark fabrics.

Keep this thread comparison guide handy, and you'll never be at a loss when choosing thread.

Winding Ways

Thread must feed smoothly off the spool for proper sewing tension. For best results, place *parallel-wound* threads on a vertical spool pin and *cross-wound* threads on a horizontal spool pin. Use a spool cap to keep spools in place while sewing.

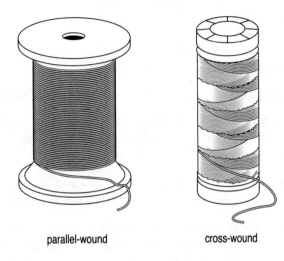

parallel-wound   cross-wound

Remember "straight on, straight off" when placing thread spools. Straight- or parallel-wound thread should unwind from the spool. Cross-wound thread should be pulled off the top.

Estimating Project Needs

Garment manufacturers use mathematical formulas to calculate thread consumption and cost per unit. Stitch type, stitches per inch, stitch length, number and length of seams, seam thickness, and fabric type are all factors for estimating thread needs. Most home sewists don't need that much detail!

Look for yardage on the spool end or outer packaging, and use the following table as a general guide for determining how much thread you'll need for common projects.

Thread Estimates

Thread Yardage	Project
50 to 100 yards	Small items such as a baseball cap, simple hand bag or tote, kitchen mitt, man's T-shirt or tank, child's shirt
100 to 200 yards	Man's shorts, suit coat, shirt; woman's blazer, dress, skirt, blouse, pant, shorts; child's jeans, pants, jacket, shirt, dress
200 to 300 yards	Man's slacks, sweatshirt; woman's coat, jeans, robe; simple bed roll or larger home décor items

The simplest estimate is to buy a small spool for making a single garment such as a blouse or skirt and a large spool for making coordinating pieces or a larger project. Very large items, such as quilts, or items with a lot of seams or stitched embellishment require additional thread yardage. Once you've settled on a thread, purchase an extra spool if you're unsure of the project's needs. You don't want to run out of thread when sewing inspiration strikes!

Thread Tips

Keep these quick tips in mind when choosing thread for your next project:

- Choose a fabric-friendly thread with the same or similar fiber content as your fabric.

- Choose a thread similar in weight to individual fabric fibers if you'd like your stitching to blend in and be less noticeable. Lightweight thread works well with thin, gauzy fabrics. Heavy denim or canvas calls for stronger, thicker thread.

- Audition color choices by unrolling a length of thread from the spool and laying it across your fabric. The color will seem less intense when viewed as a single strand.

- Some threads are not colorfast. Check for colorfastness by wetting several strands of thread in hot water and placing them on a white paper towel. If the color migrates or bleeds onto the paper towel, it will do the same on fabric.

- Test thread strength by holding a short length between your hands and pulling until the thread breaks. If thread breaks easily, you may not want to use it for construction seams. Use this same technique to test stretch or *elongation*. Threads with greater stretch are good for sewing with knit fabrics.

SEW SURPRISING

Usually expressed as a percentage of the original length, **elongation** is the amount a thread is extended at its breaking point. For example, a thread that is 100 inches long, and stretches to 110 inches before breaking, has 10 percent elongation. This is different from elasticity, which is the ability to stretch and recover to the original length.

- Check for uniformity by sliding a length of thread between your finger and thumb. Lumps and bumps indicate thick and thin places in the thread that can cause sewing problems.

- Snip thread ends to check fray. A thread that untwists too easily may be prone to breakage or be difficult to thread through the needle.

Project: Create a Cord

What can you do with a cord? The better question is, what *can't* you do with a cord? Using your sewing machine's bobbin winder, you can quickly twist cords from thread and lightweight yarn to use as drawstrings, decorative trims, and so much more.

Make your own unique cords from a variety of thread colors and weights to use as shoestrings, jewelry, and whatever else you can think of.

Finished size:

Approximately 30 inches, depending on twist

Tools and materials:

20 to 30 yards of thread

Sewing machine with bobbin winder

Extra bobbin

Scissors

PINPRICK

Designate a specific bobbin for making twisted cords, and don't use that bobbin in your machine. The uneven stress from twisting cords may distort the bobbin's edges, and that could harm your machine.

Cutting:

1. Cut 10 to 15 (2-yard) lengths of thread. The more threads, the thicker your finished cord will be.

Construction:

2. Knot one end of thread strands around the bobbin's hole. Trim the short end of the tied strands to avoid tangles.

3. Place the bobbin on the bobbin winder and hold threads taut about 18 inches above the winder. Keep the remaining thread away from the section to be wound.

4. Turn on the bobbin winder for 1 or 2 seconds and then pause to work the twist up the thread. The threads should twist but not kink. Continue twisting the thread until the entire length of thread is twisted.

5. Holding the unknotted thread ends in one hand and using your other hand to find the center of the twisted strands and keep the thread taut, bring the unknotted and bobbin ends together, folding the thread bundle in half. Let the folded strands twist around each other to make a thicker cord. Knot the ends to secure.

This fast, fun technique is a great use for extra threads and lightweight yarns.

The Least You Need to Know

- The needle and thread you choose for your machine and your project are small yet essential elements.
- Choose a needle type according to the fabric and sewing technique you'll be using.
- The fabric and thread weight you use determine the size needle you need.
- Select a thread according to the final effect you want and the sewing task at hand.

Ready, Set, Sew!

In This Chapter

- Preparing fabric for sewing
- Tips for accurate cutting
- Simple steps to sew a seam
- The importance of pressing

Now that you've mastered your machine and know more about needles and threads than you ever thought possible, you're ready to get serious about sewing. Start with a few easy but essential fabric facts and basic seaming techniques and then move on to the importance of pressing. Quality counts, and as you'll soon see, these simple skills can make the difference between homemade and professionally handcrafted results.

Fabric First

When the urge to start sewing hits, it's easy to forget fabric preparation and dive right in. Although projects often don't include instructions on prewashing and straightening the grain, fabric prep plays an important part in how a finished garment feels, fits, and drapes.

Prewashed Is Prewarned

Wash, dry, and press your fabric before cutting project pieces to guard against shrinkage and bleeding dyes. Straight or zigzag stitch around the raw edges to prevent raveling, and launder the fabric as you would the finished project.

Dry clean or steam-shrink any dry-clean-only fabrics you choose. Steam-shrink yardage by steam-pressing from the wrong side of the fabric with a damp *pressing cloth*. You can also steam-shrink fabric by hanging yardage over a shower curtain rod in a steamy bathroom and allowing it to dry. With either method, be sure to test an inconspicuous area of the fabric for water spotting before continuing. If the fabric discolors when water spots dry, consider it dry clean only.

SEWING SENSE

A **pressing cloth** is a piece of plain fabric placed between the iron and the item to be pressed to protect the item from heat damage. Pressing cloths may be dampened with water to help shape the item being pressed. Make your own pressing cloth by stitching the raw edges of an 18-inch square of muslin, or purchase a ready-made press cloth in the notions aisle of your fabric store.

Test machine-washable fabrics for colorfastness by washing with a scrap of white cotton. If the cotton comes out of the wash with a color tint, add a commercial color fixative or 3 tablespoons of vinegar to the water and rewash the yardage to remove excess dye. If the color still bleeds, consider choosing a different fabric.

Hand wash notions such as zippers or trims in warm water, and let them air dry or press them dry with a warm iron.

To determine whether the fabric will shrink, measure and cut a 3-inch square of fabric. Wet the sample swatch and then steam-press the swatch until dry. Remeasure the fabric to see if the swatch size has changed. If the swatch shrinks, preshrink all the fabric before cutting, or choose a different fabric that doesn't shrink.

The Right and Wrong of It

Fabric has two sides. The *right side* (or face) is intended for the outside of a garment or project. The *wrong side* (or back) is meant to be hidden inside a garment or project. It's easy to determine right from wrong on some fabrics; the wrong side of a print appears more muted or faded than the right side, and textured fabrics have a different look and feel on each side. However, other fabrics appear identical on each side—and some really are!

There are subtle clues to the right side of any fabric, but here's the reality: if you can't tell the difference between the right and wrong side of your fabric, chances are no one else can either! Choose and mark one side as the fabric right side and be consistent while constructing your project. Subtle differences, such as the way a fabric reflects light, may be more apparent in a finished garment, so it's best not to mix right and wrong sides.

Hip to Be Square

Woven fabrics are created on a loom from two sets of threads running perpendicular to each other. *Warp* threads run lengthwise along the loom, while *weft* threads run crosswise, over and under the lengthwise threads. Most woven fabrics have a selvage (a narrow, firmly woven border) along each lengthwise edge that prevents the fabric from raveling. It's this construction that gives woven fabric its grain.

Grain refers to the direction threads run in a fabric. The lengthwise (or straight) grain runs parallel to the selvage, along the warp threads. There's little stretch along the strong *lengthwise grain*, and most garments are cut with the lengthwise grain running top to bottom to support the garment and hold its shape. The *crosswise grain* (or crossgrain) runs perpendicularly, along the weft threads. Crosswise grain has slightly more stretch and is not as strong as the lengthwise grain.

Bias refers to a grainline running at a 45-degree angle to the lengthwise and crosswise grains. Woven fabrics stretch considerably along the bias grain. Some garments, such as skirts, are cut on the bias to take advantage of the stretch and softer draping that occurs.

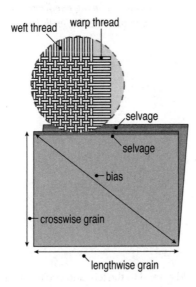

Once you identify the selvage, it's easy to determine the lengthwise and crosswise grain lines.

Before cutting any project pieces, straighten the fabric grain along each crosswise (nonselvage) edge. On some woven (not printed) designs, such as plaid or striped fabrics, you may be able to clearly see a crosswise thread. If so, you can simply follow that thread to cut away the uneven fabric edge. This works best on coarse weaves.

If you can't clearly see a crosswise thread, snip through the selvage near the fabric edge and slightly fray the cut edge. Gently pull one or two crosswise threads to create a flaw in the fabric weave. Don't worry if the thread breaks. Cut along the flaw line, and repeat until you've trimmed the entire edge.

Quilters have a quick way of creating a cleanly cut edge with a rotary cutter, ruler, and mat. Although this method isn't as precise as pulling threads, it saves time, especially with tightly woven fabrics. Here's how to do it:

1. Fold the fabric in half lengthwise, aligning the selvages. Place the folded fabric flat on the cutting mat with the folded edge closest to you. Smooth out any wrinkles, keeping the selvages together; don't worry if the crosswise edges don't align. Be sure the fold is smooth and flat.

2. Fold the fabric in half lengthwise again, aligning the first fold with the selvages. Smooth away any wrinkles, making sure both folded edges are flat.

3. Align a horizontal line on the rotary ruler with the folded fabric edge closest to you. The uneven fabric edges should extend past the right edge of the ruler.

4. Holding the ruler with your left hand, cut the fabric with the rotary cutter along the ruler's right edge.

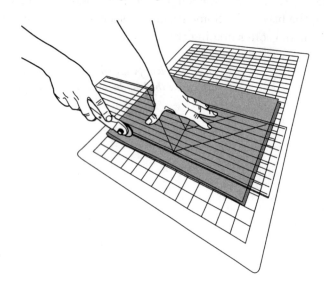

Rotary cutters are sharp! Keep fingers away from the cutting edge and "anchor" your left hand by placing one finger on the fabric to keep the ruler from shifting.

 PINPRICK

If you're left-handed, the uneven fabric edges should extend to the left, and you'll hold the ruler with your right hand.

After straightening, the fabric's grainlines should be perfectly perpendicular. If not, gently pull the fabric along the bias, in the opposite direction of the distortion, taking care not to stretch the fabric out of shape.

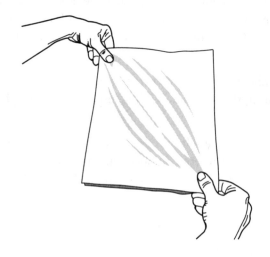

Pull gently along the bias grain to realign and straighten the lengthwise and crosswise threads.

Knit fabrics are made by interlocking loops of thread. A lengthwise row of loops is called a *rib*. A crosswise row of loops is called a *course*. Knits are inherently stretchy, with the greatest stretch along the course or fabric width. Although knits don't have a bias grain or grainline, you can straighten a cut knit end by folding the fabric along the center rib and smoothing away wrinkles. Align a rotary ruler along the fold, and rotary cut the fabric edges.

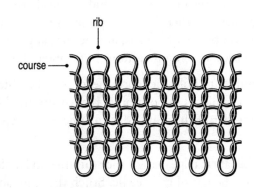

Knit fabrics usually have more stretch along the courses, or rows of crosswise loops, as shown in this close-up view.

PINPRICK

Occasionally, knit fabrics are distorted during finishing. If prewashing doesn't allow the ribs and courses to relax into their perpendicular positions, the distortion may be permanent and will affect a garment's fit and drape.

Careful Cutting

We talk more about patterns in Chapter 16, but for now, we want to point out that accuracy is essential when cutting pattern pieces. Miscut projects won't fit together properly! For best results, place fabric flat on a protected surface and pin pattern pieces in place, following the pattern layout guide. Place pins inside the cutting lines, and keep the fabric flat as you cut. Avoid moving the fabric, and be sure to follow the cutting lines or measurements exactly.

Bent-handled dressmaker's shears work well for cutting fabric. The angled handle allows you to hold the shears comfortably while making long, smooth cuts with the bottom blade resting against the flat surface. This translates into smoother, more accurate cutting.

Rotary cutters with 45mm or larger blades work well for long straight or large curved cuts. Use a small (18mm) rotary cutter to negotiate smaller curves. Flat flower head pins can be used alongside rotary rulers to keep patterns and fabric aligned.

Match, Pin, Sew

Most sewing patterns instruct you to stitch one pattern piece to another along a specific edge to construct a garment or project. It's assumed you'll know how to match, pin, and then sew the seam.

To match pieces, align the specified edge, and be sure the seamline ends match. In general, position pieces with their right sides together so the resulting seam is hidden inside the project. Occasionally a seam will be sewn with wrong sides together; if so, the project instructions will advise you. Pay attention to seamline markings on printed patterns, and be sure any pattern notches, clips, or dots align between the two pieces. (More on patterns in Chapter 16.)

Place pins along and perpendicular to the seamline to hold the fabric pieces together. Start by placing one pin at each seam end and then pin the pieces in position at the pattern markings. Use additional pins as needed to hold the remainder of the seam edge together and keep the fabric from shifting.

Using the stitch plate guidelines to position the fabric edges, align the seamline under the machine needle with the bulk of the material to the left of the needle. Stitch the seam according to the pattern instructions, backstitching as needed to secure the ends.

PINPRICK

Don't sew over pins! Stop sewing and remove pins as you come to them to avoid breaking the needle or damaging your machine.

Pressing Matters

Pressing, not to be confused with ironing, is persuading the fabric to maintain a certain shape. Ironing, the dreaded household task of removing wrinkles, involves sliding the iron across the fabric, while pressing uses an up-and-down motion that doesn't distort the fabric or seam.

A thermostat controls the iron's temperature, and temperature accuracy can vary as an iron ages. Always test press on fabric scraps before you press good fabric, and unplug an iron when it's not in use. To test press, set the iron temperature according to fabric type and press a fabric scrap to be sure the iron won't scorch the fabric.

Use steam to quickly set seams, but be sure the heat and moisture don't discolor, add shine, or change the fabric's texture. Press from the wrong side when possible, and use a pressing cloth under the iron to protect delicate fabrics.

Press seams to set stitches, push seam allowances open or to one side, flatten finished edges, or coax smooth curves from flat pieces of fabric. "Press as you sew" is a common saying among serious stitchers, and pressing each seam after it's sewn is a great way to get professional results.

Teflon-coated ironing board covers are made to reflect an iron's heat. This double dose of heat increases cooling time and can cause some fabrics to shine. Opt for a 100 percent cotton cover over a wool or cotton pad for a breathable ironing surface.

If space is limited, consider purchasing a portable pressing pad you can fold away when not in use, or make your own from heat-resistant, insulated batting.

In addition to an iron and ironing board or surface, you may find a *seam roll* or *pressing ham* helpful for shaping certain seams and curves.

> **SEWING SENSE**
>
> **Seam rolls** and **pressing hams** are firmly stuffed shapes covered in cotton on one side and a heavy fabric such as wool on the other. The shapes of these pressing tools make it easier to shape garment pieces when pressing seams.

An Open and Shut Case

To press a seam, place the stitched piece flat on your ironing surface. Set the stitches by pressing the seam just as it was sewn (see the following figure). This smoothes away tiny puckers and helps the stitches merge into the fabric. Let the fabric cool slightly, and open the stitched piece, placing it seam side up. Use your fingers and the point of the iron to open the stitched seam. Be careful not to burn your fingers! Press the seam open, moving the point of the iron up and down along the seam. Let the pressed seam cool before turning the piece over and pressing lightly from the right side.

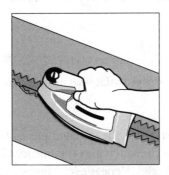

Press the seam as sewn to set the stitches and then use the point of the iron to press the seam allowance open or to one side.

Some pattern instructions indicate that a seam should be pressed to one side. This is especially common in quilting, although some garment seams are also pressed to one side. A seam that's pressed closed is generally stronger than one pressed open, and pressing to one side allows the seam to be covered by a yoke or facing. If pressing to one side is called for, simply press the seam allowances to one side together after setting the seam.

If pressed seams imprint, or show through on the right side, place a seam roll or tightly rolled towel beneath the fabric before pressing seams open. The seam roll's rounded surface helps prevent imprints and is handy for pressing sleeves and pant legs. By contrast, a pressing ham's curved shape is helpful for pressing darts and shaped seams.

SNIP IT

Mineral deposits can build up on your iron and transfer to fabric and clothes. Regular cleaning keeps your iron in top condition. Check your owner's manual for instructions or look for iron cleaner at your local fabric store.

Finger Pressing

Finger pressing is a quick alternative for setting short seams—and saving yourself multiple trips to the ironing board. Use your fingers to apply pressure and push seams open or to one side. Run your fingernail down the seam to set stitches, and crease fabrics with the edge of your fingernail. Alternatively, you can use a wooden iron or plastic finger presser (small hand tools found among sewing notions) to save your manicure.

Rip It! Rip It!

"As we sew, so shall we rip."

One of the cool things about sewing is that you can fix your mistakes. Unsew or remove errant stitching with a seam ripper or sharp-pointed scissors. Most fabrics are forgiving, and needle holes will disappear after the stitching is removed and the weave realigns. Nonwoven fabrics, such as leather, suede, or vinyl, are the exception; needle holes are permanent in those materials.

SNIP IT

Steam-pressing after stitches are removed helps reset the fabric grain so needle holes disappear.

To remove stitches with a seam ripper, place the stitched pieces flat on a smooth surface and slide the sharp, curved blade between the stitch and the fabric. Gently pull the stitch away from the fabric, letting the blade cut the thread. Repeat every few stitches until the unsewn seam pulls apart easily. Use a small piece of painter's tape to quickly remove the cut threads before resewing the seam.

You can also use sharp-pointed scissors to cut through the stitching. Starting at one end, gently pull the stitched seam slightly apart so the stitches are visible between the fabric pieces. Be careful not to stretch the fabric. Clip the first few stitches, making sure you don't cut through the fabric. Repeat along the length of the seam.

Use a seam ripper or scissors to snip apart errant stitching. Try each technique to see what works best for different sewing situations.

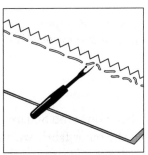

Project: Handy Hip Bag

We've sized this slim cross-body bag to carry a notebook or sketchpad. You can easily change the dimensions to vary the bag size.

Create a cute cross-body catch-all with this basic lined box-bottom bag project.

Finished size:

10×13×2 inches (excluding shoulder strap)

Tools and materials:

⅝ yard of light- to medium-weight woven fabric* for outer bag and strap

½ yard of light- to medium-weight woven fabric* for bag lining

Thread

1⅜- to 2-inch buttons for closure

Basic machine-sewing tools

Suitable woven fabrics include quilting-weight cottons or lightweight home décor fabrics. Stretchy fabrics are not suitable for this project. Yardage is based on 45-inch-wide fabric with at least 40 inches of useable width.

Cutting:

1. Follow the basic rotary cutting instructions in the "Hip to Be Square" section earlier in this chapter to square the fabric edges. Refold the outer fabric with the wrong sides together and cut edges aligned. Trim away one selvage edge, rotate the folded fabric 180 degrees, and use the ruler markings as a guide to cut two lengthwise 5×22½-inch strips for the straps.

2. Refold the remaining outer fabric yardage in half lengthwise, and cut two 13×15-inch rectangles for the bag front and back at the same time.

3. Fold the lining fabric in half lengthwise, and cut two 13×16-inch rectangles for the bag lining.

4. Cut one 2×10-inch rectangle from either fabric for the button loop.

Construction:

Use a ½-inch seam allowance, unless otherwise noted.

5. With right sides together, align the short ends of the strap pieces, and stitch to form one long strap. Press the seam open.

6. Fold the strap in half lengthwise with right sides together, and pin the long raw edge. Stitch the long edges together, removing the pins as you sew. Press the seam open, centering it within the strap width.

7. Use a turning tool to turn the strap right side out. If you don't have a turning tool, attach a large safety pin to one open end of the strap and push the pin inside the strap. Use your fingers to inch the pin along, pulling and turning the fabric to the right side through the fabric tube. Remove the pin before pressing.

8. Press the strap flat with the seam centered on the back. *Topstitch* ¼ inch away from each long edge.

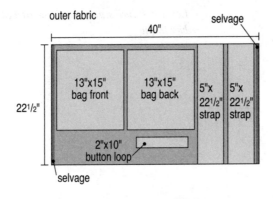

Follow this cutting layout for the Handy Hip Bag.

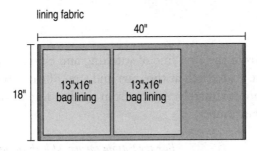

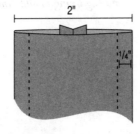

Topstitch along the strap edges to strengthen the strap and keep the fabric from rolling.

SEWING SENSE

Stitching on the right side of a project is called **topstitching.** Spaced an even distance from a seam or edge, topstitching can be decorative as well as functional.

9. Place the outer bag pieces right sides together. Pin the pieces together along 3 sides, leaving one 13-inch edge open for the bag top. Stitch along the pinned edges, backstitching at the beginning and end and pivoting at the lower corners. Press the seams to one side.

10. Repeat step 9 to stitch the bag lining together, but leave 4 inches of one side seam unstitched.

11. At one bottom corner, pinch the bag bottom and side together, aligning the side and bottom seams to form a triangle of fabric. Measure 1 inch from the triangle point and draw a line perpendicular to the seams. Stitch along the line boxing the bag to form a 2-inch-wide bag bottom.

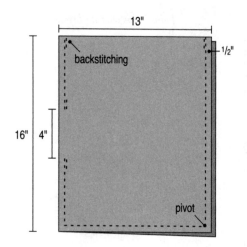

Leave a 4-inch seam section unstitched on the bag lining.

12. Stitch a second seam, ¼ inch away from the first line of stitching and closer to the triangle point, to reinforce the seam. Backstitch at the start and stop of each line of stitching. Trim the triangle points approximately ¼ inch from the last line of stitching, and press the seam toward the bag bottom.

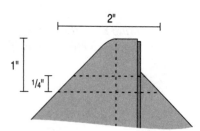

Box the bottom corners of both the outer bag and bag lining to add dimension to your bag.

13. Repeat *boxing* for the remaining bag corner and for both corners in the bag lining.

SEWING SENSE

Boxing is the portion of the fabric that gives a project depth. It can be created from the main fabric pieces, as in the Handy Hip Bag, or by attaching a separate *boxing strip*.

Create a closure:

14. With wrong sides together, fold the 2×10-inch button loop in half lengthwise. Press the fold, and open the pressed strip. Fold the two long edges to the center fold, and press again. Finally, fold the pressed strip in half lengthwise, enclosing the raw edges, to make a strip approximately ½ inch wide. Press.

15. Edgestitch along each long edge of the folded strip, approximately ⅛ inch from the strip edge, to secure the strip layers together.

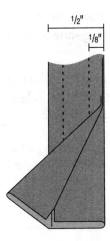

Edgestitch the long edges of the button loop strip.

Assemble the bag:

16. Turn the outer bag right side out. Choose one side as the bag back, and pin-mark the center of the bag top edge. Fold the button loop in half and align the loop's short raw edges with the bag top edge at the center pin, right sides together. Pin one short end of the loop on either side of the marking pin. Secure the button loop to the bag back with two lines of stitching, ¼ inch and ⅜ inch from the raw edge.

17. With right sides together, center one short strap end over one bag side seam. Pin in place, aligning bag and strap raw edges. Secure the strap to the bag with two lines of stitching, ¼ inch and ⅜ inch from the raw edge.

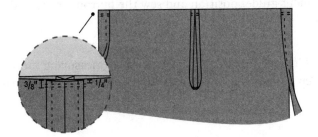

Stitch the straps to the outer bag at the side seams.

18. Repeat for the opposite end of the strap, making sure the strap isn't twisted.

19. With the outer bag right side out and the bag lining wrong side out, place the outer bag inside the bag lining so the right sides are together. Matching the side seams, pin the bag and lining together around the top edge, making sure the strap and button loop are tucked between the fabric layers. Stitch the bag's upper edge, ½ inch from the raw edge. Stitch again ¼ inch closer to the raw edge.

20. Reach through the gap in the bag lining seam to turn the bag right side out. Use needle and thread to slipstitch the opening closed.

21. Press the top seam, straps, button loop, and lining away from the body of the bag. Tuck the lining inside the bag, letting ½ inch of the lining show at the top edge of the bag. Press the lining in place along the upper edge.

22. Edgestitch around the upper edge of the bag, ⅛ inch from the top seam, to hold the lining in place, catching the strap and loop in the stitching. Edgestitch again along the folded top edge to further anchor the strap and loop, if desired.

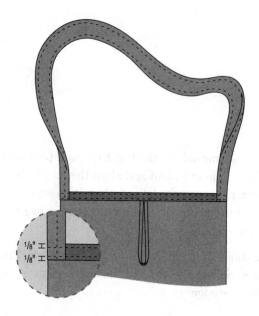

Edgestitch to anchor the strap and button loop to the top edge of the bag.

23. Using the button loop as a placement guide, position and sew the button (or stacked buttons) in place for bag closure.

Don't limit yourself to a slim-sized tote. Create a deeper but shorter bag by measuring more than 1 inch from the triangle point in step 11. Just be sure to make the same change on all the boxed corners!

The Least You Need to Know

- Prewash fabrics to avoid possible problems. Some fabrics may shrink, or colors may bleed.
- Go with the grain! Identify lengthwise, crosswise, and bias grainlines of woven fabric and cut project pieces accordingly to ensure garments hold their shape.
- Press as you sew to set seams, shape fabrics, and get professional results.
- Everyone unsews! Learn to use a seam ripper and sharp-pointed scissors to quickly undo errant seams.
- A "tuck and turn" lining and boxed bottom are two terrific construction techniques to have in your arsenal of sewing knowledge.

Beyond Basic Machine Stitches

In This Chapter

- Straight and zigzag stitches
- Working with decorative stitches
- Stretch stitch applications
- Stitches for specific construction tasks

The number and types of stitches available on high-end sewing machines can be mind-boggling, and even basic machines offer a multitude of stitches. With all those choices, how do you know which to use?

Some stitches are meant to be seen; others are almost invisible. Construction seams—those that hold garment or project pieces together—often use stitches that blend into the fabric. Decorative stitches may be added to projects as pure embellishment. The stitches you have available depend on your machine's capabilities, and some stitches require specialty presser feet.

But before we get stitching, an understanding of the basic stitch types will help you choose the best stitch for any job.

Standard Machine Stitches

Most home sewing machines have straight and zigzag stitch capabilities. By varying the stitch length and width of these two basic stitches, you can accomplish almost all your sewing tasks!

Straight Stitch

A balanced *straight stitch*, also called a *lock stitch*, is essential to machine sewing. This simple stitch is used for almost everything. In addition to sewing seams, variations of the straight stitch are used for basting, backstitching, *topstitching*, and *edgestitching*, as well as for more advanced sewing techniques.

Most machines enable you to adjust the straight stitch length from 0 to 5mm or longer. When stitch length is set at 0, the machine stitches in place without moving the fabric—useful for securing seam endings. Stitch lengths of 5mm or longer, or 5 or fewer stitches per inch, are used for gathering or basting. The standard setting for a straight stitch is a 2 to 2.5mm stitch length, or 10 to 12 stitches per inch.

A *basting stitch* is a long, straight stitch (4mm or 6 stitches per inch) used to temporarily hold fabrics together. The long stitch length makes it easier to remove stitches after the permanent seam is sewn. Use a basting stitch to test garment fit or when creating gathers and ruffles.

Use a strong, lightweight thread for basting. The stitches will be easier to remove later.

Topstitching is straight stitching sewn on the right side of a project, using a slightly longer stitch length. Used as a construction seam or as a decorative accent, topstitching usually runs parallel to a seam. Multiple rows of topstitching may be used together. A topstitching needle may be needed to penetrate multiple fabric layers or to accommodate heavier thread. Use the presser foot width or a seam guide to align parallel rows of stitching, or move the needle position to sew closely spaced rows. Don't backstitch at the seam ends; instead, leave the thread ends long enough to thread a hand needle and pull the thread tails to the wrong side or between fabric layers.

Edgestitching is a variation of topstitching. Sewn very close to the fabric edge (⅛ inch or less), edgestitching is used to hold a facing or seamline in place, prevent an edge from rolling, keep a tiny folded edge from raveling, or just for decoration. A blindstitch or edgestitch foot can help to guide your stitching.

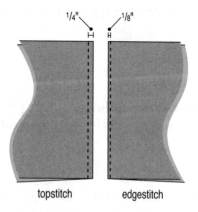

topstitch   edgestitch

Topstitching and edgestitching are two of many possible uses for the straight stitch.

Your machine should make uniform stitches that don't pull or pucker the fabric. Heavier fabrics may require longer stitch lengths, while a shorter stitch length may work better on fine, lightweight fabrics.

SNIP IT

To prevent lightweight fabrics from flagging, or being pulled down through the stitch plate opening, temporarily place a piece of masking tape over the needle hole. The needle will pierce the tape to form the stitch, but the fabric won't follow.

Zigzag/Satin Stitch

A *zigzag stitch* is made just as the name indicates—the machine takes one stitch to the left and one stitch to the right then repeats, creating a zigzag line of stitching. Because the needle moves left and right, this stitch requires a presser foot and stitch plate with wide needle holes.

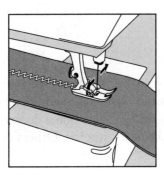

The machine needle moves left and right of center to form a zigzag stitch.

Altering the stitch width and length changes the zigzag stitch's appearance and function. A narrow zigzag used on knit or stretch fabric adds flexibility to seams. Wider zigzag stitches may be used to hem knits or hold (couch) decorative threads, yarns, or elastic in place. (Learn more about couching in Chapter 13.) A zigzag stitch can be used to encase gathering thread and cord or to attach buttons.

A zigzag stitch with a very short stitch length is called a *satin stitch*. Satin stitching appears as a solid line of thread, with no fabric showing between the stitches. The exact stitch length varies with the fabric and thread weight used. Satin stitching is commonly used to attach appliqués, with the satin stitch covering the edge of the appliqué and extending onto the base fabric.

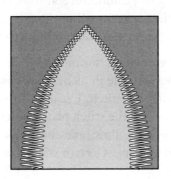

Gradually increase stitch width to create a tapered satin stitch.

Zigzag stitching should lie flat, without distorting the fabric. If the fabric tunnels, or bunches up beneath the stitches, use spray starch to stiffen the fabric or layer a lightweight *stabilizer* beneath the fabric to help hold fabric flat. Reduce the top thread tension to create a more rounded stitch and to help keep the bobbin thread hidden.

SEWING SENSE

A **stabilizer** stiffens and supports the fabric while stitching. Most often placed on the fabric wrong side, stabilizers are available in a variety of weights and types. Some stabilizers are permanent (meant to stay in the final project), while others should be removed after the stitching is complete. Choose a stabilizer according to the fabric you're using and the intended use and care of your project.

Decorative Machine Stitches

In addition to straight and zigzag stitch options, many machines offer decorative stitches. Most decorative stitches are used as embellishments and not in seam construction, and the number and type of stitches vary with machine models and manufacturers. Some decorative stitches, such as a blanket or feather stitch, replicate hand-embroidery stitches. Others create unique floral, geometric, or serpentine designs.

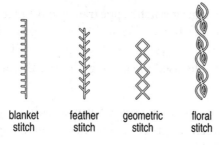

blanket stitch   feather stitch   geometric stitch   floral stitch

Modern machines often include a variety of decorative stitches.

Decorative stitching is perfect for projects that need a little extra embellishment. Use decorative stitching as topstitching around collars and cuffs, or position several rows of stitching along hemlines. Stitch trims in place with coordinating or contrasting threads, and experiment with thread weights and types. Alter stitch length and width to create a library of stitch accents.

It may be helpful to draw a temporary guideline (or guidelines, for multiple lines of stitching) on your fabric. Align the presser foot, not the needle, with the guideline, because the needle may move right, left, or backward while you're creating the stitch. Use a slow to medium speed to better control your stitching. Use a *seam guide* or follow the stitch plate guides to create parallel rows of stitching. Depending on the stitch density, fabric, and thread used, a stabilizer may be required to keep the fabric from pulling or distorting. Certain stitches may require a specific presser foot, too.

SEWING SENSE

A **seam guide** is a simple, adjustable machine accessory that attaches at the right or left of the machine needle. Some guides are simple metal rods; others have scales for more accurate measurements. Set the guide a specific distance from the needle or align the guide with a previous line of stitching to create parallel rows of stitching.

Advanced Utility Stitches

Some stitches are designed for specific sewing tasks, such as creating seams that stretch or finishing seam edges. Special presser feet or machine attachments may be required for such stitches.

Stretch Stitch

Stretch stitches are used for—you guessed it—sewing stretchy fabrics. Stretch stitches have built-in "give" that allows seams to stretch with the finished garments; straight stitches are more likely to "pop" or rip under stress.

Stretch stitches are variations of a zigzag stitch or straight stitches with a back-and-forth triple motion and are optimized for use with particular types of stretch fabric. Some machines have a number of stretch stitches available for a variety of fabric types, while others have none.

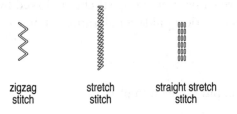

zigzag
stitch

stretch
stitch

straight stretch
stitch

Stretch stitches are indicated by icons like these on your machine. Test stretch stitches on fabric scraps before sewing the project seams.

On most machines, the straight stretch stitch is indicated as three lines. To form this extra-strong stitch, the machine takes a series of stitches, forward and back, to create a line of triple stitches. Increase the stitch width to create the zigzag variation of this strong, stretchy stitch. It takes a bit longer to sew seams with this stitch, but the results are worth it, as skipped stitches now and broken seams later are both avoided. Baste and test-fit garments before committing to triple stitch seams because they are difficult to remove.

If your machine doesn't have a stretch stitch, use a very narrow, medium-length zigzag (0.5mm width, 2.5mm length) to stitch seams. Hold the fabric taut while sewing, but be careful not to stretch it.

SNIP IT

When working with knit fabric, you can add a little "give" to straight-stitched seams by slightly stretching the fabric as it moves beneath the machine needle. Don't pull too hard, though, or the seam will ripple instead of lying flat.

Overlock Stitch

An *overlock stitch* uses a combination of straight and zigzag stitches to sew a seam and finish the fabric edges in one stitch. Sometimes called an *overcast stitch*, it's used with both stretch and woven fabrics to reinforce standard seams, to hem raw edges, and as a decorative stitch.

Overlock stitches require a special presser foot with a pin. Place the fabric under the foot and align it with the pin, as directed in the machine's owner's manual. As you sew, the needle swings to the right to wrap the thread around the fabric edge, while the pin prevents curling and tunneling. This encases the raw fabric edge to prevent raveling and adds extra strength to the seam.

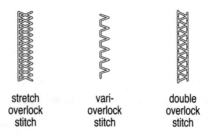

stretch overlock stitch

vari- overlock stitch

double overlock stitch

Variations of the overlock stitch are used on different weights and types of fabrics.

Blind Hem Stitch

Use the *blind hem stitch*, or *blind stitch*, to quickly sew invisible hems in medium- to heavyweight fabrics. This stitch uses a pattern of four or five straight or zigzag stitches followed by one wide zigzag and requires a special presser foot with a vertical guide for aligning stitches along the fabric edge.

To create a blind hem:

1. Finish the raw edges first, and fold and pin the hem in place.

2. Fold the hem back against the garment right side, leaving a ¼-inch margin of the hem's finished edge showing beyond the new fold. Pin in place.

This special folding technique makes the blind hem stitch almost invisible on the garment's right side.

3. Select the blind hem stitch and place the folded fabric wrong side up beneath the presser foot, aligning the guide against the new fold. Adjust the stitch width if necessary so the needle just pierces the fold when the one wide zigzag is stitched. The four or five

straight or zigzag stitches should fall near the finished raw edge, entering only the hem fabric.

4. Stitch the hem and press the hem flat along the first fold, releasing the temporary fold from step 2. The stitching should be nearly invisible from the fabric's right side.

Bar Tack

A *bar tack* is essentially a wide zigzag sewn in one place. Bar tacks are used to reinforce stress points on garments, such as pocket edges, belt loops, and buttonholes on jeans. Some sewing machines have bar tacks as a stitch selection, or a button-attaching stitch can be substituted. If your machine does not offer either stitch, set the machine for a zigzag stitch with a stitch length of 0 and a medium to wide stitch width, and take several stitches in place.

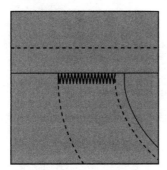

Adjust the stitch width and length as necessary to make a bar tack fit your needs.

Project: Easy-Peasy Apron

Rows of decorative stitching take this easy apron from drab to dynamite!

Quickly stitch this apron from 2 yards of fabric.

Finished size:

>   35×29 inches (excluding apron tie)

Tools and materials:

>   ⅞ yard of outer fabric*
>
>   1⅛ yards of lining fabric*
>
>   Thread
>
>   Basic machine-sewing tools

Suitable woven fabrics include light- to medium-weight cottons or lightweight home décor fabrics. Stretchy fabrics are not suitable for this project. Yardage is based on 45-inch-wide fabric with at least 40 inches of useable width.

Cutting:

1. Cut one 36×30-inch rectangle from the outer fabric.

2. Cut one 36×30-inch rectangle from the lining fabric.

3. Cut three 2-inch × wof (width of fabric) strips from the lining fabric for the apron ties.

Construction:

Seam allowance is ½ inch unless otherwise noted.

4. Remove the selvages and sew the short ends of the apron ties together. Trim the seam allowances and press the seams open to reduce bulk. Press ½ inch to the wrong side at each short tie end.

5. Fold the tie in half lengthwise with wrong sides together. Press the fold, and open the pressed strip. Fold the two long edges to the center fold and press again. Refold the strip along the center crease, enclosing the raw edges, to make a strip ½ inch wide, and press.

Fold and press the pieced strips to encase the raw edges of the apron tie.

6. Add rows of decorative stitching to the apron lining and outer fabric as desired, keeping the ½-inch seam allowance in mind. Test stitches on fabric scraps and use a temporary stabilizer if needed while stitching.

7. Position any waistline embellishments on the lining within 4 or 5 inches of the waistline seam. Remember that the lining will be turned over the ties when the apron is worn, and take that into account when stitching and for directional motifs.

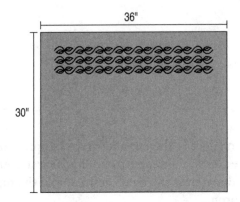

Stitch along the upper apron edge to add a waistline accent, or place parallel rows of stitching along the hem.

8. Pin the apron lining and outer fabric right sides together, matching the outer edges. The fabrics should lie flat against each other. Straight stitch around all four edges, leaving a 4-inch opening in the waistline for turning. Press.

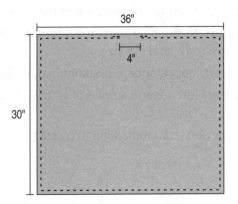

With right sides together, stitch around the apron's outer edge.

9. Trim the corners diagonally to reduce bulk. Use the seamline gap to turn the apron right side out, smoothing the corners and seams. Use a point turner or similar tool to work the corners gently into crisp points. Press, tucking the unstitched seam allowance inside the opening. Slipstitch the opening closed.

10. Center the pressed tie on the apron front, 4 to 5 inches below the apron top edge, and pin in place. Edgestitch the outer edges of the tie to secure it to the apron, and continue edgestitching all the way to the tie ends to finish the tie edges.

11. Reinforce the apron tie by bar tacking the ties at the apron edges.

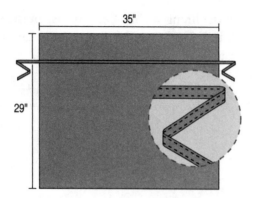

Pin the apron tie in place, and topstitch to finish.

To wear your Easy-Peasy Apron, hold the apron edges at the ties and wrap the apron around your waist. Cross the ties at the back, bring the ties to the center front of your waist, and tie in a bow, allowing the top of the apron to fold down over the tie. If desired, fold the top of the apron down over your waist before tying the apron.

The Least You Need to Know

- Almost every sewing task can be accomplished with some variation of the straight stitch.
- The zigzag is a versatile stitch. Use it as a stretch stitch on knits; as a hem stitch; as a satin stitch; or to couch down decorative threads, trims, and elastic.
- Changing a stitch's width and length alters its appearance and, sometimes, its function.
- Stretch, overlock, blind hem, and bar tack are just a few examples of stitches designed for specific sewing tasks.
- Use a seam guide or follow a stitch plate or presser foot marking to create perfectly placed parallel rows of stitching.

Great Seams

In Part 2, we take an in-depth look at seams, the basic construction tool in sewing. Standard, flat-felled, French, and zigzag—who knew there were so many ways to join two pieces of fabric together? We also explore seam finishes: traditional and trendy techniques for preventing (or promoting) frayed edges.

Not all seams are sewn in a straight line. In these chapters, you learn to smoothly navigate curves and corners and to stitch curved shapes to straight edges, join same-shape curves, and different curved shapes.

Sound impossible? Trust us. You can do this! We show you how.

Each of the projects in Part 2 provides simple, step-by-step instructions, illustrations for you to follow, and plenty of practice for learning these techniques. Fine tune your seaming skills on a Sweet Seamed Wrap, go green and girly with a Lettuce-Edge T-Shirt Scarf, and revive a retro look—while conquering curves!—with an easy Half-Circle Skirt from a pattern you draft yourself!

Soon, you'll be sewing like a pro!

Sewing Seams

In This Chapter

- Sewing standard seams
- An easy explanation of seam allowances
- Trimming and grading seams
- Three common seam types

When you stitch two or more pieces of fabric together, you're sewing a *seam*—the basic construction element in sewing. Seams give shape to garments and projects, turning flat pieces of fabric into functional clothes and accessories. Some seams are almost invisible, while others highlight and enhance a project's design. Fabric type and weight—and the desired result—determine the type of seam you sew.

The Standard Seam

A *standard*, or plain, seam is the most common method of joining two pieces of fabric. Used on many weights and types of fabric, a standard seam is sewn with the right sides of the fabrics together, and the raw edges of a finished seam may need to be trimmed to reduce bulk or finished to prevent fraying.

Woven fabrics are sewn with a plain straight stitch, and stretch fabrics are sewn with a short straight stitch (for "give"), a tiny zigzag, or a stretch stitch. (See Chapter 5 for more on machine stitches.)

Here's how to sew a standard seam:

1. Place fabric right sides together, aligning the edges and matching the pattern notches or construction marks. Pin the pieces together along the seam, placing the pins perpendicular to the seamline.

2. Machine stitch along the seamline, backstitching at the beginning and end of the seam to secure the ends, if necessary, and removing pins as you sew.

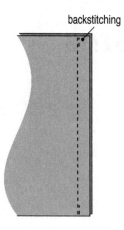

backstitching

Place fabrics right sides together, matching marks and edges. Stitch the seam, backstitching at the ends as needed.

3. Press the fabric as sewn to set the stitches, and press the finished seam open or to one side. If necessary, trim or finish the raw edges of the seam allowance.

PINPRICK

It's better to finish raw edges after the seam is sewn rather than before because finishing techniques can affect the accuracy of the seam allowance.

Seams often overlap, intersect, or cross in the construction of a garment or project. Always trim or finish the seam allowances (see Chapter 7) of the first seam (or seams) before joining the next pieces together. If intersecting seams were pressed to one side, nestle the seams together so the seam allowances lie flat in opposite directions, and pin to hold seams in place while sewing. If intersecting seams were pressed open, insert a pin through both seams to keep seams aligned.

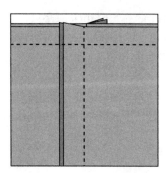
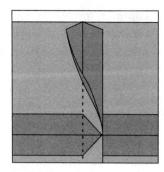

Press intersecting seams in opposite directions to reduce bulk. If intersecting seams were pressed open, clip the crossed seam allowances at an angle.

Seam Allowances and Guides

The *seam allowance* is the distance between the stitching line and the edge of the fabric. It's important to sew seams with a consistent width; otherwise, the project pieces won't fit together properly! Most garments are sewn with a standard ⅝-inch seam allowance, allowing a tiny bit of space for "letting out" if a garment fits too snugly. Home décor projects use ½- and ⅝-inch seam allowances, and quilt projects often use ¼-inch seams. Always check pattern pieces and instructions for seam allowance information before you start to sew.

Standard seam allowances are engraved on the stitch plate, the flat metal plate directly below the presser foot. The measurements indicate the distance from the needle to the engraved line. When stitching a seam, align the fabric edge with the appropriate engraved guideline to sew seams with a consistent width. Some machines include an optional accessory that clips onto the sewing table and acts as an extended seam guide.

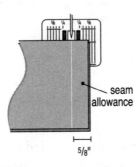

Use a seam guide or follow the stitch plate guidelines to sew consistent-width seams.

seam allowance

5/8"

SNIP IT

Make a temporary seam guide by layering painter's tape at the desired distance from the center needle position. Align the fabric edges against the layered tape to keep them aligned. When finished stitching, peel away the tape and remove any sticky residue with a cotton ball dampened with rubbing alcohol.

Some patterns may instruct you to sew a *scant* ¼- or ⅝-inch seam. This means to sew with a slightly narrower seam allowance than the given seam measurement. Instead of stitching directly on the seamline, stitch one or two threads (0.5 to 1mm) into the seam allowance to sew a scant seam. An easy way to do this is to align fabric edges against the stitch plate guide as usual, but move the needle position to the right a single step.

As suggested by the location of guides on the throat plate, seams are normally sewn with the seam allowance to the right of the needle and the bulk of the project to the left.

Trimming Seam Bulk

Sometimes seam allowances get in the way. That extra bit of material can create unwanted bulk and prevent seams from lying flat. Certain seams or seam finishes may require seam allowances to be trimmed, or graded, to reduce bulk.

After sewing and pressing a seam (and testing fit, if necessary), use shears to trim the seam allowances to a specified width. Be careful not to cut too closely to the stitched seam or into other fabric layers. If instructions don't specify a trim width, cut away about half the existing seam allowance width; be very careful if trimming seam allowances to ⅛ inch.

Grading a seam allowance creates beveled layers that lessen the chance of leaving a visible imprint of the seam on the fabric right side. Collars and cuffs, or any other spot that has multiple fabric layers, are graded to reduce bulk.

To grade, trim the seam allowance layers to different widths. The seam allowance closest to the garment or project exterior should be slightly wider than the inside seam allowance. Most trimmed and graded seams are enclosed and top- or edgestitched, so frayed and raveled fabric isn't a concern.

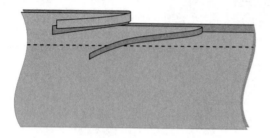

Trim and grade seam allowances to reduce seam bulk.

Uncut corner seams can create lumps and bumps in turned pieces. To reduce fabric bulk, snip off corners at a 45-degree angle, about ⅛ inch away from the seam. Make an additional 60-degree cut along each seam edge to grade the seam allowances and gradually decrease the amount of fabric in the corner area.

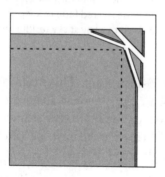

Trim and grade corners and points to reduce bulk in turned pieces.

Seams So Fine

Flat-felled, French, and zigzag are three common alternative seams. Flat-felled and French seams are self-finishing, or enclosed, seams with the raw fabric edges safely sewn inside. Zigzag seams are used on stretch fabrics, in places where fabric must have a little "give."

Flat-Felled Seam

The strong, self-finishing, nonfraying flat-felled seam, familiar to all from its presence on jeans, is used on medium- and heavyweight fabrics. Denim jeans, jackets, and other garments are constructed with flat-felled seams for durability. The finished seam is visible on the garment's right side. This seam can be bulky; use a topstitching or jeans/denim needle to pierce multiple layers of heavy fabric.

Here's how to sew a flat-felled seam:

1. Pin fabric pieces with *wrong* sides together, aligning the edges and matching any pattern construction marks. Stitch a ⅝-inch seam.

2. Trim one seam allowance to ¼ inch. Fold the remaining seam allowance in half, bringing its raw edge to meet the seamline, encasing the trimmed edge. Press and pin.

3. Straight stitch along the folded edge of the seam allowance, keeping the seam as flat as possible and the stitches parallel to the original seam.

Use contrasting thread to highlight the two lines of stitching on a flat-felled seam.

1/4"

✂ SNIP IT

Sewing over thick seams can be a challenge. The presser foot and feed dog work together to feed the fabric past the needle, so when the foot angles up over a thick seam, the feed dog can't grip the fabric, and a jam results. A height-compensating tool, such as a Jean-a-ma-jig, keeps the presser foot level when sewing over thick seams. Place the tool either in front of or behind the needle, beneath the presser foot, to keep the foot level. Stitch slowly over the bulky seam and place the needle in the down position before removing the tool.

French Seam

French seams are used on delicate light- and medium-weight sheers and other fabrics where seams and raw edges might show through the finished piece. This seam encloses fabric edges, so raw edges won't fray. Straight seams on lacy eveningwear, sheer tops, lingerie, and baby clothes are a few common candidates for French seams. The finished seam is on the fabric wrong side but may show as a darkened seamline on lightweight fabrics.

Here's how to sew a French seam:

1. Place fabrics wrong sides together and straight stitch a scant ¼ inch inside the final seamline.

2. Trim both seam allowances to a scant ⅛ inch. Fold the fabrics, right sides together, along the just-stitched seam, encasing the trimmed seam allowances. Press, and pin if necessary.

3. Straight stitch ¼ inch from the edge (the previous seamline, now folded), encasing the seam allowances. Press the finished seam to one side.

The French seam technique encloses the fabric edges for a fine, secure seam.

SNIP IT

French seams don't work on curves. As an alternative, stitch a plain seam with right sides together and stitch again, ⅛ inch from the first seam, inside the seam allowance. Trim the seam allowances close to the second row of stitches and zigzag over the raw edges to prevent fraying. The entire seam should measure less than ¼-inch wide when complete.

Zigzag Seam

Stretch fabrics are sewn with a zigzag seam, allowing the seam to stretch with the fabric. Standard, straight-stitched seams aren't as elastic and are more prone to rip or "pop" when stressed. Zigzag seams are sewn like standard seams, substituting a narrow zigzag, special stretch, or three-step zigzag stitch for the straight stitch. The zigzag is usually very narrow, but when aligning the fabric under the presser foot, be sure the stitch doesn't extend beyond the specified seam allowance. It may help to first test-stitch on a scrap of fabric and temporarily mark a new seam guideline, measuring from the needle in the zigzag's far left position.

Here's how to sew a zigzag seam:

1. Place fabrics right sides together, aligning the edges and matching any pattern notches or construction marks. Pin pieces together along the seam, placing the pins perpendicular to the seamline.

2. Select a zigzag, stretch, or triple zigzag stitch and sew along the seamline, backstitching at the seam beginning and end to secure the ends, if necessary, and removing the pins as you sew.

3. Press the fabric as sewn to set the stitches and press the finished seam to one side so the seam lies even and flat. Finish the seam allowance edges as desired.

Press zigzag seams carefully so you don't stretch or distort the fabric shape.

Project: Sweet Seamed Wrap

Mix silk, satin, and lace remnants to make an elegant evening wrap, or snuggle into a cozy cotton or lightweight flannel warmer. French or flat-felled seams make this a fun finished-edge project!

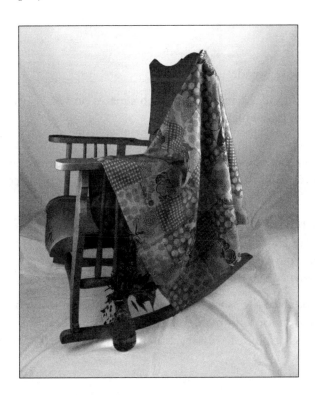

Practice seam techniques on a collection of 5-inch charm squares, sweet silks, or lovely lacey remnants.

Finished size:

Approximately 74¾×40¼ inches (flat measurement, depending on seams used)

Tools and materials:

91 5-inch squares of light- to medium-weight fabric* in a variety of colors, textures, and prints (or about 1½ yards of fabric total)

Thread

Basic machine-sewing tools

Suitable woven fabrics include light- to medium-weight cotton, flannel, lace, or silk. A lightweight knit may be used if it's not too stretchy. Yardage is based on 45-inch-wide fabric with at least 40 inches of useable width.

SEW SURPRISING

This project is "charm pack friendly." Charm packs are stacks of precut 5-inch fabric squares, usually coordinating prints from a single fabric collection.

Cutting:

1. If working with remnants or yardage, use rotary cutting tools to cut fabrics into 5-inch squares.

Construction:

Use a ½-inch seam allowance unless otherwise noted.

2. Using the following illustration as a guide, arrange the 5-inch squares on your work surface, and determine placement of individual squares.

3. Using a ½-inch French or flat-felled seam, join the 5-inch squares together in rows. You can use another seam type, but the raw edges will be visible on the inside of the wrap. Note the arrows on the illustration that indicate the pressing (or folding) direction for each seam.

   For a ½-inch French seam, place the fabrics wrong sides together and stitch ¼ inch from the raw edge. Trim both seam allowances to ⅛ inch, fold the fabrics along the seam with right sides together, and pin or press if necessary. Stitch ¼ inch from the first stitched seam, encasing the raw edges. Press the finished seam to one side.

   To piece a ½-inch flat-felled seam, place the fabrics wrong sides together and stitch a ½-inch seam. Trim one seam allowance to ¼ inch, fold the other seam allowance around the trimmed edge, and press or pin if necessary. Stitch along the folded edge to finish the seam.

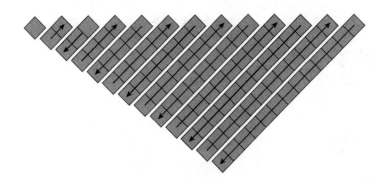

Alternate the direction of seam allowances when piecing rows of 5-inch squares.

4. Stitch the pieced rows together, matching the seams of the pieced squares and nestling the alternating seam allowances together. Align the squares' raw edges at the wrap's outer edges.

5. Place the wrap flat on a cutting surface, and align a ruler along the valleys formed by the squares along the wrap's front edge. Using a rotary cutter, trim the points, creating a straight edge.

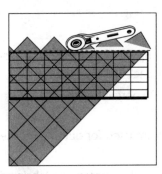

Use rotary cutting tools to trim excess fabric from the wrap's long front edge.

6. Hem the outer edges of the wrap using a double-fold hem. Prepare each edge by folding ¼ inch of raw edge to the wrong side of the wrap, and press. Fold another ¼ inch to the wrong side, encasing the raw edge, and press again, being sure to crease the fabric forming the acute angles at the two front points.

   To trim the excess fabric at the acute angles, unfold the pressed hem at one front point. Using the innermost pressed crease as a guide, mark two lines falling at 30-degree angles from the innermost point. Mark a second notched line ¼ inch closer to the outer edge. Trim along this second line, notching the point as shown, and fold the fabric to the wrong side along the first marked line. Refold the pressed hem, following the original creases. Pin if necessary. Repeat for the remaining point. The right angle at center back will not need to be trimmed.

   Straight stitch the folded hem in place close to the inner fold around the entire edge of the wrap.

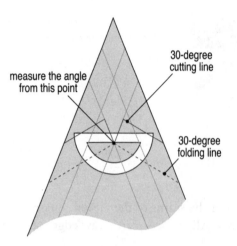

measure the angle from this point

30-degree cutting line

30-degree folding line

Using the pressed hem creases as a guide, mark folding and cutting lines at each front point.

Wear your wrap over your shoulders for an elegant evening out, or belt it like a blouse for a casual event. Add decorative stitching or button trims for an extra accent.

The Least You Need to Know

- You have many options when it comes to seaming fabrics together. Choose a seam according to the fabric type and garment or project use.
- You'll use the simplest seam, a standard seam, 90 percent of the time to stitch garments and projects.
- Standard seam allowances of ¼, ½, and ⅝ inch are used for quilting, home décor projects, and garments.
- French and flat-felled are two examples of seams that encase raw fabric edges. The fabric you choose determines which of these two seams you use.
- Zigzag seams add extra elasticity to stretch fabric seams. This helps prevent seams from "popping," or ripping out when stressed.

Fun Finishes

In This Chapter

- Simple seam finishes
- Stitched edge options
- Turned and bound edgings
- Alternatives to standard seam finishes

Have you ever heard the phrase "falling apart at the seams"? Leaving even a properly sewn seam unfinished in ravel-prone fabric will cause exactly that. Woven fabrics are prone to fraying, and seam allowances in knit fabrics can roll, making garments uncomfortable to wear. Seam finishes reduce the risk of raveling and make a finished piece look professionally made. Let's look at how it's done.

Common Seam Finishes

Seam finishes can be done in many different ways. Some completely enclose raw edges, while others leave the edges exposed. Which finish you choose depends on the type and weight of fabric you're using. Does the fabric ravel easily? How often will the finished project or garment be laundered? Will the item need to withstand a lot of wear and tear? Test seam finishes on fabric scraps to determine which one is suitable for your project.

Ordinary Cut or Raw Edges

Ordinary cut or raw edges are just what they sound like—the raw edge of the fabric is exposed on the wrong side of the seam. Sometimes this isn't a problem. If the fabric doesn't ravel easily or if the seam will be protected by a lining or encased between fabric layers, you may not need to finish the seam allowance edges. Simply stitch the seam and press the seam allowances open or to one side.

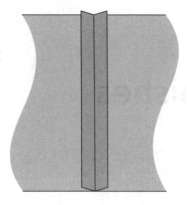

Ordinary cut edges don't always require additional finishing after the seam is stitched and can be pressed open or to one side.

Pinked Edges

Trim seam allowance edges with *pinking shears* or a wavy rotary blade to create a pinked edge. The uneven zigzag cut of the pinking shears reduces—but doesn't absolutely prevent—the risk of raveling and makes the seam allowance less likely to imprint or show on the garment right side. Pinking works well on most fabrics except lightweight knits, and is often used on dry-clean-only items. Pink seam edges on very lightweight fabrics when a sewn seam edging would add too much bulk or weight to the seam.

SEWING SENSE

Pinking shears are specialty scissors with saw-tooth blades that create a zigzag cut in the fabric. Pinked edges are less likely to ravel than smooth cuts and can be used as seam finishes or a decorative edge.

For extra antiraveling insurance, straight stitch ¼ inch from the raw edge before trimming with pinking shears. The stitching will stop any raveling, and a slightly shortened straight stitch makes the edge even more unlikely to fray.

Most pinked seam allowances are pressed open rather than to one side.

Stitched Edges

Stitched edge finishes use straight, zigzag, or overlock stitches to reduce the risk of raveling. They can be used on a variety of fabric types and weights.

If using a straight stitch, reduce the stitch length to create a tighter stitch. For a zigzag finish, choose a narrow to medium stitch width and a short stitch length. If using a medium-width plain or triple zigzag stitch, be sure the seam allowance edge doesn't tunnel, curl, or pucker under the stitches; a tension adjustment may be needed. Zigzag or straight stitch along seam allowance edges, stitching close to, but not over, the fabric edge.

An overlock stitch encases the raw fabric edge and is the stitched edge finish most likely to prevent raveling. A blind hem stitch may be substituted for the overlock stitch. Test stitch your machine's overlock and blind hem stitches on fabric scraps to see which edge finish you prefer. As with zigzag finishing, choose width and tension settings that prevent tunneling.

Choose a stitched edge finish according to fabric type, weight, and "fray factor."

straight   zigzag   overlock

Trimmed seam allowances on knit fabrics are often *serged* or overlocked together and then pressed to one side to create a neater edge. Double-stitched seams are also common on knit fabrics. The seams are stitched twice—once at the seamline, and again about $1/8$ inch into the seam allowance. Excess seam allowance is then trimmed away.

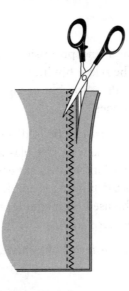

Stitch trimmed seam allowances together or double-stitch seams to keep knits under control.

SEWING SENSE

A **serger** is a type of sewing machine that stitches and trims seams at the same time. Sergers use 2, 3, 4, or 5 threads to sew seams and encase seam edges. They're often used for sewing or finishing knits as well as woven fabrics.

Turned Edges

Turned edges include clean-finished and edgestitched seam finishes. Both types of turned edges can be used on light- to medium-weight fabrics where the doubled fabric won't add too much bulk to the seam. Turned edges are best used on straight rather than curved seams because the extra fabric in the turned edge causes puckers and prevents pressing the seam allowance flat.

To stitch a clean-finished edge, press ¼ inch to the wrong side along each seam allowance edge, and straight stitch through the seam allowance only ⅛ inch from the folded edge. For an edgestitched seam finish, press ⅛ inch to the wrong side along each seam allowance edge, and straight stitch through the seam allowance only close to the folded edge. Press the turned-edge seam allowances open so the wrong side of the seam allowance isn't visible.

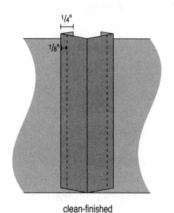

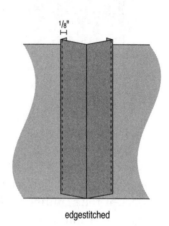

Press open clean-finished and edgestitched seam allowances.

clean-finished

edgestitched

Bound Edges

Bind seam allowances with bias tape or seam binding for a very professional look. Use sheer bias tricot binding on lightweight fabrics. Gently pull the tricot binding to determine which way it curls, and fold it around the seam allowance raw edge. Straight or zigzag stitch near the binding edge, catching all the layers with one row of stitches.

Seam binding and hem tape are stable, woven-edge tapes that can be folded in half lengthwise and applied to medium- and heavy-weight fabrics in the same way. Use bias binding instead of seam binding on curved seam allowances. The extra "give" in the bias cut eases this binding around curves, but be careful not to stretch the seam as the binding is applied. Purchased or custom-made single- and double-fold bias binding can be used on medium- and heavyweight fabrics. (Learn more about bias tape and binding in Chapter 13.)

A *Hong Kong finish* is a special type of binding that uses bias strips of lightweight silk or cotton batiste to encase the seam allowance edge.

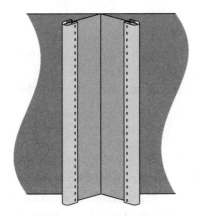

Both edges of seam binding or bias strips are turned under or finished, leaving no visible raw edges on the encased seam allowance.

Here's how to make a Hong Kong finish:

1. Align the raw edge of a bias strip with the raw edge of the seam allowance. Pin the bias strip in place.

2. Stitch the bias strip to the seam allowance, ¼ inch away from the raw edge. Be careful not to stretch the bias strip; this could distort the seam.

3. Fold the bias strip over the seam allowance, encasing the raw edge. Press, and *stitch in the ditch* of the binding seam, catching the binding on the underneath side.

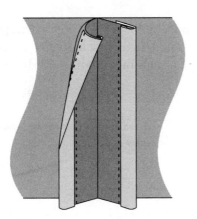

The underneath edge of the bias strip in a Hong Kong finish is left unfolded to reduce bulk.

SEWING SENSE

Stitch in the ditch means to stitch very close to, or exactly on top of, a stitched seam. With seam allowances pressed to one side, stitch along a seamline so the stitches lie on the opposite side of the seam from the seam allowances; with seam allowances pressed open, stitch exactly on the seam so the stitches disappear into the ditch. This almost-invisible stitching is used to secure facings and fabric layers.

Edgy Alternatives

If standard seam finishes are too fussy for your taste, don't despair. Alternatives to the tried-and-true ways of finishing a seam exist. While some of these suggestions might not merit your mother's approval, in some sewing situations these fast and fun ideas provide the perfect sewing solution.

Frayed Edges

Don't be afraid to fray. We know, this sounds completely contradictory to the ravel risks we've been warning you about, and ... well ... it is. Any time a frayed edge or element is introduced, you limit the life of a stitched piece. But the truth is, not all garments or projects are destined to be family heirlooms, and you can control the fray.

One way to control the fray is to add an extra line of shortened straight or zigzag stitching $1/8$ to $1/4$ inch into the seam allowance, as you would for a stitched edge finish. Use this double-stitched seam technique in places where you want the seam allowance and frayed edge to show on the garment or project's right side. Pant hems, sleeve edges, or skirt endings of edgy, grunge-look or 1970s-inspired garments are great candidates for frayed seam edges. You can take this a step further by purposely constructing garments seam side out (wrong sides together) so all seam allowances are exposed. (We did say your mom probably wouldn't approve!)

Exaggerate a frayed seam allowance by adding extra width before cutting pattern pieces and purposely fraying 1 or 2 inches of fabric to create a thin fringe. Double-stitch the seam to help control the fray, and if the fringe is long enough, tie groups of strands in overhand knots, if desired.

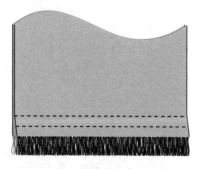

An extra line of stitching helps secure a frayed seam allowance.

Fusible Tape

Fusible tape is a fast way to control a seam finish. Made from fusible web—a fibrous, man-made adhesive material that melts and sticks when heated—fusible tape is available in a variety of widths and weights and requires no sewing. When placed between two pieces of fabric and heated with an iron, the tape melts and fuses the fabrics together.

Some fusible tapes are wrapped in release paper that keeps the tape from sticking where you don't want it. Cut the tape and paper to the needed length and place it, web side down, on the wrong side of the seam or hem allowance. Follow the manufacturer's instructions to adhere the first surface. Peel off the release paper and fold the seam or hem allowance smoothly over the tape. Place a thermal pressing sheet, press cloth, or parchment paper over the work to protect the fabric and fuse with a heated iron, following the manufacturer's instructions.

PINPRICK

Fusible web can quickly gunk up an iron! When working with fusibles, use a thermal pressing sheet or parchment paper to protect your pressing surface and keep your iron clean. Afterward, use an iron cleaner to remove residue and avoid transferring "glue gunk" to other surfaces.

Use fusible tape to stabilize a seam allowance, secure a quick hem, or make quick repairs. (See Chapter 11 to learn how to apply this technique to appliqué.) Always test fusible tape on fabric scraps before using on a garment or project. Some fusible products can show through and stiffen or darken fabrics.

Lettuce or Celery Edges

Named for its crinkled, ruffled look, this edge technique is often used at the neckline, cuff, or hem of children's clothing, nightwear, and special occasion garments. A tight zigzag, satin, or overlock stitch is used to finish the stretched fabric edge. Knit fabrics that return to their original shape after being stretched are the best candidates for this technique, but you can lettuce the bias edge of some woven materials, too.

Use a tight stitch length, such as a satin stitch length of less than 0.5mm, to cover the fabric edge, or a longer stitch to let the fabric show through. The edge finish works by putting enough thread in the fabric to push the material's fibers apart, so a shorter stitch length produces more ruffles. However, too short a stitch may make the finish too stiff, so be sure to experiment with fabric scraps before trying this technique on a garment or project.

Here's how to lettuce an edge:

1. Use the same thread in the needle and bobbin. Choose a 3mm or wider stitch width and a stitch length of your choice. Place the fabric edge under the presser foot so the right swing of the stitch falls just past the fabric edge.

2. Hold the fabric in front and in back of the needle, stretching the fabric as you sew, to create the ruffled edge. Be sure the fabric isn't pushed through the stitch plate needle hole. The edge of the fabric may roll slightly, adding to the finish's frilly appearance.

3. Restitch the edge two or three times, if necessary, to completely cover the fabric and prevent the fabric from fraying. Work the thread tails back through the stitched edge with a hand needle when sewing is complete.

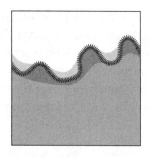

Give a girly twirl to refashioned T-shirts with fun lettuce edging.

Stretching thin strips of knit fabrics causes the knit to curl in on itself, creating a cord that won't ravel or fray. Use this fast, fun technique to create quick fringed ends on T-shirts and fleece knit afghans.

Project: Lettuce-Edge T-Shirt Scarf

Create a two-tone effect with coordinating T-shirt colors. A contrasting thread color accents the lettuced edge.

Create a lettuce-edge scarf from upcycled Ts or abandoned knits.

Finished size:

    Approximately 8×70 inches, depending on T-shirt size

Tools and materials:

    2 light- to medium-weight adult-size T-shirts in coordinating colors*

    Thread

    Basic machine-sewing tools

*T-shirts should be in good condition without excess wear or holes. Additional fabric may be needed if cutting around printed elements.

Cutting:

1. With one T-shirt pressed flat on a cutting surface, use a rotary cutter and ruler to trim away the hemmed bottom edge and cut the upper shirt just below the sleeves to remove the sleeves, shoulders, and neckline.

2. Cut 8-inch-wide strips across the T-shirt body from one side fold to the other. Adjust strip width, if necessary. You'll need at least two strips for one side of the scarf.

If desired, adjust cuts to spotlight a logo or other printed element on the shirt.

3. Cut through one side fold on each strip, or trim the sewn side seam from one edge of each cut piece, creating long, flat, single-thickness strips.

4. Repeat steps 1 through 3 with the second T-shirt.

Construction:

Use a ½-inch seam allowance, unless otherwise noted.

5. Place two cut strips wrong sides together, aligning one short edge. Pin and sew along the short edge using a flat-felled or French seam (see Chapter 6), enclosing the seam allowances. Repeat for the remaining two cut strips.

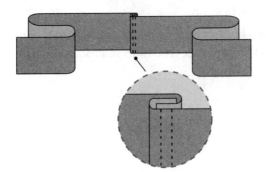

Piece cut strips together along their short edges to create the scarf front and back.

6. Press the seams and place the strips wrong sides together, aligning the edges. Pin the strips' long edges together. If one strip is longer than the other, use a rotary cutter and ruler to trim the excess length.

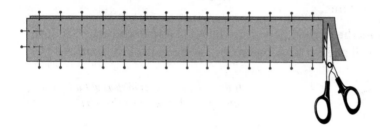

Pin strips together, being careful not to stretch or distort the fabric.

7. Lettuce edge along the scarf's outer edges, creating a ruffled edge and stitching the two sides of the scarf together.

SNIP IT

For a masculine look, substitute these instructions after step 2: pin the scarf front and back with right sides together, trimming any excess length. Straight stitch ¼ inch from the long edges. Turn the scarf to the right side, and press to set the seams. Cut the scarf's short ends into ½-inch-wide fringe, making each cut 4 inches long. Pull each strand of fringe to curl the fringed ends, if desired.

Refashioned T-shirt scarves give extra life to secondhand shirts and make a one-of-a-kind accessory.

The Least You Need to Know

- A seam finish can extend the life of a garment or project by preventing seams from raveling. Some seam finishes give garments a couture look.
- Plain, pinked, and stitched edges are among the easiest and fastest seam finishes. Turned edges are a tidy way to finish straight seams.
- Choose a seam binding according to the fabric weight and the type of seam. Never add extra bulk to a seam with a weighty seam binding.
- Alternative methods to traditional seam finishes include intentionally frayed edges, fusible web options, and decoratively stitched finishes that embellish seams and hems.

Throw Me a Curve

In This Chapter

- Simple tricks for sewing curved shapes
- Easing seams to fit
- Clipping and notching curved seam allowances
- Techniques for sewing corner seams

Caution, curves ahead! Fitting curved pieces to straight edges or smoothly seaming two curves together may look like mission impossible to the beginning sewist. But with a few simple tips, you'll be sewing necklines, waistbands, sleeves, and shaped seams like a pro!

Curves Ahead!

Curved shapes can vary, from gentle waistband arcs to tight armhole edges. Some curved seams join identical edges, while others pair opposite shapes that must be aligned. Most curves can be classified as either *convex* or *concave* shapes. A convex curve extends outward, like the surface of a ball. The outer edge of a collar and a rounded skirt hem are convex curves. Concave curves extend inward, like the inside of a bowl. Armhole edges and necklines are concave curves. An easy way to remember the difference between convex and concave is to cup your hand to "make a cave." The curled palm of your hand forms a concave shape. The back of your hand forms a convex curve.

Keep these tips in mind when stitching curves:

Reduce the stitch length and sew slowly for more control. Use your hands to help the pattern pieces hold their shape.

Be careful not to stretch the fabric. This could distort the fabric, causing neck or arm openings to gap.

Focus on aligning the curved seam allowance edges at a single stitch guide point directly to the right of the needle. Don't distort the fabric by trying to align it against a long seam guide marking.

Stop and start stitching, or "pause and pivot," as needed to realign the fabric edge with the stitch guide point. The stitched seam should look like a smooth arc, not a series of straight segments joined together, so it's better to take just two or three stitches between small pivots.

Use a pressing ham to press and shape stitched curves, clipping or notching the seam allowances to help the seams lie flat.

On most sewing machines, the fabric lying against the feed dog travels faster than the fabric against the presser foot. When sewing curves, place the convex curve against the feed dog to help ease pieces together.

Same-Shape Curves

Same-shape curves are used to add facings to necklines, finish armhole edges, construct collars, and create pockets. Sewing two same-shape curved pieces together isn't hard—it just takes a little patience!

To join same-shape curves, place fabric pieces right sides together, aligning the raw edges, notches, and seam ends. Next, pin the two pieces together. The fabrics should lie flat together along the curve. Place the pinned pieces beneath the presser foot. Align the seam allowance at the beginning of the seam with the appropriate seam guide marking on the stitch plate.

Using a shorter stitch length (1.5 to 2mm, or 12 to 16 stitches per inch), stitch slowly along the seam. Focus on a single point on the seam guide mark to the right of the machine needle and keep the fabric flat against the machine bed. Guide the fabric in a gentle arc around the curve. On tight curves, stop frequently with the needle down and pivot slightly while slowly working your way around the curve. Don't try to "straighten" the curved edge by pulling the fabric edge into a straight line because that could introduce tucks and puckers into the seam.

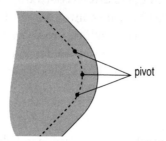

Pause and pivot around same-shape curves to stitch smooth seams.

SNIP IT

Modify the pivot point technique you learned to turn a corner in Chapter 2 to stitch smoothly around curves. Stop stitching and lower the needle down into the fabric. Raise the presser foot and slightly pivot the fabric to realign the seam. Lower the presser foot and continue sewing. For a smooth seamline, pause and pivot as often as every 2 or 3 stitches to make a series of slight adjustments rather than sharp turns.

When same-shape curves are sewn and then turned back on themselves (for example, when making a curved collar), the extra fullness or short length of the raw edge relative to the seamline becomes an issue. If the curves are convex, cut notches into the seam allowance at regular intervals to remove the excess fabric, so the seam allowance lies smooth and flat inside the turned shape.

For concave curves, the issue is too little fabric at the raw edge; clip the seam allowances at regular intervals so the edges can spread apart inside the finished shape. Avoid clipping through both layers of seam allowances at the same spot, as this could weaken the seam; instead, stagger clips between the two seam allowances.

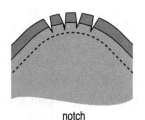

notch

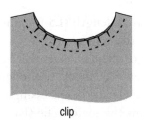

clip

Notch outer (convex) curves to eliminate full-ness; clip inner (concave) curves to allow the fabric to spread.

Easing into It

Sewing a curved piece to a straight edge is all about *easing* one piece to fit another, or "easing to fit." It's a lot like nudging or stretching slightly. The curved piece may be slightly longer than the straight edge or the seamlines may be exactly the same length, but the raw edges of differently shaped pieces won't match.

Curves sewn to straight edges, even when the seamlines are the same length, are always eased into place for a smooth join without puckers or pleats. Pressing, often with steam, is sometimes the essential finish to easing in fullness along a seam.

SEWING SENSE

In sewing terms, **ease** means "a little bit extra." It may be the extra fabric built into a pattern to allow easy movement when wearing the completed garment, or it may be the process of working a little extra fabric into a seam to accomplish fitting. An **ease stitch** is one or two lines of extra-long straight stitching, similar to gathering, used to fit a slightly longer seam edge to a shorter one.

To sew a convex curve to a straight edge, place the pieces right sides together, matching notches, seam endings, and raw edges. Pin the pieces together, first at the notches and then at the seam endings. Next, match and pin the center of each piece. Continue to pin the two pieces together, evenly distributing any fullness to ease the edges together. It may help to hold the two pieces in a slight curve while pinning, and always remember that it's the seamline that must be smooth, not the cut edge.

On longer seams, it may help to "divide and conquer" while pinning the seam. That is, pin first at the center point of the seam and then at the quarter points. Continue dividing and pinning the remaining portions of the seam into smaller and smaller sections until the excess fabric is eased into place.

In some cases, an *ease stitch* may help fit the two pieces together. Before pinning, use a longer-than-normal straight stitch length (between 3 and 5mm) to stitch along the seamline of the convex curved piece and again about ¼ inch closer to the seam allowance raw edge. Pull the bobbin threads of the two lines of stitching to very slightly gather and shorten the longer edge before matching and pinning the pieces together. The convex, or longer, piece should still be smooth at the seamline, but the gathering stitches will compress its threads, accomplishing the ease.

Once the seam is pinned, use a shorter stitch length (1.5 to 2mm, or 12 to 16 stitches per inch) to stitch the two pieces together, placing the convex piece against the feed dogs and the straight piece against the presser foot; the action of the feed dogs will help ease the curve into place. Stitch slowly, removing the pins as you sew. Be careful not to stitch any tucks or gathers into the seam. Press the seam over the curved surface of a pressing ham, notching the seam allowance if necessary to remove bulk and allow the seam to lie flat.

For easier removal of ease or gathering stitches, position the stitches just past the seamline or just inside the seam allowance. Stitches past the seamline will be visible in the finished garment, making them easy to identify and remove, while stitches in the seam allowance can even be left in place.

When sewing concave curves to straight pieces, the objective is the opposite: to gently stretch the curve to fit. The concave piece will be shorter at the raw edge than its mate, although the seamlines will be the same length. An example is sewing a circular skirt waistline to a waistband, as in the project later in this chapter.

To fit a concave curve into place, the seam allowance must be clipped almost all the way to the seamline to allow the raw edge to spread. Before clipping, *staystitch* the curve by sewing ⅛ inch inside the seamline with a shortened straight stitch. Clip the seam allowance at regular intervals, usually ¼ to ⅛ inch, snipping to *but not through* the staystitching. Pin the curved edge to its mate, and sew as before.

SEWING SENSE

Staystitching is a line of straight stitches sewn ⅛ inch inside the seamline through a single fabric layer to stabilize curves and corners that will be clipped and prevent stretching and distortion as the project is assembled. Use a short stitch length (1.5 to 2mm, or 12 to 16 stitches per inch) for staystitching.

For the smoothest curves, keep seam allowance notches and clips close together and evenly spaced. If the seam allowance is just ¼ inch wide, trim with pinking shears to make perfectly spaced notches for a fabulously smooth finish.

Use pinking shears to notch and trim seam allowances in one cut.

Complex Curves

Complex curves are made of two curves moving in opposite directions: one convex and the other concave. Set-in sleeves and princess seams in fitted tops are the most common examples of this type of curve. Complex curves add shaping to a garment or project and require extra care to join smoothly.

To fit two curved pieces together, staystitch just inside the seamline on the concave piece to reinforce the seam. Clip the seam allowance every ¼ to ½ inch, being careful not to cut through the staystitching.

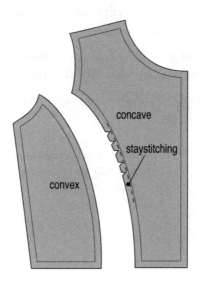

concave

staystitching

convex

Staystitch and clip the seam allowance of the concave piece before pinning two curved pieces together.

Place the pieces right sides together, matching seam ends and notches. If the curved pieces did not have notches or other markings, determine the center of each curve by folding the piece in half and marking the midpoint in the seam allowance with a fabric pencil or marker. Unfold the fabric and match the center points. The clipped curve will spread to fit the nonclipped piece at the raw edges. Add more clips as necessary and pin in place.

With the clipped (concave) piece facing up, stitch the seam, making sure the staystitching falls within the seam allowance. Check the stitched seam for any tucks or puckering, and press the seam using a pressing ham. Notch the convex seam allowance if necessary to reduce bulk and allow the seam to lie flat.

SEW SURPRISING

Curved seams with narrow seam allowances are easier to align and sew together. The narrower seam allowance is less likely to stretch or distort, and if it's no more than a fat ⅛ inch wide, it may not require clipping to lie flat.

Turning Corners

Like curves, corner seams give shape to garments and projects. As you learned in Chapter 2, you can place the needle down and pivot the fabric to stitch outside corner seams. Use the same technique, with a slight modification, to stitch inside corner seams:

1. Place fabric pieces right sides together. Lightly mark the corner point where seam allowances cross on the fabric wrong side, and pin the pieces together along the corner's inside edge.

2. Stitch along the seam edge, sewing from the far seam edge toward the corner, and stop with the needle down at the marked corner point.

3. Raise the presser foot and pivot the fabric around the needle, realigning the raw edges with seam guide markings. Lower the presser foot and finish stitching the seam.

4. Clip the inside corner, stopping just short of the stitching line, and trim seam allowances before turning and pressing the seam.

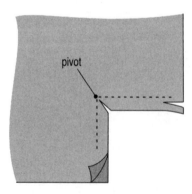

Pivot at the corner and align the next seam section. Clip the corner and trim the seam allowance as needed.

Very sharp pivot points, such as at collar corners, leave no room for seam allowances in the turned piece. Instead of making one sharp turn, stop sewing just shy of the pivot point and partially pivot the fabric. Take two or three very short diagonal stitches across the corner and pivot again to align the needle with the next seam segment. Trim and grade the seam allowance at the point. The slightly blunted point will actually appear sharper than one with a single pivot point.

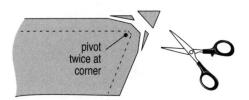

Stitch diagonally across a corner point. Trim and grade seam allowances to avoid a lumpy point.

Project: Half-Circle Skirt

Two measurements and some fabulous fabric are almost all you need to make this flattering flared skirt. Practice zipper insertion and waistband techniques, and you can wear your homework when you're finished!

Sew a curved edge to a straight waistband to make this fun, flared skirt.

Finished size:

Variable

Tools and materials:

45-inch-wide woven fabric (amount determined by measurements)

Fusible interfacing (purchase 4 inches more than your waist measurement)

One 7-inch zipper

One skirt hook-and-eye closure

Pattern drafting paper, wrapping paper, or other wide paper

Scrap of corrugated cardboard

String or yarn

Push pin

Thread

Basic sewing equipment

Make the pattern:

1. You'll need two measurements to make a pattern for this skirt. First, measure your waist, keeping the measuring tape parallel to the ground. Next, measure from your waist to the desired skirt length, passing the tape measure over the fullest part of your hips. Use your waist measurement to determine your waist circle radius using the following formula:

   (waist measurement + $1\frac{1}{2}$ inches) $\times 2 = A$

   $A \div 3.14 = B$ (round to the nearest $\frac{1}{8}$)

   $B \div 2 = C$ (waist circle radius)

2. Use a ruler or yardstick to draw two sets of lines $\frac{1}{2}$ inch apart, with each set perpendicular to the other. Be sure the lines intersect at a 90-degree angle.

3. Measuring from the point where the seamlines intersect, mark the waist circle radius along one seamline. Measuring from the marked point, mark the desired skirt length along the same seamline. Using the seamline intersection as an anchor point, draw two quarter-circle arcs with a string compass.

SNIP IT

To make an impromptu compass, tie a string around a pencil. Use a pushpin in a scrap of cardboard to anchor the string at the center point, and holding the string taut, draw the circle's arc with the pencil.

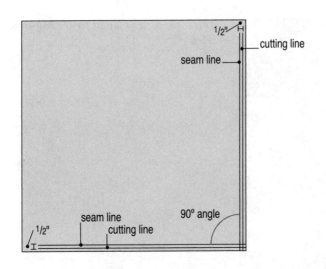

The seamlines should be ½ inch inside and parallel to the outer cutting lines.

4. Using a ruler and pencil, add ½-inch seam allowances to the waistline and hem curves. Measure from the cutting line intersection to the bottom of the hem allowance. You will need approximately twice this much fabric for one skirt.

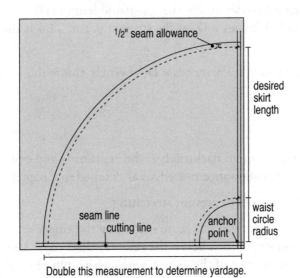

Double this measurement to determine yardage.

Plug in your calculations to draft the half-circle skirt pattern and sketch the ½-inch seam allowances.

5. Cut out the pattern along the cutting lines.

Cutting:

6. Place the fabric right side up in a single layer. Use the pattern to cut two skirt pieces, arranging the pieces as shown.

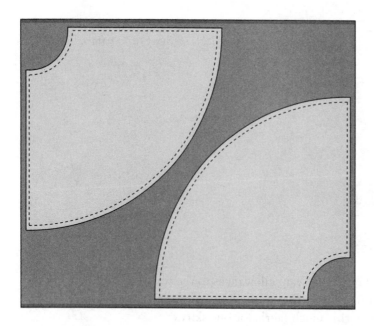

This is the pattern layout for the half-circle skirt.

7. Add 4 inches to the waist measurement to determine the waistband length (D). From the scrap fabric, cut a rectangle 3 inches × D on the straight grain. This is the waistband.

8. From the fusible interfacing, cut a rectangle 1⅛ inches × D – ¾ inch; this is the waistband interfacing.

Construction:

Use a ½-inch seam allowance unless otherwise noted. Backstitch at the beginning and end of each seam, except where indicated. Finish seam allowance raw edges as detailed in Chapter 7.

9. Staystitch ⅜ inch from the waistline curves to prevent stretching.

10. Pin the skirt pieces together along one straight side seam edge. Lay the zipper on the pinned seam allowances with the top stop 1 inch below the raw waistline edge. Mark the location of the zipper stop (at the bottom of the zipper teeth) with a pin or chalk. Remove the zipper.

11. Sew the side seam from the mark to the bottom edge of the skirt. Switch to a 4mm long straight stitch, and sew from the waistline edge to the zipper mark. Do not backstitch at either end. Press the side seam open. This is the left side of the skirt; mark the skirt front with a safety pin or piece of tape to avoid confusion later.

12. Following the instructions in Chapter 14, use the lapped zipper technique to set a zipper into the seam. Remove the basting stitches.

13. Pin and sew the right side seam and press open the seam.

SEW SURPRISING

We give instructions later in this section for applying the waistband in the traditional manner, plus alternative directions for a timesaver that requires no hand stitching.

14. Fold the waistband fabric in half lengthwise, with wrong sides together, and press. Open the fabric, and lay the waistband interfacing on the fabric wrong side, aligning one long edge of the interfacing with the center crease. Fuse the interfacing to the fabric, following the manufacturer's instructions.

15. Press the seam allowance to the wrong side along the long, noninterfaced edge. This will be the inside of the waistband.

16. Pin the interfaced long edge of the waistband to the skirt with right sides together. Leave ½ inch of the waistband free at the front side of the zipper; the waistband will extend 2 inches beyond the back side of the zipper. Sew the waistband to the skirt.

17. Fold the waistband in half lengthwise, with right sides together, and pin the short ends. Open the pressed seam allowance beyond the back side of the zipper, and pin the waistband edges together there. Sew the back end of the waistband, pivoting at the corner and continuing to stitch along the waistband extension, connecting with the previous seam. Sew the front end of the waistband even with the front side of the zipper placket.

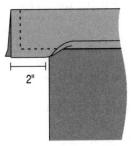

With right sides together, stitch the waistband ends, pivoting at the corner to align the stitching with the waistband seam.

18. Trim the corners to reduce bulk, and turn the waistband right side out. Use a point turner or similar notion to work the corners into place gently. Grade the waist seam allowances and press the seam toward the waistband.

19. Pin the pressed edge of the waistband to the skirt wrong side at the seamline, enclosing the seam allowances. Slipstitch the fold to the skirt, enclosing the seam allowances.

Alternative waistband:

For the alternative waistband mentioned earlier, substitute these steps:

15. Press the seam allowance to the wrong side along the long, interfaced edge. This will be the outside of the waistband.

16. Pin the noninterfaced long edge of the waistband to the skirt, placing the waistband right side against the skirt wrong side. Leave ½ inch of the waistband free at the front side of the zipper; the waistband will extend 2 inches beyond the back side of the zipper. Sew the waistband to the skirt.

Steps 17, 18, and 19 are the same.

20. Pin the pressed edge of the waistband to the skirt right side at the seamline, enclosing the seam allowances. Edgestitch the waistband fold to the skirt.

21. Sew the hook of the hook-and-eye closure to the waistband wrong side on the front end above the zipper placket. With the zipper closed, determine the position for the eye and sew the eye to the right side of the back waistband.

22. Hang the skirt by the waistband from a coat hanger and leave it overnight.

> **PINPRICK**
>
> We know you'll really want to go right to wearing your new creation. But remember: those bias edges may stretch! If you hem the skirt before allowing it to stretch and relax, the hem will become unattractively wavy.

23. Try on the skirt and have a friend mark the hem with chalk or pins by measuring from the floor to the desired hemline. Add ½ inch below the marks for hem allowance and trim any excess fabric.

24. Press ¼ inch to the wrong side twice around the skirt bottom. Edgestitch the hem to complete the skirt.

Got the clothes-making bug? Learn about patterns, measurements, and more in Part 5.

The Least You Need to Know

- Curved and corner seams are two ways to shape garments and projects. Sewing curves may be intimidating at first but can be accomplished with a little practice and patience.
- Slight differences in pattern pieces can be eased away by evenly distributing extra fullness over the length of the seam.
- "Divide and conquer" when pinning long seam sections by continually halving the excess fabric sections and pinning them to the corresponding midpoint on the shorter edge.
- "Pause and pivot" is a useful technique for sewing curves and corners. Pivot at multiple points to stitch smooth curves, or make an abrupt change in direction to turn a sharp corner.
- Seams that are stitched correctly won't lie flat if the seam allowance is rippled or strained. Eliminate bulk by cutting notches, or clip curves to allow the seam allowance to spread.

Sweet Shapes

Part

3

Part 3 is all about turning flat fabric into sculpted shapes. You learn to add textural surface treatments, such as pleats, tucks, and darts, which can also contour fabric to fit body curves. You discover the difference between gathering and ruffles, and explore a number of techniques and applications for each. Next, we examine different ways to appliqué—there are more methods than you might think!

Projects include a hip Hobo Bag accented with topstitched tucks, a Sweet Shirred Summer Dress with shirred bodice, and, for the eco-minded, a reverse appliqué Trendy Tank made from re-purposed T-shirts.

We've outlined specific techniques to make the projects in each chapter, but by all means, experiment! Prefer pleats to tucks? Go for it! Not so sweet on shirring? Substitute something else. Playing with possibilities is part of the fun of sewing, and we encourage you to strike out in your own creative direction!

Pleats, Tucks, and Darts

In This Chapter

- Contouring flat fabric
- Folding fabric into pleats and tucks
- Using darts to shape garments
- Texturizing fabric

Fabric is flat, but we aren't! So to shape and contour flat fabric into comfortable clothes that fit the curves of your body, or to add function to home décor projects, use pleats, tucks, and darts. Accurate marking and stitching is a must for these techniques.

Pay attention to fabric type. These shaping methods yield best results in light- to medium-weight fabrics, while heavyweight fabric can become stiff and bulky. Some techniques may detract from boldly printed designs, and extra yardage may be needed. Stitch purely decorative pleats and tucks before cutting to avoid distorting pattern pieces.

Pleats Are a Kick

A *pleat* is a measured fold that creates and controls fabric fullness. Pleats can be flippant and fun in schoolgirl skirts, or sophisticated and tailored on the back of a business suit. Unpressed pleats have a soft, gathered effect, while pressed pleats are sharp and crisp. The space between pleats and the depth of each pleat may be consistent or vary, depending on the desired finished look.

On patterns, pleats are indicated by pairs of solid fold lines and dashed placement lines, often connected by an arrow that indicates the fold's direction. Pleat markings need to be visible on the right side of the fabric, so when marking, use a fine-line chalk marker or other completely removable tool to transfer the lines to the fabric. Consider using two different colors to differentiate between the dashed and solid pattern lines. Mark accurately; errors multiply quickly across a row of pleats! For pleats that are topstitched, also indicate a release point (the spot where stitching stops and fabric falls freely from the fold) for each pleat.

To form a pleat, work with one set of lines (one pleat) at a time. Fold the fabric, wrong sides together, along the fold line and bring the fold to meet the pleat-placement line. Pin the fabric layers in place. A second fold is created by default when the pleat is made. Baste the folded pleat in place or temporarily secure the folded fabric with several large diagonal hand stitches. If the finished pleat will be edgestitched, keep the basting stitches away from the fold.

SNIP IT

Whether the pleats will be crisp or soft, edgestitched or not, always baste or pin them in place for a few inches along the length of the fold. If left unsecured, the pleats will shift and hang unevenly.

A line of stitching inside the seam allowance permanently anchors the pleats in place. Depending on the finish you want, you can leave the pleats unpressed for a casual look or press and stitch them for a sophisticated feel. The outer and inner folds of a pleat may be edgestitched to permanently hold a sharp crease, or the securing stitches may be hidden inside the fold. Complete hems before finishing pleats and press pleats before stitching the folded edges.

Crisp pleats require firm pressing. Cover the fabric with a damp press cloth to add crease-setting moisture and to avoid making the fabric shiny when steam-pressing pleats. If necessary, pressure-set the folds by covering warm, just-pressed pleats with a tailor's *clapper*. Apply pressure to the clapper and leave it in place until the pressed piece cools.

SEWING SENSE

A **clapper** is a wooden block tailors use to pressure-set folds and creases. The clapper is placed over an item immediately after it's been steam-pressed, and pressure is applied. The wooden clapper absorbs the heat as the fabric cools, creating a more permanent fold or crease.

To set unpressed pleats, pin the pleated fabric to a padded ironing surface and steam pleats in place by holding a hot steam iron just above the fabric. The steam should penetrate the fabric to set its shape without any weight or pressure from the iron. Allow the fabric to cool before moving.

Knife or Side Pleat

Knife, or side, pleats are a series of folds facing the same direction and usually uniform in size. The folds lie flat at the seam and flare out below, making this pleat a favorite for many skirt styles. Girl's school uniforms, cheerleader skirts, and Scottish kilts feature knife pleats.

Knife pleats are made using a 3-to-1 ratio. That means 3 inches of fabric yields 1 inch of finished pleat. A 45-inch length of fabric will make a 15-inch pleated piece.

Construct knife pleats as directed earlier in this chapter, using the fold and placement lines from the pattern. For ½-inch-deep pleats, the fold line will be 1 inch away from the corresponding placement line. The spacing between pleats is usually at least ½ inch, or the width of one pleat, to avoid the thickness of overlapping pleat layers.

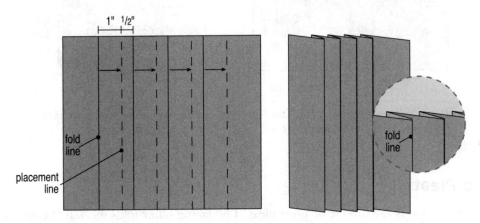

With knife pleats, 1½ inches of fabric yields a ½-inch pleat.

Box Pleat

A *box pleat* is actually two knife pleats, side by side, facing in opposite directions. On the right side of the project, the visible folds face away from each other. On the wrong side, two inner folds face each other, meeting at a center line beneath the outer folds. This pushes the pleat outward for more dimension than knife pleats alone. Box pleats add fullness to skirts, shirts, and blouses and are often used for upholstery, window treatments, and home décor projects. Like knife pleats, box pleats follow a 3-to-1 ratio: every 3 inches of fabric yields a 1-inch pleat.

To make a box pleat, place fabric right side up and mark the center line of the box pleat plus two fold lines equal distances apart on each side of the center line. The two marks closest to the center line are outer fold lines. The outermost marks indicate the inner folds.

Form one side of the pleat by folding the fabric, wrong sides together, along the outer fold line. Next, fold the fabric, right sides together, along the inner fold line, bringing the inner fold to meet the center line. Pin in place and repeat on the opposite side to complete the entire box pleat.

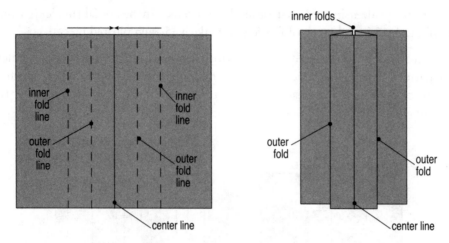

To quickly form a box pleat, pinch the inner fold lines together beneath the center line, folding the fabric at the outer fold lines.

Inverted Pleat

An *inverted pleat* is the reverse of a box pleat. The facing outer folds meet at the pleat center point on the fabric right side, while underneath, the inner folds point in opposite directions. This pushes fullness to the inside of the pleat, creating a hidden panel that's perfect for showcasing contrasting fabric. When a row of box pleats is placed side by side, inverted pleats automatically form between them. Like box pleats, inverted pleats are used for garments, window treatments, and home décor projects.

To make an inverted pleat, mark the center and fold lines, just as you would for a box pleat. The two marks closest to the center line are inner fold lines for the underneath folds, and the outermost marks are outer fold lines for the top, facing folds. Fold the fabric, wrong sides together, along the outermost lines. Bring the outer folds together, aligning them at the center line and allowing the fabric to fold along the inner fold lines. Pin the folds in place. Finish inverted pleats by pressing and stitching along the edges of the two top folds, securing the folds together at the bottom line of stitching.

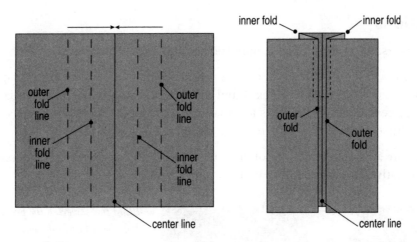

To finish inverted pleats, press folds and secure pleats in place by partially stitching down the folded edges.

Tucks

Tucks are stitched folds of fabric. Tucks vary in width and spacing, from narrow accents on heirloom garments to wide, functional bands that double as built-in bag pockets. Decorative tucks are completely stitched along their length. Partially stitched tucks, called *released tucks*, control fabric fullness in a manner similar to pleats but are stitched either inside or outside garments rather than simply folded and pressed. Released tucks are used to add extra room at the front waist of pants and skirts.

Like pleats, tucks require extra yardage. As a general rule, you'll need yardage twice the finished fabric width for equally spaced tucks, and three times the finished width if tucks touch each other. Tucks are usually folded along the firmer lengthwise grain but can be placed crosswise instead.

SNIP IT

Horizontal (crosswise) tucks can be used to extend the life of children's clothes. Simply remove tucks to lengthen the hems as children grow.

To make a single tuck, place the fabric right side up and mark two lines *twice* as far apart as the desired tuck depth. For example, to create a $1/2$-inch tuck, mark two lines 1 inch apart. Fold the fabric wrong sides together, aligning the two marked lines. Pin and press along the folded edge. Stitch along the marked line, unfold the fabric, and press the tuck to one side.

Tuck Variations

Modify the versatile tuck to create a multitude of interesting variations.

Blind tucks are a series of tucks sewn close together so the fold of one tuck overlaps and hides the stitching line of the previous tuck. Blind tucks can be any width; the essential characteristic is that the space between the tucks is less than the tuck depth. Some blind tucks are spaced so the tuck width appears to gradually increase (or decrease).

Spaced tucks are arranged so an area of plain fabric is visible between tucks. Spaced tucks are used as decorative elements on shirt bodices, skirts, and sleeves.

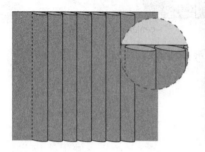 

blind tucks   spaced tucks

Blind tucks overlap the previous tuck's stitching. Spaced tucks do not.

Snip-fringed tucks are made by repeatedly cutting the folded tuck perpendicular to the stitching line. Cut the fringe as wide or narrow as you like, at same or varied intervals. To make a double-layered fringe, cut the tuck apart at the fold before fringing. Woven-fabric fringed tucks will fray with repeated washings.

Go a step further by removing the lengthwise threads along the fold to create a *raveled fringe tuck*. Use a long pin or needle to pick and pull threads from the weave. Stabilize the fringe and prevent further raveling by adding a line of zigzag stitching at the base of the fringe.

Snip or fringe tucks to create textural accents.

snip-fringed tucks

raveled fringe tucks

Topstitched and Tied Tucks

The folded fabric edges that tucks create can be manipulated in a number of ways. *Topstitched* (or cross-stitched) tucks are made by sewing over tucked fabric. Alternate tuck direction between rows of topstitching to make undulating folds that seem to ripple back and forth.

The folded fabric edges of *tied tucks* are hand tacked by bringing the needle up at the stitched edge and then through the folded layers of the tuck to emerge through the folded edge. The thread is pulled tight to gather the tuck and secured in place with whipstitches.

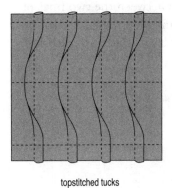

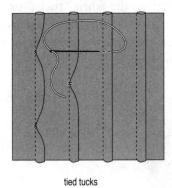

Topstitch or tie the folded edges to add interest to plain tucks.

topstitched tucks   tied tucks

SEW SURPRISING

Want to add tucks to a pattern that doesn't include them? Rather than altering the pattern, embellish the fabric first. Begin with a block of fabric larger than the pattern piece, add the tucks, and lay the pattern piece on the embellished fabric. Mark around the pattern piece, and staystitch ¼ inch inside the marked line to stabilize the tucks. Cut out the pattern pieces, and make the project according to the pattern instructions.

Pintucks

Pintucks are very narrow tucks that are "only as wide as a pin." These delicate ¹⁄₁₆- to ⅛-inch tucks are often combined with lace insertions on heirloom garments, but they can be made in any lightweight fabric. Work along the straight grain of the fabric for best results.

Because pintucks are so small, they're usually marked with a single line to indicate the fold. To create a pintuck, fold the fabric, wrong sides together, along the desired tuck line. Pin and press if necessary. Straight stitch ¹⁄₁₆ to ⅛ inch from the fold, using a blind hem presser foot to guide the stitching if desired. Repeat for each pintuck.

Zigzag machines and twin needles can be used in combination to create mock pintucks. Twin needles have two needles attached to a single shaft. The needle makes two parallel lines of stitching in a single pass. Pintucking feet have grooves in the bottom of the foot that help guide parallel rows of stitching. Previously stitched tucks ride in the grooves, and the foot acts as a spacing guide.

> **SEW SURPRISING**
>
> Two size numbers are listed for twin needles: the first number indicates the distance in millimeters between the needles and the second number indicates needle size. The smaller the space between the needles, the tinier the pintuck will be.

Refer to your machine's manual to position two spools of thread for the twin needle. The threads should unwind in opposite directions to avoid tangling.

Test stitch on fabric scraps before stitching your project. You may need to tighten thread tension and/or shorten the stitch length so the fabric "tucks" or rises between the two lines of stitching. Grasp all three thread tails at the beginning of a pintuck and hold the fabric taut in front of and behind the presser foot. Don't press stitched tucks, as this can flatten the fabric; instead, use a steam iron to gently steam away any wrinkles.

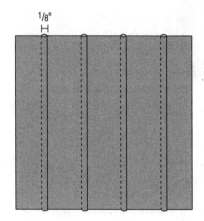

Pintucks are usually ⅛ inch deep or less.

Darts

More than mere decoration, *darts* are key construction elements for sculpting form-fitting garments. Darts shape flat fabric to fit body curves, and although it seems counterintuitive, bigger body curves need deeper darts.

Darts may be curved or straight, and the length, width, shape, and position of a dart depends on the garment's design. Most darts are found at the bust, hip, and waistline of fitted garments. Vertical darts shape bodices and skirt waists. Horizontal or angled darts shape bust areas. Unless used as a decorative element, darts are made on the wrong side of the fabric.

Accuracy is essential, so take care when transferring dart markings from the pattern to the fabric. Most patterns indicate dart ends with a small dot, with dashed lines indicating angled stitching lines. Some patterns include a center fold line or additional dots for matching. It may be helpful to lightly mark the stitching line on the wrong side of the fabric.

V-Shape Darts

V-shape, or open, single-point darts, are indicated as a triangular shape on patterns. Two angled sides, or legs, of the dart meet at a single point. When the sides of the dart are sewn together, the fullness at the dart point is controlled and diminished at the seamline. Single-point darts are often used at the bust or waistline to shape garments to natural curves.

To stitch a single-point dart, fold the fabric with right sides together along the center of the dart, matching the angled stitching lines. Pin the folded dart, marking the point. Backstitch at the wide dart end (at the cut edge) and sew from the wide end to the point. Reduce the stitch length as you near the point, and position the stitches to approach the point gradually, ending almost parallel to and just one or two threads away from the fold. Continue stitching right off the fold at the dart point. Hand-tie the thread ends to secure, taking care not to squeeze the fabric at the point, and use a needle to hide the thread tails inside the dart.

Stitched darts should lie smooth, with no cupping or puckering at the point. Tying a knot at the point, rather than backstitching, discourages puckering by allowing a little give in the final stitch at the point. As an alternative to knotting, try this method: stitch off the end of the dart point, making a ½-inch thread chain. Turn the fabric 180 degrees, and sew along the dart fold for ½ inch. Backstitch and cut the thread.

Press darts flat, as they were stitched, being careful not to crease the fabric past the stitched point. Then press darts open or to one side, as directed in the pattern, using a pressing ham to help shape the dart. Deep darts may be slashed (cut along the fold) and pressed open to distribute fabric bulk. Vertical darts are usually pressed toward the center of a garment. Horizontal darts are pressed down.

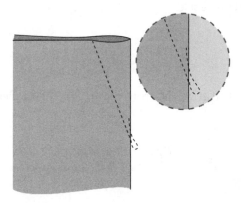

A short chain of stitches at the dart end provides the necessary give as well as tying a knot would.

Double-Ended Darts

Double-ended or closed darts are indicated as elongated diamond shapes on patterns. Sewing the dart sides together reduces the amount of fabric between the dart points while leaving the fullness at the dart ends intact.

To stitch a double-pointed dart, fold the fabric with right sides together along the dart center fold line, matching all markings. Pin the folded dart and mark both dart ends. Start at the center and stitch toward one point, reducing stitch length and stitching off the fold, as for a single-point dart. Repeat for the opposite dart end, overlapping stitching at the dart center.

Clip double-pointed darts so they lie flat when pressed. Darts with very deep folds should be slashed open to a point about ⅝ inch above the dart end. Press the dart open, and overcast the raw edges by hand if the fabric is prone to fraying.

Stitch double-ended darts from the center to the point.

SNIP IT

Reinforce curved darts with a second line of stitching ⅛ inch closer to the folded fabric edge. Clip along the curve, and press the dart to one side.

Project: Hobo Bag

This fun Hobo Bag is a snap to make. You can texturize the front fabric panel with pleats, tucks, or darts to make your bag unique!

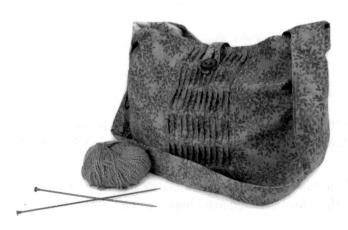

Topstitch tucks in alternate directions to create fabric folds that seem to ripple back and forth.

Finished size:

16×12×4 inches (excluding shoulder strap)

Tools and materials:

1 yard of light- to medium-weight woven fabric* for outer bag (Additional yardage may be needed if another method is used to texturize the front panel.)

1 yard of light- to medium-weight woven fabric* for bag lining

Button for closure

Thread

Basic machine-sewing tools

Suitable woven fabrics include quilting-weight cottons or lightweight home décor fabrics. Stretchy fabrics are not suitable for this project. Yardage is based on 45-inch-wide fabric with at least 40 inches of useable width.

SEW SURPRISING

A light-colored lining fabric makes it easier to see what's in the bag.

Cutting:

1. From the outer fabric, cut:

   Two 5½-inch × wof strips for the strap

   One 16×17-inch rectangle for the bag back

   One 25½×18-inch rectangle for the bag front

   One 2×10-inch rectangle for the button loop

2. From the lining fabric, cut:

   Two 5½-inch × wof strips for the strap

   Two 16×17-inch rectangles for the bag front and back

3. Fold the bag back rectangle, right sides together, to form an 8½×16-inch rectangle. Use a small round plate as a guide to mark and cut curved edges as indicated in the following illustration. Before unfolding the fabric, mark the center top and bottom edge on the fold, between the two curved corners, with an erasable fabric pencil.

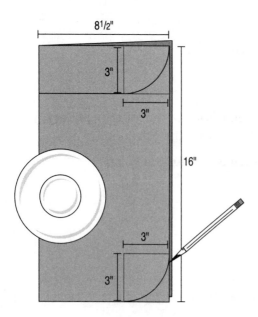

Use a small plate to mark the curved top and bottom bag corners.

4. Using the outer bag back as a guide, trim the lining front and back. Mark the center top and bottom edge on each.

Construction:

Use a ½-inch seam allowance unless otherwise noted.

5. To make the bag front tucks, place the bag front panel right side up and use an erasable fabric pencil to mark a vertical fold line 7¼ inches from the left edge. Mark 10 additional lines, each 1 inch apart, to the right of the first marked line. Fold the fabric wrong sides together along the fold line at the far right. Keeping the edges of the fabric aligned, press the folded edge. Straight stitch ¼ inch away from the folded edge. Press the tuck as stitched to set the stitches. Unfold the fabric and press the stitched tuck to the right. Repeat to make the remaining 10 tucks.

6. Measure and mark a line across the tucks ⅜ inch from the bottom edge of the tucked panel. Mark 5 more lines, 2 inches apart, across the tucks, and a sixth line 2½ inches above the fifth line. Anchor the tucks in place by stitching across every other line, leaving 4-inch thread tails and keeping the tucks pressed to the right. For the remaining marked lines, flip the tucks to the left and stitch across them, leaving 4-inch thread tails. Pull the thread tails to the wrong side, and tie to secure.

7. Place the outer bag back on top of the textured panel, aligning the bottom edge and centering the tucks. Using the outer bag back as a guide, pin or mark the bag front on the textured panel, and cut out the bag front. Transfer the center top and bottom marks to the bag front.

8. Trim the selvages from the outer fabric strap pieces. Pin the strap ends right sides together, and stitch one short end to make one long strip. Press the seam open.

9. With the right sides together, align the strap seam with the bottom center of the bag front. Pin in place. Continue pinning the strap around the bottom and side edges of the bag front. Sew the strap to the bag front. Stitch again, ⅛ inch into the seam allowance, to reinforce the seam. Press the seam toward the strap.

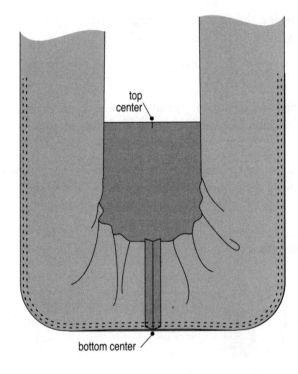

top center

bottom center

Centering the strap seam at the bag bottom, pin and stitch the strap to the bag front. Reinforce the seam with a second line of stitching within the seam allowance, if desired.

10. Repeat step 9 to sew the strap to the bag back. Be sure the top edges of the front and back align across the strap.

11. Repeat steps 8 through 10 to construct the bag lining.

Create a closure:

12. With wrong sides together, fold the 2×10-inch button loop in half lengthwise. Press the fold and open the pressed strip. Fold the two long edges to the center fold and press again. Finally, refold the strip along the center, enclosing the raw edges, to make a strip approximately ½ inch wide. Press. Edgestitch along each long edge of the folded strip to secure the strip layers together.

13. Fold the button loop in half, aligning its short raw edges. With right sides together, pin the loop to the bag back at the center mark, matching the raw edges, with the fold toward the bottom of the bag. Secure the loop to the bag with two lines of stitching, ¼ inch and ⅜ inch from the raw edge.

Assemble the bag:

14. With right sides together, tuck the outer bag (right side out) inside the lining (wrong side out). Pin the outer bag and lining together along the bag front upper edge between the side seams. Stitch the bag and lining together along the pinned edge. Press the stitched edge.

15. Repeat step 14 to sew the outer bag and lining together along the back upper edge, being careful to catch only the loop's raw edges in the seam.

16. Turn the bag right side out through one of the strap openings, and press the bag upper edges.

17. Trim the strap ends to make the bag and lining straps the same length, if necessary. With right sides together, stitch the outer bag strap ends together. Repeat for the lining strap ends. Press the seams open.

18. Press under ½ inch on both long edges of the bag and lining straps. Pin the straps with wrong sides together, and topstitch along the outer edges, continuing across the top edges of the bag.

19. Create a slimmer center section of the strap by folding 17 inches of the bag strap in half, with lining sides together, centering the strap outer edges on the underside of the strap. Press and topstitch in place.

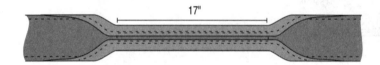

17"

Fold a 17-inch center section of the bag strap in half, with the outer edges meeting at the center underside of the strap.

20. Using the button loop as a placement guide, sew a button to the bag center front. Slip-stitch 1 to 2 inches of the loop together to make a tighter closure.

Trying new techniques on small projects like this hip Hobo Bag is a great way to get a maximum amount of fun without investing a lot of time and materials.

The Least You Need to Know

- Use pleats, tucks, and darts to shape flat fabric into fitted garments that follow body curves or as decorative elements that create visual texture.
- Accuracy is essential for each of these techniques. For best results, take your time when marking, folding, and stitching the fabric.
- Pleats control fabric fullness with a formal flair when gathering might look too casual. Experiment and combine types of pleats to vary the look of a project.
- Tucks can be fun and functional at the same time. Master several types of tucks for terrific embellishment potential.
- Single- and double-point darts shape flat fabric to fit body curves.

Gather Together

In This Chapter

- Making a basic ruffle
- Tips for perfect gathers
- Alternative gathering and ruffle techniques
- Shirring shortcuts

Fun flounced skirts, pretty peasant blouses. Frilly ruffles and gentle gathers add instant appeal to feminine fashions, and are surprisingly easy to accomplish! Read on to discover several different methods for gathering fabric and making ruffles.

Gathering and Ruffles

What's the difference between ruffles and gathering? It's easy to confuse the two terms. Gathering controls and creates fullness by compressing fabric with rows of stitching. Ruffles are gathered strips of fabric. Unlike ease (see Chapter 8), which fits fabrics together without puckers or tucks, gathers are obvious in the finished piece.

There are a number of ways to gather fabric. Hand gathering draws fabric together on hand-sewn running stitches. Machine gathering uses multiple lines of basting, elastic, or corded techniques. Specialty presser feet and attachments gather and seam fabric in a single step. In all these techniques, stitch length determines fullness: longer stitches equate to deeper, fuller folds.

Choose light- to medium-weight fabrics for ruffles and gathers. Most heavyweight fabric is too bulky for the tight folds required, and stiff fabric may yield undesirable results. And as always, test new techniques on fabric scraps before starting a project.

Ruffles 101

There are many different types of ruffles!

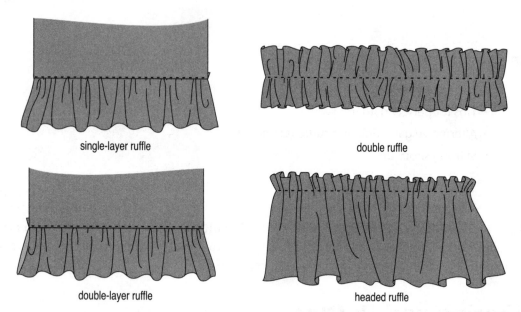

single-layer ruffle

double ruffle

double-layer ruffle

headed ruffle

Different types of ruffles add interest, movement, and shape to flat fabric.

Single-layer ruffles are finished on one edge and stitched to a garment or project piece along the gathered edge. *Double-layer ruffles* are made from folded fabric. The fold is used as the lower edge, and the two raw edges are gathered and seamed, so there's no need for finishing. The extra layer of fabric makes the ruffle stronger than a single-layer ruffle, but it also doubles the fabric's effective weight.

Ruffles can be gathered within the ruffle width, instead of at the fabric edge, and stitched to a base fabric. Both the upper and lower edges must be finished before gathering the ruffle. A ruffle that's gathered in the center of the ruffle strip, creating an equal ruffled width on both sides of the gathering line, is called a *double ruffle*. A *headed ruffle* is gathered off-center, forming a short ruffled head above a deeper lower ruffle.

Here's how to make a basic single-layer ruffle:

1. Cut fabric strips to the desired width plus the necessary seam allowances. The length of the strips depends on the amount of fullness you want as well as the fabric weight. In general, a fabric strip 1½ to 3 times the finished ruffle length is required. Join fabric strips along the short edge, pressing seams open, to make one long strip of fabric. Finish one long edge of the strip.

PINPRICK

Finish first! It's much easier to apply an edge or hem finish to the flat fabric strip before the strip is gathered. If necessary, test edge finishes to learn how weight and firmness affect the ruffle.

2. With the fabric right side up, machine baste along the unfinished long strip edge as directed in the pattern. Usually, one row of gathering stitches is positioned inside the seam allowance with the other on the seamline or ⅛ inch from the seamline, outside the seam allowance. When gathering fine, lightweight fabrics such as batiste and voile, use a standard 2.5mm or slightly longer stitch length. For medium- to heavyweight fabrics, lengthen the stitch to 4mm. Leave thread tails at least 3 inches long at both ends of the ruffle fabric, and don't backtack.

3. At one end of the stitched lines, pull the needle thread ends from each stitching line to the wrong side and secure them to the bobbin threads with an overhand knot tied close to the fabric.

4. At the opposite end of the stitched lines, place a pin perpendicular to the long, raw edge and wrap the needle thread ends in a figure eight around the pin to secure.

5. Gently pull the bobbin threads to gather the fabric along the basting lines, reducing the gathered strip to the needed length. Hold the thread ends taut, and slide the fabric along the thread, a little at a time, to create gathers. Pin-anchor the bobbin threads and evenly distribute the gathers along the ruffle length.

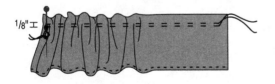

Gently gather the fabric along the basting threads.

SNIP IT

If the fabric to be gathered is very long—for example, for a highly gathered skirt waist—work the gathering threads from both ends. You can also pick up and pull the bobbin threads at the center of the gathered fabric and work outward from the center to meet the gathers from the ends.

6. With right sides together, pin the gathered section to the appropriate pattern piece, matching centers, sides, and raw edges. To help evenly distribute the ruffled fabric, mark center, quarter, and eighth points along the fabric strip before gathering the edge. After gathering, match those marks to corresponding points along the flat fabric edge, and pin in place. Evenly distribute fabric between the pinned marks, being careful not to shift the fabric beyond the pinned points, before sewing the strip in place. If you prefer, pin the fabric to be gathered to the base fabric at the ends, centers, and other marks before gathering the edge.

7. With the gathered piece on top, straight stitch along the seamline to secure the gathers in place. Reinforce the seam with a second line of stitching within the seam allowance, if necessary. Remove any gathering stitches that show on the project right side, and press the seam allowances away from the ruffled edge, pressing only the seam allowances so the ruffle isn't flattened.

Thoughts on Gathering Stitches

Are two rows of gathering stitches really necessary? In a word … *yes.* The two rows keep the gathers aligned, giving a professional look to the finished project. The second basting line is more than a backup in case the first line of stitching fails. Two basting threads make it easier to control spacing and give the gathered fabric a tighter, rounded appearance instead of a flat, folded look.

Placing a row of basting stitches on either side of the seamline helps control and create even gathers without the hassle of gathering stitches on the seamline that must later be removed. Weigh that benefit against the potential for needle holes in the garment when deciding where to position the second row of stitches.

The extra fabric layer at perpendicular seam allowances may create a thick or stiff section in the ruffle. To avoid possible problems, notch the seam allowances before sewing the gathering lines, or stop and start stitching on each side of the seam, leaving long thread tails on each end and allowing the seam allowances to remain flat rather than gathered.

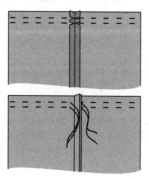

Notch seam allowances or interrupt the basting lines to avoid unwanted thickness variations along the gathered edge.

Cord or Channel Gathering

This technique offers an alternative to basting. Sometimes called zigzag machine gathering or a "fishing line" ruffle, cord or channel gathering tolerates lengthy ruffles and heavier fabrics when even strong threads might snap. Instead of gathering the fabric on a basting thread, the fabric slides on a cord, heavy thread, or monofilament attached to the wrong side of the fabric in a channel of zigzag stitching.

Here's how to make a cord gather:

1. Cut a length of cord twice the length of the fabric to be gathered, plus 6 to 10 inches. Fold the cord in half, and place it on the wrong side of the fabric, near the raw edge, with the cord halves ⅛ to ¼ inch apart.

2. Using a grooved presser foot to help keep the cord aligned, stitch over the cord's folded end to anchor it to the fabric. Zigzag stitch over one cord half, ensuring that the needle doesn't pierce the cord. It may be helpful to hold the cord end up in front of the foot as you sew. Repeat for the other half of the cord.

3. Pull the cord ends to gather the fabric, adjusting fullness as needed. Pin or stitch the cord ends in place to secure. If you want, you can remove the cord after the gathers are anchored in the seam.

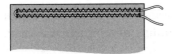

Zigzag stitching encases each side of the gathering cord.

Shirr Pleasure

One of the fun things about sewing is that it's okay to break the rules occasionally. What if you didn't evenly distribute those gathers, or forgot to finish that edge? We wholeheartedly endorse playing with fabric, just for the sheer joy of it. To get you started, here are a few fun techniques for cranking up those creative gears!

Random Ruffle

What *would* happen if gathering went gonzo and didn't end up evenly distributed along a ruffled edge? Chances are, not a thing! Experiment and embrace the unevenness by purposely pushing gathers around. Use the asymmetric look to highlight an edge or accent a certain area.

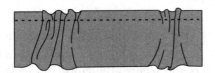

Randomly gather ruffles for a unique effect.

Before permanently stitching the random ruffle in place, check to be sure the uneven shift of fabric doesn't adversely affect other pattern pieces or cause undesired drag due to the uneven weight.

Fuzzy Ruffle

Remember those edgy alternatives from Chapter 7? The ones that might not merit your mom's approval? This fuzzy raw-edge ruffle fits right in with those frayed-edge finishes.

Here's how to create a fuzzy ruffle:

1. Using a shortened straight or zigzag stitch, sew ½ inch from the raw edge along the seam allowance of the pattern piece you'll be sewing the ruffle to.

2. Machine baste the ruffle strip edge as usual.

3. Add an extra line of shortened straight or zigzag stitching to the ruffle strip within the seam allowance between the gathering stitch lines. Be sure the added stitch line doesn't interfere with the gathering stitch line, and gather the ruffle to the desired length.

4. Pin the gathered edge to the flat fabric with *wrong sides* together, matching sides, edges, and center points. Adjust gathers as needed, and stitch to secure the seam. Remove the gathering stitch lines.

5. On the fabric right side, press the seam allowance away from the ruffled edge. Add a second line of stitching ¼ inch from the seamline to reinforce the seam.

6. Use a pin to gently fray the raw upper ruffle edge, if desired.

Shirring

Now here's a technique Mom might like! Shirring was all the rage back in the day, and it's been revived and refreshed with fast, fun fashions. Pretty and practical, shirred sections are used as decorative elements and, when paired with elastic thread, shirring is functional, too. Soft, lightweight fabric such as voile or batiste works well for all-over shirring. Use a matching thread that blends into the fabric, and sew on the crosswise grain.

SNIP IT

Keep this in mind while planning your project: shirring reduces fabric width by about 50 percent and may slightly decrease the fabric length.

Traditional shirring methods involve marking and sewing multiple basting lines and then gathering and securing the fabric along each line of stitching. A quicker approach is to use a specialty presser foot, the shirring foot, that gathers and secures the fabric in one step.

An easy way to shirr fabric with a standard presser foot is to use *elastic thread* (or shirring elastic) in the bobbin. Not only is the fabric gathered and secured in one step, the finished fabric stretches! It's a quick, easy, and practical solution for fitting garments; plus, it's a lot of fun.

SEWING SENSE

Elastic thread, or shirring elastic, is found in the notions section of most fabric stores. Used in gathering and shirring lightweight fabrics, the polyester-wrapped rubber is available in a limited number of colors. Elastic thread is usually not seen from the garment right side.

Here's how it works:

1. Hem or finish fabric edges before shirring. Mark temporary stitching guidelines ½ inch apart on the fabric right side.

2. Wind the elastic thread onto the bobbin by hand, taking care not to stretch the thread. Do not use the machine's bobbin winder; that will stretch the elastic. Load the bobbin in the machine as usual, and use a standard sewing thread that matches the fabric as a top thread.

3. Set the stitch length to 3.5mm. As with other gathers, a longer stitch length creates deeper folds. Test-stitch on a fabric scrap and adjust as needed. It may be helpful to reduce the top tension. The goal is to allow the elastic thread to lie on the wrong side of the fabric, with the top thread looping around it to hold it in place.

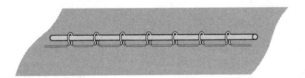

The elastic thread should lie on the wrong side of the fabric, with the top thread looping around it to hold it in place.

4. Place the fabric right side up beneath the presser foot, and stitch along the first marked line, holding both thread tails and backstitching one or two stitches at the beginning and end of the line to secure. When the line of stitches is complete, tie the thread tails together on the wrong side. Repeat for subsequent rows, holding the fabric flat as it travels beneath the needle.

5. Press from the right side of the shirred piece to avoid excess heat affecting the elastic. Hold the iron just above the fabric and allow the heat and steam to set the gathers without flattening them. In some instances, pressing may slightly tighten the shirring.

Yo-Yos

Yo-yos are circles of fabric gathered along the outer edge. Easy and fun to make, yo-yos are portable and great for using up fabric scraps. Single yo-yos can be used as quick embellishments and appliquéd flowers. Stitch yo-yos together to create festive garlands, garments, table toppers, and bedspreads.

Here's how to make a yo-yo:

1. Use chipboard or light cardboard to make a pattern: draw and cut a circle twice the desired size of the finished yo-yo, plus ½ inch. For yo-yos 5 inches or less, add just ¼ inch.

2. Using the pattern as a guide, mark the circle on the wrong side of the fabric, and carefully cut along the marked line.

3. Thread a hand-sewing needle with a doubled thread long enough to stitch the circle circumference, plus 3 or 4 inches. Knot the thread ends.

4. Fold ¼ inch of fabric to the wrong side along the circle outer edge. Using a ¼-inch running stitch, sew completely around the circle, stitching close to the folded edge and ending with your needle on the right side of the fabric. (For a tighter center circle on the finished yo-yo, use longer gathering stitches.)

5. Gently pull the threads to gather the stitched edge at the circle center. Secure the gathers with a few quick stitches in the gathered edge, and bring the needle through the center opening to the wrong side of the fabric. Knot and trim the thread ends. Press the yo-yo flat or leave it unpressed.

Yo-yos are circles of fabric hand-gathered along the outer edge.

Join yo-yos together by hand or machine. With gathered sides facing, use a double-threaded needle to whipstitch the yo-yos together along one edge. Sew about five stitches, knot, and clip the thread close to the fabric. Machine stitch yo-yos together with a narrow zigzag stitch, making sure the left needle swing stitches through one yo-yo and the right needle swing stitches through the other.

You can also tack yo-yos to a base fabric by either hand or machine.

Project: Sweet Shirred Summer Dress

This lightweight summer dress is made with 54-inch width cotton voile. The attached lining is a sweet surprise, peeking out from under the dress hem.

A shirring shortcut leads to a quick and easy summer dress.

Finished size:

Fits bust sizes 28 to 38 inches; length is approximately 28 inches, excluding straps

Tools and materials:

1 yard cotton voile for outer dress*

1⅛ yards cotton voile for lining*

1 spool of elastic thread

Thread

Basic machine-sewing tools

Suitable fabrics include light- and medium-weight fabrics that drape well. Stretchy fabrics are not suitable for this project. Yardage is based on 54-inch-wide fabric with at least 52 inches of useable width.

Cutting:

1. Using a rotary cutter and ruler, square the upper and lower cut edges, and trim selvages from both the outer dress and lining fabric. Place a pin parallel to the trimmed selvage edge to mark the lengthwise grain on each piece of fabric.

2. Cut a 4-inch × wof (width of fabric) strip from the outer dress fabric for the dress straps.

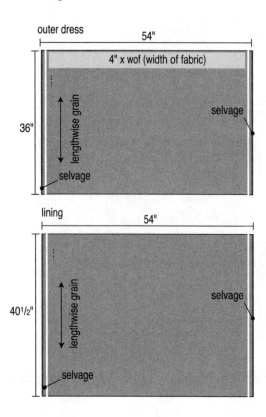

Follow this cutting layout to prepare the outer dress and lining fabrics.

Construction:

Use a ½-inch seam allowance unless otherwise noted.

3. With right sides together, fold the 4-inch × wof strip in half lengthwise. Pin, and stitch the long raw edge. Press the seam open. Use a turning tool to turn the strip right side out. Press, centering the seam on the back of the strip.

4. Cut the strip in two equal lengths for the straps. Zigzag stitch across the raw edges of each short strap end to prevent fraying.

5. With both fabrics facing right side up, layer the lining fabric on top of the outer dress fabric, matching the top crosswise grain edges. Pin, and stitch the layered fabrics together along the top edge. Press the seam flat, fold the lining fabric wrong side up over the seam, and press the seam open. Fold the joined fabrics on the seamline to encase the seam allowances. Both fabrics should be right side up, with the outer dress fabric on top. Press, and edgestitch along the seamed edge. If one fabric is slightly wider than the other, trim the excess amount.

6. Pin the layered fabrics together along each side, 10 inches below the top edge. Referring to the shirring instructions earlier in this chapter, mark and shirr 9 inches of fabric along the dress upper edge, beginning ½ inch below the stitched upper edge.

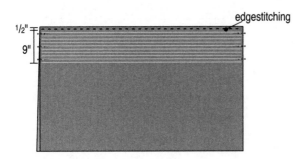

Shirr the upper edge of the dress to form a stretchy bodice.

SNIP IT

Save time by using a seam guide instead of marking the shirring lines. Set the guide to the right at a ½ inch distance from the needle. Align the stitched upper edge with the seam guide to stitch the first row of shirring. For subsequent shirred lines, align the previous line of stitching with the seam guide to position the next row of stitches.

7. Temporarily fold the bodice and outer dress out of the way, and use a French seam (see Chapter 6) to join the lining side edges together from the bodice lower edge to the hemline.

8. Fold the lining out of the way and use a French seam to join the outer dress edges together from the bodice lower edge to the hemline.

9. Fold both skirts out of the way and use a French seam to join the bodice side seams together.

10. With the dress right side out and the seam at one side, pin the straps inside the bodice at front and back. The top three shirring lines should overlap the strap ends, with the strap outer edges 2½ inches from the side seam and opposite side fold.

11. Test-fit the dress, and adjust strap placement and length. If necessary, trim the strap ends and replace the zigzag stitches. Secure the straps to the bodice by stitching just below each of the shirring lines.

12. Test-fit the dress again and mark the desired hemline. Use a double-fold hem to finish the lower edges separately. Prepare each edge by pressing ¼ inch of raw edge to the wrong side. Fold and press another ¼ inch to the wrong side, encasing the raw edge. Straight stitch the folded hem in place close to the inner fold.

If extra-wide fabrics aren't available or you need a larger size, piece fabric panels together to achieve the needed fabric width. For a longer dress, purchase additional yardage and make the dress as directed.

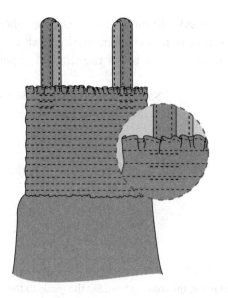

Stitch below the shirring lines to secure the strap ends to the bodice.

The Least You Need to Know

- You can make a variety of ruffles by hand or machine stitching rows of basting lines. Speed up the process with specialty presser feet that gather and seam in one step and other time-saving twists on traditional methods.

- Cord gathering is a stronger alternative to traditional basting techniques. Zigzag stitches form a channel for a gathering cord or thread.

- Add texture and stretch to shirred fabric with a quick-and-easy elastic thread technique.

- Yo-yos are a perfect portable project. Fabric scraps, scissors, needle, and thread are all you need to go and sew!

- Sewing should be fun! Don't be afraid to bend the rules a bit. Experiment and explore new techniques, and find out where those "What if …?" questions lead.

All About Appliqué

In This Chapter

- Embellishing with appliqué
- Traditional and trendy appliqué techniques
- Working with raw-edge appliqué
- Adding texture with appliqué

Appliqué—the process of applying a smaller, shaped fabric piece to a larger foundation fabric—is basically sewing a patch onto a base fabric. An appliqué can be practical, covering worn sections or hiding fabric flaws, or it can be a purely decorative element.

There are many methods of appliquéing one fabric to another, and the one you choose often depends on the fabric you're working with and the intended use of the finished project. Turned-edge appliqué creates a clean finish by securing fabric edges that may fray. Nonfraying fabrics, such as leather or felted wool, are good candidates for raw-edge appliqué. Securing stitches may be nearly invisible or a prominent part of the overall project design. Appliqué is a very versatile technique!

Appliqué Essentials

Regardless of which appliqué method you use, it's a good idea to prewash and press both the patch and foundation fabrics. Prewashing guards against shrinking and bleeding dyes and may also tighten the fabric weave, resulting in a stronger finished piece.

Most appliqué methods use templates the exact size of the finished piece. Seam allowances, if needed, are cut by eye. You can make your own multiuse templates from sturdy, reusable materials such as thin cardboard or template plastic. For single-use templates, try fusible web or freezer paper. Whatever type of template you use, be sure to label it and indicate whether it's right-reading or a mirror image of the final piece. Where pieces overlap, extend the shapes underneath with a ¼-inch seam allowance.

SNIP IT

Freezer paper is often stocked next to the plastic wrap and aluminum foil in most grocery stores. One side of the paper has a shiny plastic or wax coating that temporarily adheres to fabric when heated with an iron. Trace template shapes on the uncoated side for fast and easy appliqué.

Trace carefully around cardboard or plastic templates, or iron freezer paper templates to fabric as indicated for individual techniques. Allow extra room between patches if seam allowances are required. Match foundation and appliqué grainlines so the fabrics can move together without puckering.

Turned-Edge Techniques

In traditional turned-edge appliqué, seam allowances are folded beneath the patches, creating smooth, finished edges. Use turned-edge appliqué with woven fabrics that ravel or when you need a strongly stitched edge that holds up to regular laundering.

Needleturn Appliqué

Needleturn appliqué uses tiny, almost invisible hand stitches to secure patches to a foundation. With this technique, the needle is used to turn under small sections of the seam allowance immediately before sewing the turned edge in place.

Here's how it works:

1. Trace and cut right-reading patch templates. Place the templates right side up on the right side of the appliqué fabric. Using a temporary marker or fabric pencil, trace and then cut the marked patch ⅛ to ¼ inch outside the marked line. Place the patch on the base fabric, and pin in place.

2. Thread a straw or milliners hand-sewing needle with an 18-inch length of fine, light-weight thread that matches or blends with the appliqué. Knot one end of the thread.

3. Beginning on a straight edge of the patch, stroke the needle point along the appliqué edge to turn under a ½-inch section along the marked line. Hold the folded edge in place, and insert the needle through the underside of the fold, hiding the knot beneath the folded edge. Using a ⅛-inch slip stitch (see Chapter 1), sew the folded edge to the foundation. Stitching carefully so the thread is barely visible, continue turning and sewing ½-inch sections around the entire patch.

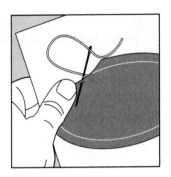

Take tiny stitches through the edge of the appliqué so the stitches are almost invisible.

4. Take extra care when sewing curves, corners, and points on appliqué shapes. Clip and notch seam allowances as necessary (see Chapter 8), stopping a few threads shy of the sewing line.

   Clip the seam allowance to but not through the outline at inner points, stopping a thread or two shy of the sewing line. Turn the seam allowance under, and take tiny $1/16$-inch stitches near the corner, adding a stitch or two in the corner itself to secure the patch edge.

   Construct outer points by stitching to the point and folding the intersecting seam allowance under. If excess fabric creates a lump, trim the seam allowance before folding. Take one stitch exactly at the point to secure the folded edge; it will even give the point a sharper appearance.

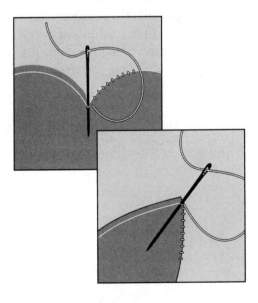

Clip and trim seam allowances to create smooth curves and sharp corners.

SEW SURPRISING

Most gentle appliquéd curves won't need clipping if the seam allowance is no wider than a scant ¼ inch.

5. To end stitching, bring the needle to the back and knot the thread close against the foundation fabric. Reinsert the needle at the exit point, and pull the knot between the fabric layers before trimming the thread tail.

Invisible Machine Appliqué

Invisible machine appliqué uses a small blind stitch and invisible or matching thread to replicate the look of hand appliqué in half the time:

1. Trace the mirror image of the patch pattern on the dull side of the freezer paper. Cut the freezer paper template on the drawn line.

2. Using a hot, dry iron, adhere the freezer paper template to the wrong side of the fabric. Let fabric and paper cool. Cut out the appliqué patch, adding a $^3/_{16}$- to $^1/_4$-inch seam allowance.

3. Use a fingertip or small brush to apply liquid starch to the seam allowances, taking care not to moisten the paper template. Fold the seam allowances along the template edge and press. When cool, peel the freezer paper away from the pressed patch, and press the seam allowances again. Pin the pressed patch to the foundation fabric.

4. Using a matching or *invisible thread*, choose an appropriate machine stitch (see the following figure) and align the patch under the presser foot. Appropriate stitches swing to the side for one in every three or four stitches, so the majority of the stitches fall in the foundation fabric close to the folded patch edge while the swing stitch bites into the appliqué itself. Reduce the stitch width so the "bite" stitch reaches just over the folded patch edge; a 1 to 1.5mm stitch width is optimal. Stitch around the outer patch edges, pivoting as needed around any curves. Pull the thread ends to the wrong side of the fabric, and tie off.

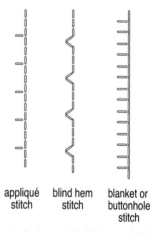

appliqué
stitch

blind hem
stitch

blanket or
buttonhole
stitch

The "bite" stitch anchors the patch to the foundation fabric.

Raw-Edge Appliqué

Raw-edge appliqué is just as the name implies—the edges of the patch are unfinished. Fabric selection affects results; nonfraying felted wool is a favorite for the basic technique.

Here's how to do it:

1. Cut right-reading patch patterns and place the templates right side up on the patch fabric right side. Using a temporary marker or fabric pencil, trace and then cut on the marked line. Pin the patch to the foundation fabric.

2. Machine or hand stitch ⅛ to ¼ inch from the patch edges, using a straight or running stitch.

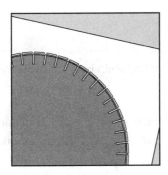

Blanket or buttonhole stitching is commonly used to anchor felted wool patches in place.

Variations of this technique include allowing woven fabric edges to fray for a casual, raggy look or taming unturned edges with decorative topstitching.

Ragged-Edge Appliqué

Fast, easy, and fun, when used with woven fabrics, this technique produces a softly frayed edge that's perfect for a worn, casual look:

1. Prepare right-reading templates and trace the templates, right side up, on the patch fabric right side with a temporary marker or fabric pencil. Cut on the marked line. Pin the patch to the foundation.

2. Using a straight stitch, sew ¼ inch inside the cut edge of the patch, pivoting at curves and corners and backstitching at the beginning and end.

3. To promote gentle fraying rather than unsightly raveling, clip into the raw edges before washing and drying the finished project as usual.

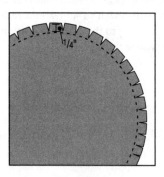

Stitch ¼ inch from patch edges to anchor the appliqué in place.

Satin-Finish Appliqué

This variation controls raw edges with a line of straight stitches hidden beneath a satin-stitched edge. Here's how:

1. Prepare right-reading templates and trace the templates, right side up, on the patch fabric right side with a temporary marker or fabric pencil. *Rough cut* the appliqué, and pin it in place on the foundation fabric.

> **SEWING SENSE**
>
> **Rough cut** means an inexact cut. Cut appliqué patches freehand, about ¼ inch outside the marked line.

2. Straight stitch on the drawn line, pivoting at curves and corners as needed. Trim the excess appliqué fabric as close to the stitched edge as possible without cutting the stitches.

3. Using a wide satin stitch (2.5 to 4mm wide and 0.3 to 0.4mm long), sew along the patch edge, covering the straight stitching and the fabric raw edge.

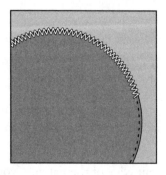

Satin stitch over the straight stitching, and encase the raw edges.

This technique is easy to adapt and experiment with. Vary stitch width, substitute another decorative stitch in place of satin stitching to secure raw edges, or extend stitches into the background fabric. By varying stitch width and length and choosing matching or contrasting thread, you can define or distort shapes, using the stitching as a design element.

The Fuss About Fusing

Fusible web can be used with raw edge appliqué techniques to control fraying fabrics and add strength to patch pieces. Use fusible web—that fibrous man-made adhesive material that melts and sticks when heated—to adhere patches in place on foundation fabrics.

Here's how to use fusible web with raw-edge appliqué:

1. Trace the mirror image of the patch onto the fusible web's paper backing. Rough cut the marked patch, and follow manufacturer instructions to adhere the fusible web to the fabric wrong side. Let the fused fabric cool completely before cutting the patch on the marked line.

2. Peel the paper backing from the patch, and place the patch adhesive side down on the right side of the foundation fabric. Following manufacturer's instructions, fuse the patch in place. Let the fabric cool completely.

3. Use a thread and a stitch of your choice to hand or machine stitch along patch edges.

PINPRICK

Be sure the fusible product you choose is meant for sewing. Heavy-duty and no-sew options use a more powerful adhesive that leaves a deposit on needles and breaks threads after only a few stitches. To keep your iron and pressing surface free of fusibles, use a thermal pressing sheet or parchment paper between the fabric and pressing surface or iron. Remove adhesive residue from the iron with an iron cleaner, found among the notions at the fabric store.

Reverse Appliqué

Unlike traditional appliqué, reverse appliqué puts the foundation on top. Two or more fabric layers are stitched together before the top layers are trimmed away to reveal the fabric underneath. Knits and nonfraying fabrics work best for this technique.

Here's how to create a reverse appliqué:

1. Using a removable fabric pencil, mark the right-reading appliqué design on the right side of the top layer of fabric.

2. Layer the patch fabric (or fabrics, if you're working with more than one layer) right side up with the marked layer on top. Pin or tack the layers together to hold them in place.

3. Being careful to cut the top fabric layer only, cut ⅛ to ¼ inch inside the marked shape, removing the inner portion of the design and revealing the second layer of fabric.

4. Clip or notch curved sections as needed, and turn the ¼-inch seam allowance to the wrong side along the marked line, tucking the seam allowance between the layered fabrics before slipstitching. Alternatively, stitch on the marked lines before cutting out the shapes and leave the seam allowance raw for a more casual look.

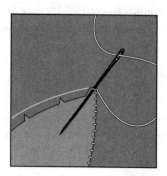

Hide the seam allowance between the fabric layers, and slipstitch along the folded edge to secure.

Project: Trendy Tank

Use reverse appliqué to transform readymade T-shirts into a trendy textured tank. Adding your favorite text message or characters makes it uniquely yours!

Text a readymade tank with raw-edge appliqué.
(Photo by Jessi Butler)

Finished size:

Variable

Tools and materials:

Two light- to medium-weight T-shirts, in coordinating colors*

Thread

Template material of your choice

Basic hand- or machine-sewing tools

T-shirts should be new or in good condition, without excess wear or holes.

Marking and cutting:

1. Prior to cutting, wash and press the T-shirts.

2. Layer the T-shirts one inside the other, and test the fit. Pin-mark the center point for a lowered neckline. Pinch and pin excess fabric together along each side seam for a fitted silhouette. Place two pins on each shoulder seam to indicate shoulder strap width and the altered armhole edge.

3. Remove the shirts and note the edge-to-pin measurements in the following figure.

Average side seam measurements, if necessary, so the side seams mirror each other when stitched.

4. Remove the pins and separate the shirts. Place the outer shirt flat on the work surface. Cut off the hemmed bottom edge, and cut an additional 1¾-inch strip from the bottom edge. Reserve this strip for armhole and neck edge binding.

5. Cut through the side and underarm seams on the outer shirt, and place it flat on the work surface. Referring to the measurements recorded in step 3, mark a new front neckline, shoulder strap, armhole edge, and side seams. Mark a slightly higher neckline on the shirt back, matching the front at the shoulders.

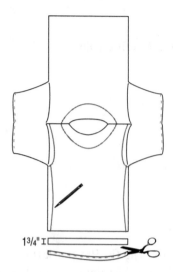

Mark the cutting and sewing lines for the tank top edges.

6. Fold the outer shirt in half along the center front and center back. Cut the new neckline edge along the marked line. Refold the shirt along the shoulder seams, matching side edges, and trim the armhole edges.

7. Trim the hemmed bottom edge, and cut the side and underarm seams of the lining T-shirt. Place the shirt right side up on the work surface, and layer the trimmed outer shirt right side up on top of the lining. Match shoulder seams, and pin the shirts together.

Appliqué:

8. Use a computer word processing or graphics program to compose and print text messages approximately 2¼ inches tall. Print and cut right-reading templates. Follow the instructions for reverse appliqué earlier in this chapter to embellish the T-shirt material, referring to the photograph to position the appliqués. If desired, add decorative stitching to accent the appliqués.

Construction:

Use a ½-inch seam allowance unless otherwise noted.

9. Baste ¼ inch from the outer shirt edge around neckline and armhole openings, stopping 1 inch from marked side seams. Trim the excess lining from the basted neckline and armhole edges.

10. Trim the side seam edges of the outer shirt ½ inch outside the marked fitting line. Using the outer shirt as a guide, trim the lining side seam, armhole, and neckline edges.

11. With right sides facing, sew the outer shirt side seams together. With wrong sides facing, sew the lining side seams together. Press the seams open.

12. Align and pin the outer and lining seams at the underarm edge. Straight stitch the outer and lining shirts together along the neckline and armhole edges, sewing ⅜ inch from the raw edge.

13. Cut the reserved binding along a side seam to form one long strip. On the T-shirt right side, align one long edge of the binding strip with the raw neckline edge, beginning at one shoulder seam. Pin the strip in place, trimming and overlapping the short strip ends at the shoulder seam. Use a ½-inch seam allowance to stitch the strip to the neck edge.

14. Fold the strip to the T-shirt wrong side, encasing the neckline raw edges. The binding raw edge will extend slightly below the seam. Pin the strip in place, and stitch in the ditch along the neckline seam to secure.

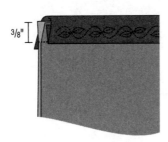

3/8"

Use decorative stitching to secure the binding strip in place along the neck and armhole edges.

15. Repeat steps 13 and 14 to bind the armhole edges, piecing a 1¾-inch binding strip from the T-shirt scraps, if necessary.

16. At the hemline, cut the lining T-shirt even with the outer shirt. Fold and press ½ inch of fabric to the inside along the bottom edges of both the lining and outer shirt. Align the shirt side seams, and pin the bottom edges together. Straight stitch close to the folded hem edge to secure.

Upcycling old T-shirts into uniquely textured tops is a great way to test appliqué techniques.

The Least You Need to Know

- Freezer paper is an affordable alternative to standard cardboard or plastic appliqué templates. Translucent enough for easy tracing, freezer paper can be peeled away to use again.
- Needleturn and invisible machine appliqué are two turned-edge techniques that create a crisp, durable finished edge. Turned-edge techniques are a good choice for working with fabrics that ravel.

- Some raw-edge techniques result in frayed, ragged edges, while others have a smoothly stitched, controlled look. Raw-edge appliqué is also good for working with felted wool or other nonfraying fabrics.

- Reverse appliqué removes sections of upper fabric layers instead of applying patches to a foundation. Edge options include both clean finishes and casual frayed edges.

Textiles and Trims

In Part 4, you learn fabric fundamentals—how fabric is made, what fibers are used, and how this affects the yardage you choose to sew. We cover standard and specialty fabrics—those materials that are made for a specific purpose—and special considerations you must give to certain fabric types and designs. We walk you through buying off the bolt and point out where to find important fabric information.

We also explore trim types and teach you how to make your own binding and piping—two techniques you'll use for many years and projects to come. You learn to create unique accents by layering different trim types and couching cords and yarns. Finally, we take a look at some simple fasteners—snaps, buttons, elastic, and zippers, to name just a few.

Projects include a Pop-Up Storage Cube, Double-Bind Pillow, and Backpack Bag—practical, easy-to-make items that you'll create over and over again for yourself and as gifts for family and friends.

Fabric Fundamentals

Chapter **12**

In This Chapter

- Common fabric fibers and properties
- Working with prints, plaids, and stripes
- Special-purpose fabrics
- Fabric-buying tips

One peek inside a fabric store reveals yards of project possibilities: colorful cotton prints, slinky synthetics, plush piles of fleece, and so much more. With so many options, selecting a single fabric for your particular project may seem overwhelming.

Help is here! In this chapter, we help you narrow the number of candidates by choosing fabric according to intended use. By following pattern recommendations and paying attention to those "Not suited for ..." notes, you'll be that much closer to finding the perfect fabric for your project.

Cloth Considerations

Most fabrics are made with a particular purpose in mind. Heavyweight home décor textiles are intended to be used as upholstery or drapery fabrics. Fashion fabrics are manufactured for specific garment types. Fiber content, fabric construction, weight, drape, and design are a few factors to consider when selecting fabric for projects.

That said, we believe some rules are made to be broken, and sometimes the "wrong" fabric may be exactly right for your project. It's still important to know the ins and outs of fabric selection, however, so you can bend the rules appropriately and avoid unpleasant surprises.

Content and Construction

Put simply, fiber content and fabric construction indicate what a fabric is made of and how it is made. Content and construction affect everything about a fabric, from strength and shrinkage to laundering and looks. Natural fibers, such as cotton, linen, silk, or wool, come from plants or animals. Synthetic, or man-made, fibers are manufactured from chemical compounds or reprocessed materials. Different fiber types have their own strengths and weaknesses and are often combined, or blended, to create fabrics with specific qualities.

Natural Fibers

Cotton fabric absorbs moisture, dries quickly, is nonallergenic, and is easy to work with and care for. Prewash cotton fabric before using; it can shrink and does wrinkle. Available in a wide range of weights and textures, cotton is a good choice for beginning projects. Special finishes can make it flame-, water-, stain-, and shrink-resistant.

Linen is made from flax. Like cotton, linen is sturdy, durable, and absorbent. It has a crisp, clean look but can wrinkle. Linen can feel stiff but softens with repeated washing. Some linens are prone to abrasion.

Ramie is a linenlike fiber made from nettle. Strong, durable, and easy to wash, ramie has a silky luster and resists wrinkling. Ramie does not dye as well as cotton and can become brittle with age, so it's most often found in blended fabrics.

Silk is a strong, somewhat wrinkle-resistant fabric made from silkworm cocoons. Silk is warm in winter, cool in summer, and takes dye well. Silk is absorbent, dries quickly, and is often blended with other fibers. Some silks must be dry cleaned.

Made from sheep's fleece, *wool*'s natural insulating qualities retain warmth in winter and coolness in summer. Wool is water-repellant and flame- and wrinkle-resistant. Some wool garments may stretch during wear, and care must be taken while cleaning so the fabric doesn't felt and shrink.

Synthetic Fibers

Nylon was originally created as a synthetic replacement for silk. Lightweight and strong, nylon is used for sportswear and swimsuits. Nylon is heat-sensitive and may "pill" with excessive laundering.

Polyester is woven or knit from synthetic fibers; resists wrinkling; and is durable, strong, and warm. Polyester tends to "pill" and have static cling.

SEW SURPRISING

Plastic soft drink bottles and synthetic fabric have a lot in common. Recycled drink bottles can be used to make synthetic polymers for fabrics and stuffing.

Rayon is neither a truly synthetic nor a wholly natural fiber. Made from regenerated wood pulp, rayon mimics the look and feel of natural fibers. Rayon is soft, smooth, cool, and absorbent; does not insulate; and can be weak when wet. Rayon dyes beautifully but wrinkles unless treated.

> **SEW SURPRISING**
>
> Eco-friendly fibers, such as bamboo and hemp, are becoming more readily available. Bamboo fabric is noted for its softness, absorbency, and naturally antibacterial qualities. Prewashing is a must because bamboo shrinks significantly. One of the strongest natural fibers, hemp is insulating, absorbent, breathable, and blends well with other fibers. Hemp can be coarse, but new processes have created knit and woven apparel fabrics that soften with repeated washings.

Fibers are spun into thread or yarn and then woven, knitted, or matted together to make fabric. Woven fabrics (detailed in Chapter 4) are generally stable and easy to sew, but can fray at cut edges. Knit fabrics are stretchy and resilient, returning to their original shape after being distorted. Knit fabrics don't fray, but can run and curl along the cut edges.

Nonwoven fabric is neither woven nor knit. Fibers are matted together using heat, pressure, moisture, or chemicals, and cut edges are as stable as the rest of the cloth. Many interfacings are nonwoven. Wool felt is a nonwoven fabric; the fibers lock together when washed in hot water, creating a dense, textured fabric. Synthetic felts are created by needlepunching fibers into a nonwoven base.

Weight, Hand, Drape, and Count

Weight, hand, drape, and count describe different fabric properties. All can be important points to consider when selecting your fabric.

Formulas are available for figuring out a fabric's *weight*, or the number of ounces or grams per yard of cloth, but most sewists use a "touch test" to loosely categorize fabrics as light-, medium-, or heavyweight. Simply pinch a bit of fabric between your finger and thumb to determine fabric thickness. Don't worry about being too precise; the lines between weights are often blurred!

While you're pinching, pay attention to how the fabric feels. Is it flexible between your fingers? Is the surface rough or smooth? The way fabric feels is called the fabric *hand*. A number of factors are considered when characterizing fabric feel and quality, but for most, it's a subjective assessment based on whether or not the fabric feels good to the touch. Most would consider the sensation of repeatedly washed cotton an exceptional fabric hand, while stiff or scratchy fabrics get a thumbs down. That's why prewashed jeans are so popular!

Drape refers to the way a fabric flows. Stiff fabrics such as heavy denim or light cotton organdy have less drape, while cotton voile and wool crepe have more. To determine drape, hold a length of fabric against your body while standing in front of a mirror. Does the fabric flow over your curves or stand stiff as a board beside you? Examine the fabric folds to get a general idea of how it will look in garment form.

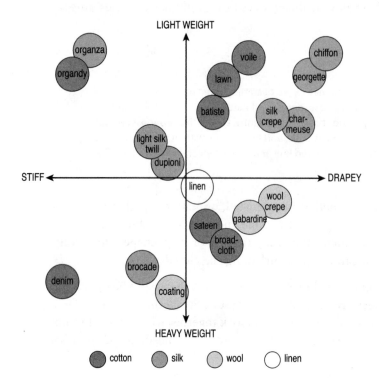

Drape and stiffness vary among fabric types.

Count, or *thread count*, applies to woven fabrics and is defined as the number of threads, both vertical and horizontal, contained in one square inch of fabric. A high thread count (180 or above) is desirable for certain fabrics, while other factors, such as fiber quality, thread size, and finishing, can greatly affect overall fabric quality. Overly dense weaves, for example, can be difficult to sew through.

SNIP IT

Match fabrics to intended use, and consider care requirements when selecting textiles for specific projects. If you're in love with linen but hate ironing, consider substituting a ramie blend instead.

Prints, Plaids, and Directional Designs

Luscious large florals. Bright, bold stripes. Small, busy prints. Most fabrics are designed as a series of repeated patterns. A *pattern repeat* is the distance from the starting point of a design to the place where the design begins again and can range from as little as 2 inches to 36 inches or more. Home décor fabrics often list the pattern repeat (in inches) on the selvage.

Some pattern repeats are directional designs: imagery that has an obvious orientation. Uneven stripes are one example of a directional design; novelty prints can be another. Place pattern pieces so the pattern repeat runs in the same direction throughout the finished project.

Extra yardage may be needed to match repeated patterns, especially when working with large-scale designs. Most patterns provide "with nap" and "without nap" yardage requirements and pattern layouts. Follow "with nap" recommendations for matching repeated patterns, and purchase additional yardage if needed. Plan ahead before cutting to ensure patterns align along major seamlines.

SNIP IT

Napped fabrics, such as velvet or faux fur, have a raised surface texture that makes the fabric look and feel different when viewed or touched from different directions. Place pattern pieces carefully; the nap should run in the same direction on each pattern piece to avoid odd color variations in the finished garment.

To match large pattern repeats between fabric panels, press the seam allowance to the wrong side along the edge of one panel. Align the pressed edge with the second panel, matching the pattern repeat exactly. Baste or use fusible web tape to secure the folded edge in place, and stitch along the inside of the fold to secure the panels together.

fold

Match pattern repeats along the folded edge.

To match plaid fabrics, determine if the plaid is an even (balanced) or uneven (unbalanced) design. Fold the fabric in half lengthwise, and fold one corner back at a 45-degree angle. If the colors and spaces line up along the horizontal and vertical edge of the turned back corner, the design is even. If the design doesn't match, it's uneven.

Even or balanced plaids can be folded for cutting. Take care to fold the fabric through the center of a dominant stripe within the plaid, align selvages, and pin the fabric together at matching points throughout the plaid. Position pattern notches and markings on dominant stripes within the plaid, and match the plaid from one piece to the next.

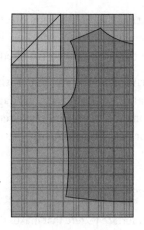

Check the alignment of even plaids by temporarily folding back the top fabric layer.

Cut uneven plaids as a single layer, remembering to flip pattern pieces where needed.

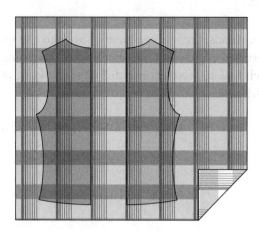

Duplicate and flip pattern pieces as needed for a single-layer cutting layout.

SNIP IT

Match plaids precisely along seamlines by inserting pins along the edge of a dominant design stripe in the top fabric layer. Align the pin with the same stripe in the lower fabric layer, and pin the fabrics together perpendicular to the seamline. Use a walking foot to feed both layers evenly under the presser foot, maintaining the match as you sew.

Specialty Fabrics

Specialty fabrics are created for specific applications. They may be woven or nonwoven, knit or not. Fiber content often relates to intended use. Some specialty fabrics are coated or covered with thin layers of wax, rubber, or other substances to create certain characteristics. Other fabrics are made to fill very specific needs, such as interfacing that adds support or Kevlar that stops bullets.

Fun and Functional Finishes

Fabric finishes (or coatings) can render fabrics wrinkle-resistant; colorfast; water-resistant, water-repellent, or waterproof; flame retardant; or fire-resistant. Some finishes add gloss to fabric surfaces, repel dirt and stains, or protect against UV rays.

Read care requirements before prewashing such fabrics because laundering can remove some finishes. Always test stitch on specialty fabric scraps; stitching through some finishes leaves permanent holes!

Polyvinyl chloride (PVC) coated fabrics, known as oilcloth or laminates, are woven cotton with a semisoft protective vinyl bonded to the fabric right side. Do not machine wash; instead, wipe clean with a damp cloth. Unless treated with a UV inhibitor, the fabric may fade with prolonged exposure to sunlight. Use these fabrics for raincoats, tablecloths, shower curtains, placemats, or tote bags.

Indoor/outdoor fabrics are treated to withstand strong sunlight and repel mold, mildew, soil, and stains. These durable fabrics "breathe," meaning that air passes through the weave, which helps them to dry quickly. Use these fabrics for outdoor awnings, sun umbrellas, and chair cushions. Check care requirements; many wipe clean with soap and water.

SNIP IT

It's great fun to shop standard fabric sources—fabric stores, quilt shops, and outlets—but don't overlook alternate origins. Check specialty stores, such as army surplus markets, drapery shops, and art supply stores, for fabric possibilities, and explore online or mail-order options as well. Pick up fabric for pennies at thrift shops and garage sales. You can also scout alternate origins right in your own home. There may be yards of vintage fabric in out-of-date clothes. It's a great way to clean out your closet and repurpose items you never wear.

Inside Stories

Some specialty fabrics are not meant to be seen. Interfacings, stabilizers, and stuffings are sewn inside other fabrics to provide support and structure to garments and projects.

Interfacing is placed between fabric layers to add stability and support to collars, cuffs, waistbands, and facings. Buttonholes also benefit from the extra strength interfacing provides. Interfacing is available woven, nonwoven, and knit in a variety of weights and colors. Fusible interfacings have heat-activated adhesive on one side and can be bonded to fabric with a household iron. Sew-in interfacing is secured to garments in construction seams.

Consider the base fabric when selecting interfacing. Choose interfacing that's similar in weight to the fabric it will support, and consider black interfacing on dark fabrics to avoid a show-through sparkle. The interfacing and fabric must have similar care requirements. Preshrink knit or woven interfacing by soaking it in warm water and laying it flat to dry; the adhesive on fusible interfacing will not wash off.

Like interfacing, *stabilizers* provide structure and support. Stabilizers are used in machine embroidery to support fabric under dense, multidirectional machine stitching. Most machine embroidery stabilizers provide temporary support and are removed when the embroidery is complete. Heavyweight, ultra-firm stabilizers shape and support accessories, crafts, and home décor projects and can be permanently sewn or fused in place.

Stuffing is used to fill pillows, pincushions, and stuffed toys. Polyester fiberfill is a popular option; alternative eco-friendly fibers are becoming more available, too. Polystyrene microbeads are used for filling pillows and bean bags. Old-time alternatives include dried beans, rice, sawdust, or wood shavings, but polystyrene won't attract bugs and is usually washable.

Linings add support and conceal inside construction seams. Most linings are made from smooth, slippery fabrics that facilitate sliding garments on and off. Flannel and fleece linings provide extra warmth. Garments may be fully or partially lined.

Buying Off the Bolt

Fabric is measured, cut, and sold by the yard or in fractions of a yard. Yardage is cut from *bolts* of fabric, or stores may sell precut pieces in 1-yard, ½-yard, or smaller specialty cuts. Fat quarters (18×22-inch pieces) and fat eighths (11×18-inch cuts) are popular precut sizes in quilt shops. Some stores provide sample swatches for a minimal fee, and *remnants* are often sold at a reduced rate. Remnant size varies; some pieces may be large, while others are ⅛ yard or less. Bags of remnants can be used for small projects and appliqués, while larger pieces may be perfect for small garments and accessories.

SEWING SENSE

A **bolt** is a roll of fabric, usually 15 to 100 yards long. Fashion fabrics are folded onto flat cardboard blanks, while home décor and upholstery fabrics are rolled on to cardboard tubes without folding. A **remnant** is the fabric that remains after the bulk of the yardage has been used or sold.

Purchase yardage requirements at one time. Fabrics are seasonal and often sell out. Even if a fabric is reprinted or the store is able to reorder, different dye lots may result in noticeable color differences.

Finding Fabric Information

When purchasing yardage, check fashion fabrics' bolt ends for information. Home décor and upholstery materials list information on stickers or tags attached to the cardboard tubes. Most manufacturers note the company and fabric collection name, fiber content, yardage width, and care requirements, as well as price, pattern, and dye lot numbers.

To help keep track of your fabric information, carry a small notebook in your purse and record in it the care requirements for each fabric you buy. When you're home with your purchases, snip a small swatch from a selvage or one cut end, and tape it into the notebook for a lasting reminder of your fabric purchases and their care. Printed care requirements and application instructions are folded into bolts of interfacing and stabilizer sold by the yard. Take the instruction sheet home with the textile, and use it to make an envelope or folder for storing the interfacing or stabilizer. The instructions for application and care will always be handy when you need them!

Standard Fabric Widths

Although fabric width can vary, most yardage is made in standard widths: 36, 44/45, 52/54, and 58/60 inches. The *usable* fabric width is what's left after selvages are removed and grain aligned. This width varies with individual fabrics, but it's a safe guess that the usable width will be 2 to 4 inches less than the stated fabric width.

If yardage requirements don't list an amount for a fabric width you select, consult a yardage conversion chart (see Appendix C).

To determine the number of yards needed for fabric requirements given in meters, divide the metric measurement by 0.9144 and round up. For example, 3 meters equals 3.2808 or $3\frac{3}{8}$ yards. One word of warning: conversions are inexact. Take care when converting metric seam allowances to fractional equivalents, as rounding for conversions will change the final size of a project with a lot of seams. Better yet, have both metric and imperial rulers on hand so there's no need to convert pattern measurements.

SNIP IT

If you prick your finger and get a spot of blood on your fabric, spit on it. Your saliva helps dissolve the stain before it sets. (We know it sounds gross, but it works.) If you simply can't spit on your fabric, dab the spot with a cotton swab soaked in peroxide. Test on a fabric scrap first, though, because peroxide may bleach the fabric dyes as well.

If you're an iPhone user, check out the Apple iTunes store for Guleno Consulting's Yardage Calc application. With it, you can estimate yardage at different widths, convert yards to meters, and vice versa. Fabric Calc, by the same developer, also compares fabric prices.

Project: Pop-Up Storage Cube

Storage is always at a premium. This foldable basket pops up to hold fabric, magazines, or miscellanea and folds down so it's easy to store itself! What's more, it's a perfect fit for inexpensive storage cubes, changing them to drawer space in a flash.

Pop-up storage cubes are a great way to stash stuff in plain sight. Make several coordinating cubes to corral project pieces.

Finished size:

> 11×11×11 inches

Tools and materials:

> ¾ yard 45-inch-wide cotton print (main)
>
> ¾ yard 45-inch-wide cotton print (contrast)
>
> *(Note: Choose nondirectional prints.)*
>
> 1½ yards 15-inch-wide ultra-firm stabilizer such as Floriani Stitch N Shape
>
> 3-inch length of ¼-inch-wide ribbon
>
> Ruler
>
> Marking pen or pencil (removable)
>
> All-purpose thread
>
> Scissors
>
> Straight pins

Cutting:

> 1. From the main fabric, cut the following:
>
>> 2 side panels 11½×22½ inches
>>
>> 2 bottom panels 11½×11½ inches
>>
>> 1 handle 4×8½ inches

2. From the contrast fabric, cut the following:

    2 side panels 11$\frac{1}{2}$×22$\frac{1}{2}$ inches

    1 bottom panel 11$\frac{1}{2}$×11$\frac{1}{2}$ inches

3. From the ultra-firm stabilizer, cut the following:

    3 squares 10$\frac{1}{2}$×10$\frac{1}{2}$ inches

    4 rectangles 5×10$\frac{1}{2}$ inches

Construction:

The seam allowance for this project is $\frac{1}{4}$ inch. Be sure to backstitch at the beginning and end of each seam.

4. Fold $\frac{1}{4}$ inch to the wrong side on each short end of the handle fabric. Fold the handle in half lengthwise, with wrong sides together, and press. Open the fold, and press the two long raw edges to the wrong side to meet at the center crease. Press again. Refold the handle along the center crease, and press once more.

5. Edgestitch both long edges of the handle, enclosing the raw edges. With a removable marker, draw lines 1 inch from each short end, creating a square. Draw lines from corner to corner across each square, forming an X inside the square. These are guides for topstitching the handle in step 7.

6. Measure and mark two points on one contrast fabric side panel, 8 inches above one short edge and 2 inches in from each side. Pin the handle to the side panel with the lower corners of the handle on the marks. Pin the handle ends again 1 inch from the short ends.

Measure and mark the handle location.

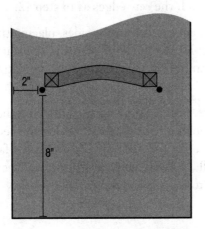

7. Sew the handle ends to the fabric. Begin by edgestitching the handle end, and pivot and stitch along the existing edgestitching to the opposite side of the square. Continue stitching along the guidelines from step 5, overlapping stitches as necessary. Repeat on the other handle end.

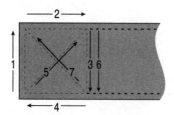

Reinforce the handle attachment by stitching an X in a square on each end.

8. With right sides together and long edges aligned, sew a main fabric side panel to each contrast fabric side panel. Begin and end the seams ¼ inch from the fabric raw edges. Press the seams open.

9. With right sides together and long edges aligned, sew the units from step 8 together, beginning and ending the seams ¼ inch from the fabric raw edges, to make a tube with alternating fabrics. Press the seams open.

10. Fold the tube in half, wrong sides together, matching the seams and raw edges, and press. The foldline will be the top edge of the storage cube, and the handle is attached to the outside surface.

11. Measure to find the center of each main fabric panel, parallel to the side seams, and mark with a removable marking tool. Straight stitch along the marked lines, dividing the main fabric panels in half. Working from the right side, stitch in the ditch along each seam between panels.

12. Insert a 10½-inch square of ultra-firm stabilizer between the layers of each contrast fabric side panel, pushing the stabilizer all the way up to the fold. Pin the raw edges together, enclosing the stabilizer, and stitch a scant ¼ inch from the raw bottom edges.

13. Insert a 10½×5-inch rectangle of ultra-firm stabilizer between the layers on each side of the divided main fabric panels. Pin and stitch the raw edges as in step 12.

14. Pin one main fabric square to the bottom edges of the cube sides, placing the square's right side against the cube's outer surface. Match the cube seams to the square's corners. Pin with the square on the bottom for better visibility when pivoting at the corners.

15. Begin sewing along one side of the square. Stitch to the corner, allowing the ¼ inch left open at the end of the cube seam to open up at the corner. With the needle down precisely at the end of the cube seam, raise the presser foot and swing the fabric around to align the next side seam with the needle. Lower the presser foot, and keep sewing, pivoting at each corner, until you return to the starting point.

SNIP IT

If the stabilizer bulk makes pivoting at the corners difficult, pin and sew each side individually instead, backstitching and breaking the seam at the corners.

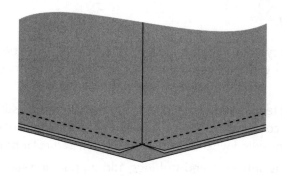

The side seams open as the fabric pivots around the corners.

16. Set the machine for an overcasting or zigzag stitch and sew the raw edges of the seam together to prevent fraying. Turn the cube right side out, and set aside.

17. Press ¼ inch to the wrong side along one edge of each remaining 11½-inch square.

18. Fold the ribbon in half, wrong sides together, and pin it to one square in the middle of the side opposite the pressed edge. Lay the ribbon loop on the square's right side with the raw edges matched and the ribbon fold toward the center of the square.

19. Pin the two squares, right sides together, along the three raw edges and stitch, leaving the pressed edges open. Be sure to catch the ribbon in the seam.

20. Trim the corners diagonally to reduce bulk. Turn the squares right side out, and press flat.

21. Slip the remaining square of ultra-firm stabilizer into the pouch you just made. Pin the pressed edges together, and edgestitch, trapping the stabilizer inside.

To use the storage cube, slip the stiffened bottom insert into the cube to hold the sides erect. To fold the cube away, use the ribbon loop to remove the bottom insert and accordion fold along the main fabric panels' central seams, tucking in the unreinforced bottom panel as the cube collapses.

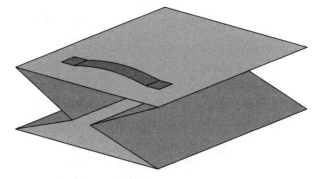

Accordion fold the sides to collapse the cube for storage.

Stitch up pop-up storage cubes for a fun and functional alternative to fabric gift bags. It's one wrapping that won't be thrown away!

The Least You Need to Know

- Fabric can be made from natural or synthetic fibers or a blend of both. Different fiber types are combined to create fabrics with qualities required for a specific use. Fabrics may be woven, nonwoven, or knit.

- Weight, hand, drape, and count are terms used to describe a fabric's thickness, its stiffness, the way a fabric feels, and how it is constructed. These qualities, as well as fiber content and care requirements, must be considered when selecting fabric for a particular project.

- Specialty fabrics, such as interfacings, stiffeners, and stuffings, add support and stability but aren't seen in finished garments and projects.

- Conversion charts take the confusion out of figuring yardage.

Trim Techniques

In This Chapter

- An overview of types of trims
- Quick tips for attaching trims
- The scoop on bias binding
- Making and applying piping
- Terrific trim techniques

Beaded, braided, twisted, or flat—whichever way you like it, trim is *in*. Strong webbing or twill tape makes a quick no-sew strap. Binding stabilizes seams and covers raw edges. Ribbons can be used as drawstring ties, and strategically placed trims can visually extend a hemmed edge. Add a fun finish to almost anything with decorative trim: glam up rubber gloves, ruffle up a cuff, or pretty up a purse. In this chapter, you learn to attach basic trim types and even create your own unique trims!

Trim Types

One visit to the trim aisle of your favorite fabric store reveals an almost overwhelming number of trims—light laces, bold braids, and thick fringe, just to name a few. Choose a trim with your base fabric in mind. The weight, drape, and care requirements must be compatible.

Some trims have headers—flat fabric flanges to sew into seams. Other trims are simply stitched directly onto the fabric. Browse the following basic trim types for tips on turning corners, negotiating curves, and finishing trim ends.

Flat trims, such as ribbon, *rickrack*, twill tape, and braids, can be stitched directly to the fabric. Simply pin the trim in place and topstitch, or hand stitch to hide the stitching. Wide trims may need to be stitched along both the top and bottom edges to secure the trim in place.

Flexible trims can be coaxed around corners and curves. Stiff, rigid trims may need to be
mitered at corners. To form a mitered corner from a light- or medium-weight trim, stitch
trim in place along both long edges, stopping at the corner. Backstitch or tie off the thread
to secure, and remove the stitched piece from the machine. Fold the trim back on itself, right
sides together, and press the fold. Fold the trim again, creating a 45-degree angled fold ending
precisely at the outer corner and aligning the outer trim edge with the first fold. Press the
angled fold, and unfold and stitch along the pressed line to secure it in place, taking care that
no stitching shows beyond the trim. Refold the trim, and stitch it in place along the edges.

To reduce bulk with heavier trims, stitch along the diagonal fold, and carefully cut away the
excess trim beneath the fold.

*Fold miters precisely for a crisp, professional
look.*

To join flat trim along a continuous edge, position the trim ends at an inconspicuous spot.
Stitch the trim in place, leaving at least 1 inch unstitched at the trim ends. Trim the ends,
leaving a ³⁄₈-inch overlap on one end. If necessary, zigzag the trim edges to prevent fraying or
treat the cut edges with liquid seam sealant. Fold ¼ inch to the wrong side on the overlapping
end and layer the folded end over the shorter edge so the raw edges are hidden. Stitch the trim
in place.

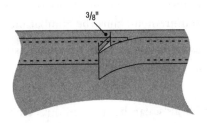

3/8"

*Fold the trimmed end to the wrong side, hid-
ing raw edges.*

Twisted *cords* are available in a variety of sizes. Some cords do not have headers and must be hand sewn to the fabric using coordinating thread and fine slip stitches. Other cords have headers and are attached within seamlines, like piping (see the "Piping" section in this chapter). Most cords are flexible and can be curved around shapes and corners. Clip headers at corners and around curves so the cords will lie flat.

Clip headers at curves and corners, and stitch close to the cord to attach.

To join cords along a continuous edge, position the ends at an inconspicuous spot and attach the rest of the cord as usual. Overlap the cord ends, tucking ends into the seam. Stitch across the overlapped ends twice to secure.

Fringed trims have brushed, beaded, or twisted fringes extending from headers that are meant to be either sewn inside a seam or topstitched to fabric. Use a cording or zipper foot to stitch hidden headers in place. Abut the ends of thick trims, and stitch in place.

SNIP IT

To preshrink trims, place the trim in a lingerie bag, or wrap trim around a plastic container to prevent tangling. If necessary, tape trim ends or treat with seam sealant to prevent raveling. Soak for 10 minutes in the same temperature water the garment will be washed in, and blot with a towel to remove excess moisture. Lay flat to dry or machine dry in a lingerie bag.

Bias Tape and Binding

Bias tape and binding are folded strips of bias-cut woven fabric. The bias-cut strips have more "give" than straight-of-grain strips, allowing them to wrap easily around curves and corners. Use bias tape and binding to finish raw edges at necklines, armholes, and other openings.

Single-fold bias tape is folded once along each long edge. As a decorative trim, single-fold bias is stitched flat, close to each folded edge. Wide single-fold bias tape is sometimes used as an elastic or drawstring casing, or as a lightweight facing that doesn't add bulk to heavy fabric. Double-fold bias tape is folded along each long edge and down the center of the strip, forming a pocket to encase fabric edges.

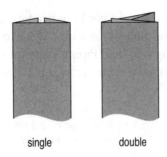

single   double

Both single- and double-fold bindings are available in many colors and widths. You can also create your own binding from light- and medium-weight fabric.

Trim and Finish with Bias

Some sewing machines have nifty attachments that make applying binding a breeze, but it's really not that hard to stitch bias tape and binding in place with ordinary tools. Follow manufacturer instructions if using prepared bias binding, or use these instructions to attach your own bias strips.

To apply single-fold bias binding, unfold the bias strip and align one binding raw edge with the raw edge of the piece to be bound, right sides together. Pin, and stitch the binding strip in place along its crease. Refold the bias, and press the binding over the raw edge. Fold the binding strip around the seam allowance raw edges, folding the remaining binding to the project wrong side where its fold meets the seamline. Hand stitch or edgestitch the binding in place.

Premade double-fold bias is available in two widths. Apply it as directed for single-fold bias. Double-fold bias has an extra crease in place to wrap over the fabric edges. Hand stitch or edgestitch it in place. For a different double-fold binding application, see the "Project: Double-Bind Pillow" section at the end of this chapter.

A double-layer binding is used in quilts and other projects where durability is a plus. The binding strips are cut four times the desired width, plus two seam allowances, and often with an extra $\frac{1}{8}$ to $\frac{1}{4}$ inch to wrap around the project's thickness. The binding strip is folded and pressed in half lengthwise with wrong sides together. With right sides together, the raw edges of the binding strip are aligned with the raw edges of the project. The strip is stitched in place, and the binding strip is folded over the stitched edge, encasing the raw edges. The folded edge is slipstitched or edgestitched in place.

single-fold binding   double-fold binding   double-layer binding

Single-fold, double-fold, and double-layer binding each offer a unique finish. (All views shown from the project right side.)

When binding a continuous edge, such as an armhole or neckline, position the binding ends at a seamline or other inconspicuous spot. Stitch the rest of the binding in place, leaving an inch unstitched at the binding ends. Trim the ends, leaving a ³⁄₈-inch overlap on one. Fold ¼ inch to the wrong side on the overlapping end, and layer the shorter end over the folded edge so the raw edges will be hidden when the binding is sewn in place. Finish the binding as usual.

To form a mitered corner in a double-layer binding, stitch the binding in place along one long edge, stopping a few stitches shy of the finished binding width from the corner. Backstitch or tie off the thread to secure, and remove the stitched piece from the machine. Fold the binding away from the next edge, forming a 45-degree angled fold at the corner. Press, and pin the folded binding in place. Next, fold the binding down, aligning the raw binding edges with the raw fabric edge and making a straight fold at the upper corner edge. Pin in place and stitch the binding along the fabric edge. The miter is formed when the binding strip is folded over the stitched seam allowance and stitched in place. Slipstitch the 45-degree fold to secure.

When slipstitching the binding fold to the reverse side, fold the corner miter in the opposite direction by tucking in the fullness as you approach the corner. Folding the miter in the opposite direction evenly distributes the fullness around the corner for less bulk.

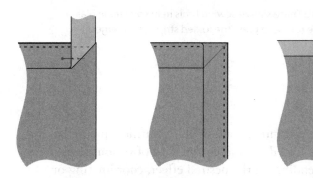

Quilters often use mitered corners when binding quilts.

SNIP IT

For instructions on mitering a double-fold bias tape, see the "Project: Double-Bind Pillow" section, later in this chapter.

DIY Bias Binding

To make your own bias strips, first determine the desired width of the finished binding. For single-fold binding, cut strips twice the desired finished width. Cut double-fold binding strips four times the desired width. Press the raw edges to meet at the center of the cut strip. For double-fold binding, press the resulting strip almost in half, wrong sides together, allowing one pressed edge to extend ¹⁄₁₆ inch beyond the other.

To cut bias strips, straighten the fabric grain and use rotary cutting tools to create a clean-cut edge. Lay the fabric flat in a single layer, and fold one corner at a 45-degree angle by bringing the cut edge parallel to the selvage. Trim ¼ inch from the folded edge. Using the cut edge as a guide, cut bias strips the desired width. Be careful not to stretch the bias fabric. (Binding doesn't have to be cut on the bias. Straight-grain strips, especially when cut crosswise, work beautifully on straight edges. Even "bias tape makers" can be used with straight-cut strips.)

To join bias-cut strips together, place two strip ends at a right angle to each other with right sides together. Draw a 45-degree line where the strips intersect, or follow the already angled edge. Pin and stitch the strips together along the drawn line. Trim the seam allowance to ¼ inch, and press the seam open. The two strips should form one smooth, long strip. Continue adding strips until the desired length is reached.

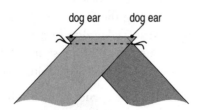

Trim the "dog ears" from the joined bias strips.

SEW SURPRISING

Check the notions aisle for bias tape makers. These simple sewing tools help you create bias tape easily. Pull cut fabric strips through the tool, and press the folded strip as it emerges from the tip.

Piping

Piping is a narrow flange of folded fabric stitched into a seam. Flat, or unfilled, piping has a soft, layered look. For corded piping, fabric is folded around cotton cord of various sizes to make a filled, rounded seamline accent. Depending on the desired effect, coordinating or contrasting fabrics may be used for the piping. Use piping to enhance borders on a quilt or highlight home décor projects. Piped seams can be stiff, making this trim unsuitable for softly draped designs.

Applying Piping

To apply flat piping, sandwich the folded flange between fabric pieces, with right sides together and raw edges aligned. Pin or baste the piping in place, and stitch the seam. Trim excess piping at seam ends.

To join flat piping around a continuous shape, place piping ends at an inconspicuous spot and stitch piping in place, leaving the ends unstitched. Trim the ends, leaving a ⅜-inch overlap. Tuck the short end inside the longer end, turning under ¼ inch on the overlapping edge to hide raw edges. Slipstitch the folded edge in place.

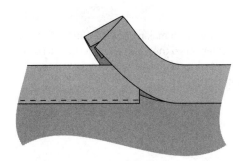

Overlap flat piping ends to hide the raw edges.

To apply corded piping, position the piping on the right side of the fabric along the seam, with the rounded cord facing away from the seam allowance. Using a cording or zipper foot, baste the piping in place. With right sides together, layer the second fabric piece on top of the piping, aligning and pinning seam allowance raw edges. Position the needle to the left of the presser foot, and stitch just past the basting line so the basting won't show on the right side of the seam.

To join corded piping around a shape, trim the fabric strip, leaving a ³⁄₈-inch overlap. Trim the cord ends so they abut each other, or you can unravel the cord ends where they overlap, trim half the cord strands from each end, and twist the ends together. Hand stitch the butted or joined cord ends together. Re-cover the cord with the fabric strip, turning under ¼ inch on the overlapping edge and slipstitching the folded edge in place.

Secure cord ends together with a few hand stitches, avoiding extra bulk in the seam.

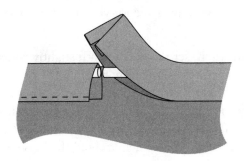

DIY Piping

To make basic flat piping, cut bias fabric strips double the desired piping width plus seam allowances. For example, for ¼-inch piping on a project using ½-inch seam allowances, cut a strip of fabric 1½ inches wide. Fold the strip in half lengthwise, with wrong sides together, and press. Apply as usual.

To make corded piping, cut bias strips wide enough to wrap the cord, plus seam allowances. Fold the strip in half lengthwise with wrong sides together. Tuck the cord inside the folded strip, snug against the fold. Using a zipper or piping foot, machine stitch the folded fabric strip together, close but not tight to the cord.

Cotton or polyester cord is available in different thicknesses. Choose one according to the desired piping size. Preshrink the cord before using to avoid possibly distorting the seam when the finished project is washed.

Trim Techniques

Individual trims are just the tip of the creative iceberg. Consider the possibilities of combining trims! Couch cord over flat trims. Layer ribbons of varying widths. Stack rickrack for a textural treat. Top off trims with button or bead embellishments. You're only limited by your imagination!

Couching

Couching is a simple embellishment technique that uses zigzag stitching to attach cord, yarn, floss, or ribbon to fabric. Use couching to add extra interest, texture, and color to fabric or to cover up a fabric flaw.

Specialty couching, cording, or braiding feet make quick work of this technique; guide holes in the feet align the couched cord with the needle. Some specialty couching feet require a straight stitch rather than a zigzag stitch. If a specialty foot isn't available for your machine, use an open toe foot for visibility and flexibility as you stitch.

To couch a yarn or cord using a zigzag foot and stitch, set the stitch width slightly wider than the cord so the stitches fall on either side of the cord edges. It's okay to catch the cord fibers slightly, but don't crush the cord beneath the stitching. With the cord on the fabric right side, center the cord beneath the presser foot. Anchor the cord end in place with a few back stitches, and zigzag over the cord, trapping it against the fabric. Stitch slowly, placing the needle down and pivoting as needed to negotiate curves and corners. It may help to hold the loose cord up as you stitch.

If the fabric puckers, use a lightweight fusible or tear-away stabilizer to support the fabric. Hide the cord ends in the seams or pull the cord and thread ends to the fabric's wrong side with a large-eye needle. If the cord is too large to thread through a hand needle, cut the cord end close to the fabric and secure in place with hand stitching.

Layering

If one trim is terrific, why not use two … or more? Layer up those lovely laces, ribbons, and rickrack for extra effect! Tuck an extra trim behind piping for a seam accent. Stack up rickrack in several sizes, offsetting peaks before center stitching to secure. Curve and coil tiny bias strips into sweet swirls. The options are endless!

Keep fabric content, care instructions, and combined weight in mind when selecting embellishment options. Stacked trims may need more than a single line of stitching to keep them in place. For instance, when layering narrow trims on top of wide ribbons, secure both ribbon edges to the base fabric first, and center stitch the narrow trim in place. It may be best to hand stitch single elements, such as buttons, pompoms, and bows.

SEW SURPRISING

Make stacked trims work for you. To give a tote bag's handles extra strength, stack two or more layers of grosgrain ribbon, joining them with decorative stitches, to create a fancy braid. Back with another layer of ribbon to hide the bobbin threads.

Project: Double-Bind Pillow

This simple pillow provides a perfect canvas for exploring embellishments, featuring a special fabric, or just creating a bit of comfort on your couch. Our model is trimmed with binding applied two different ways. It's bound to be a delight!

Binding applied two ways adds interest to a simple pillow.

Finished size:

16×16 inches

Tools and materials:

$\frac{1}{2}$ yard light- to medium-weight cotton* for main fabric

$\frac{1}{4}$ yard light- to medium-weight cotton* for contrast fabric

(Note: Choose similar fabrics for a subtle appearance, or go for drama with high-contrast options such as black and white.)

16-inch pillow form

$\frac{1}{2}$-inch and 1-inch bias tape makers (optional)

Ruler

Marking pen or pencil (removable)

All-purpose thread

Scissors

Straight pins

Suitable woven fabrics include quilting-weight cottons or lightweight home décor fabrics. Stretchy fabrics are not suitable for this project. Yardage is based on 45-inch-wide fabric with at least 40 inches of useable width.

SNIP IT

If you prefer a pillow cover with more body, fuse iron-on interfacing to the wrong side of each pillow piece before sewing.

Cutting:

1. From the main fabric, cut the following:

    1 front panel 16×16 inches

    2 back panels 16×11 inches

2. From the contrast fabric, cut the following:

    2 strips 1 inch × wof (width of fabric)

    2 strips 2 inches × wof

SEW SURPRISING

It looks as if we forgot to add the seam allowance! In fact, it's a design decision: by making the pillow cover slightly smaller than the pillow form, we ensure a plump, overstuffed look.

Construction:

The seam allowance for this project is ½ inch. Be sure to backstitch at the beginning and end of each seam.

3. Using a removable marking tool, draw lines on the right side of the front panel, 2 inches from the outer edges, to create a 12-inch square.

4. Remove the selvages from all four contrast strips. Join the two 1-inch strips at one short end, as shown in the "DIY Bias Binding" section earlier in the chapter.

5. Press ¼ inch to the wrong side on the long edges of the 1-inch binding strip. The long raw edges should meet at the center of the strip. Optional: use a ½-inch bias tape maker to turn and press the edges in one step.

6. Beginning at one corner of the marked 12-inch square, pin the outer edge of the prepared binding to the guideline. The binding's inner edge will have extra fullness at the corners.

7. Pin the binding completely around the drawn square. Where the binding meets at the first corner, fold under the unpinned end at a 45-degree angle, with the excess extending away from the pillow center. Carefully trim the excess length so the raw edges at the beginning and end are hidden under the binding, creating a miter at the corner.

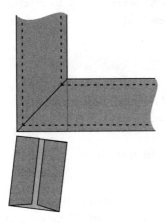

Fold and trim the binding end to create the first mitered corner.

8. Edgestitch the outer edge of the binding.

9. Miter the remaining three corners of the square by folding the excess fabric along the inner edge under the binding, creating a 45-degree fold at each corner. Tuck the extra fabric under in the same direction each time so the corners turn identically.

10. Edgestitch the inner edge of the binding. Slipstitch the miters by hand, or edgestitch them by machine to secure the folds. If you want, treat the binding's cut edges with liquid seam sealant to prevent fraying.

Create miters at each corner.

11. Press ¼ inch to the wrong side on one 16-inch edge of each back panel. Press an additional 1 inch to the wrong side on the same edges. Edgestitch the inner fold to secure the hems.

12. Lay the back panels on the front panel, wrong sides together, matching the raw edges. The back panels will overlap at the center. Pin the panels together and baste ¼ inch from the raw edges all around.

13. With right sides together, join the 2-inch contrast strips along one short edge, as in step 4. Press ½ inch to the wrong side on both long edges of the assembled binding. Optional: use a 1-inch bias tape maker to fold and press in one step. Fold the pressed binding almost in half lengthwise, allowing one pressed edge to extend ¹/₁₆ inch beyond the other when folding the tape. Press the new fold.

> **SEWING SENSE**
>
> The binding made in step 13 is double-fold binding, with an extra fold designed to encase raw edges. The binding created in step 5 is single-fold binding, often applied as trim and sometimes used to finish hems or seams.

14. Open up the binding at one end, and press ¼ inch to the wrong side. Refold the binding, and press again.

15. Beginning near the center of one side with the pressed binding end, encase the basted pillow edge inside the folded binding with the slightly longer binding edge on the pillow back. Set the machine for a zigzag stitch 1.5mm wide and 1.4mm long, and thread the needle and bobbin with thread to match the binding. Sew the binding around the pillow's outer edge, enclosing all the fabric layers, and positioning the stitch along the inner binding edge. Check frequently to be sure the underside of the binding is also caught in the seam.

To miter the corners:

16. Stitch all the way to the corner, and backstitch. Lift the presser foot and cut the thread.

17. Fold the binding back on itself, turning it inside out, and crease the binding along the pillow edge.

18. Fold the binding forward at a 45-degree angle, turning it right side out again and enclosing the next edge to be bound. The 45-degree fold tapers to nothing at the outer edge of the binding. Begin sewing at the miter fold, and continue to the next corner.

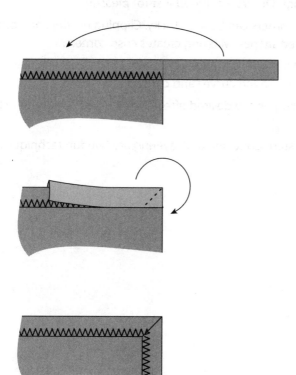

Turn the binding back on itself to create a mitered fold.

19. After turning the last corner, sew to within 4 inches of the binding start. Lay the remaining binding along the pillow edge, and mark where it meets the leading edge. Add a ¼-inch seam allowance, and cut off the excess binding. Unfold the binding, and press the seam allowance to the wrong side; refold and press again. Stitch the remainder of the binding to the pillow, ensuring that the pressed ends meet squarely.

20. Slipstitch the beginning and end of the binding together with matching thread. Slipstitch the miter fold at each corner, if desired.

21. Insert the pillow form through the overlapped back panels.

Once you've learned the basics of pillow making, have fun experimenting! Make seasonal covers and change your décor by popping the pillow form out of one cover and into another. The extras even fold flat for easy, compact storage.

The Least You Need to Know

- Trims offer another avenue for personalizing your projects. Some trims are functional, acting as handles, straps, or drawstrings. Others are added just for pleasure.
- Applying trims around curves and corners can be a bit tricky. Clipping headers or fabric flanges helps align trims with curved shapes. Mitering creates crisp corners.
- Bias tape and binding can be used to finish raw edges or as a decorative accent. Bias-cut strips stretch, making it easy to work around curves and corners.
- Piping can be flat or filled, depending on the desired effect. Pair a piped edge with rick-rack for a fun layered look.
- Attaching individual trims is just a start. Couching and layering are two fun techniques for cranking up the creativity.

Fascinating Fasteners

In This Chapter

- An overview of simple fasteners
- Button basics
- Essentials for applying elastic
- Attaching zippers

Fasteners—buttons and buttonholes, zippers, hooks, and snaps—are the endnotes of most projects, but these easy yet essential elements are much more than a "finishing touch." Many fasteners can be machine stitched in place; others are hand stitch only.

In this chapter, we show you some of the more popular fasteners and help you choose a fastener according to the project, fabric, and opening type.

Simple Fasteners

Simple fasteners are easy to apply. Most have two parts that interlock to hold sides of an opening together. Let's review some simple fasteners:

Hook-and-loop tape consists of two synthetic fiber strips: one covered in tiny flexible hooks and the other in soft loops. When the strips are pushed together, the hooks and loops intertwine, creating a surprisingly strong bond. Separate the strips by deliberately pulling them apart. Commonly called Velcro after a popular brand, hook-and-loop tape is used for quick finishes on accessories and home décor items.

Hook-and-loop tape is available in a number of colors and widths, in sew-on or adhesive formats. Purchase the tape in precut lengths or by the yard. To apply sew-on hook-and-loop tape, trim both the hook and loop strips to the needed size. Position and pin one strip in place. Using a heavy-duty needle and a zipper foot, edgestitch the strip in place. Align the second strip on the facing fabric, and edgestitch in place.

PINPRICK

Don't sew through adhesive versions of hook-and-loop tape. The glue will quickly gum your needle, break threads, and damage your machine.

Hook closures are used at stress points when you don't want the closure to be seen. Hooks and eyes consist of a blunt bent wire hook that slips through a rounded wire loop. Use these to close edges that meet but don't overlap, such as at a neckline. Use hooks and bars on waistbands or in other high-stress areas where edges overlap.

To attach a hook and eye, place the eye at the finished edge so the loop extends beyond the garment. Using a double thread, blanket or whipstitch the eye in place through the wire loops at each end, taking care to slide the needle between fabric layers so the stitching doesn't show on the garment right side. Slip the hook through the eye, align the finished edges to determine hook placement, and stitch the hook in place through its wire loops. The hook should curve away from the underlying fabric.

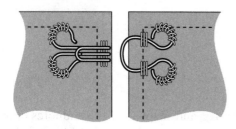

Add a few extra stitches at the base to keep the hook and eye aligned.

Sew the hook in place first to attach a hook and bar. Position the hook close to the finished edge on the underside of the overlap and blanket stitch it in place, making sure the stitching does not show on the garment right side. Slip the stitched hook through the bar to position the bar correctly. Mark the bar ends, and stitch the bar to the underneath edge.

Use *snaps* to secure overlapping edges that aren't likely to be pulled apart during wear. Snaps are made from metal, plastic, or nylon and have either two or four parts. Two-part snaps consist of a ball (male) and socket (female) that are sewn in place on opposite garment edges. Four-part snaps have posts or prongs that pierce the fabric and attach to a snap cap to hold the snap in place. Place four-part snaps correctly the first time because the prongs put permanent holes in the fabric.

Snap tape consists of multiple snaps preset into twill tape. You sew the tape to each side of an opening with the snap halves aligned instead of sewing or setting individual snaps.

Magnetic snaps house powerful magnets that hold the fastener closed. Designed as heavyweight handbag closures, the snap halves are held in place with metal washers hidden inside a lining.

To sew a two-part snap in place, position the snap halves on the fabric opening, with the socket on the underlying fabric and the ball on the overlapping piece. Align the snap halves by poking a straight pin through the fabric and snap center hole. Use a buttonhole or whipstitch to sew the snap halves in place, sliding the needle between fabric layers so the stitching doesn't show on the garment right side.

Four-part post or prong snaps may be pressed into place with rubber-tipped pliers, or they may require a specialty tool. Check manufacturer instructions before purchasing.

SNIP IT

Before tossing out worn or ruined items, reclaim buttons, sewn-in snaps, zippers, and other fasteners to save yourself a trip to the store.

Frogging is a bold, decorative form of fastener. Made of cord or thin braid, a frog has two parts: a loop and a knot. A number of designs are available for creating frogged fasteners. The stiffness of the cord determines complexity.

You can also make your own frogged closure. First, sketch the loop design on paper. Holding the cord right side against the paper, pin the cord end at the center of the design where it will be overlapped or covered. Following the drawn design, pin the cord in place. Whipstitch the looped cord together where it overlaps. Trim the cord ends and stitch to join, making sure the stitching doesn't show on the right side. Remove the loop from the paper and place it right side up on the garment, extending the button loop over the finished edge. Slipstitch the loop in place, making sure the stitches don't show.

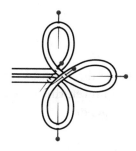

When creating frogged closures, start with a simple design.

To make a ball button, loop and interlace 8 to 10 inches of cord as shown in the following illustration. Holding the cord ends firmly, pull the loops together to form a knotted ball. Trim the cord ends, and stitch them securely to the ball bottom. Use the loop as a guide to position the ball button, and sew it in place.

Weave the end of the third loop through the first two loops to make a ball button.

Buttons

Made of almost any material imaginable, buttons come in every shape, color, and size. Some buttons are purely decorative; others are completely practical. Many buttons are a bit of both.

Keep fabric and function in mind when selecting buttons. Don't weigh down delicate fabric with large, heavy buttons or expect tiny baby buttons to hold heavyweight weaves in place. It's all right to stray slightly from recommended sizes; just be sure the size you select is compatible with your project. For example, substituting ¾-inch buttons for ½-inch buttons on a shirt front leaves too little fabric for the placket to overlap properly, but ⅝-inch buttons may work as a substitute.

Types of Buttons

There are two main button types: *sew-through* and *shank*. Sew-through buttons have holes going all the way through the button. A shank button has a loop on the back to hold the button above the fabric surface. The extra space provided by the shank makes it easier to button coats or jackets made of bulky fabrics.

sew-through   shank

Sew-through buttons traditionally have two or four holes. The loop size varies on shank buttons.

Traditionally, men's and women's fashions button in different directions. Women's garments button right over left, while men's button left over right. However, this isn't a hard-and-fast rule; most jeans button in the same direction, regardless of gender.

> **SEW SURPRISING**
>
> Use button forms to create covered buttons. Available in a number of shapes and sizes, button forms consist of an outer shape that can be covered with light- to medium-weight fabric and a button back that holds the fabric in place when the two pieces are snapped together. Stitch through the metal shank on the button back to sew the button in place.

Attaching Buttons by Hand

Hand stitch a sew-through button in place using a needle and thread. Be sure the needle is small enough to pass easily through the button's holes. Double the thread for stronger stitches. Knot thread ends, and trim the thread tails close to the knot.

Working from the right side of the fabric, take one or two small stitches where you want the button to be. Thread the button onto the needle through one of the button's holes. Hold the button in place, hiding the knot and the stitch beneath the button, and stitch through the next button hole and back through the fabric. Bring the needle and thread back up through the fabric and the first hole. Slip a pin or toothpick under the thread on top of the button to lengthen the thread loops. Stitch through the button and fabric three or four times, ending with the needle between the fabric and button. Be sure the thread is pulled evenly tight.

Remove the toothpick or pin, wrap the thread three or four times around the stitches between the button and the fabric, and pull the needle to the wrong side of the fabric beneath the button. This creates a thread shank that provides the space for another fabric layer when the button is in use; eliminate the shank when sewing decorative buttons that should lie flat against the fabric. Take a few small backstitches beneath the button to secure the thread, and trim the thread ends.

Form an X or = with your stitches to sew a four-hole button in place, or sew a decorative arrow or square.

Secure a shank button by sewing from the wrong side to the right side of the fabric, stitching through the button shank. Take several stitches, pulling the threads evenly tight to hold the shank firmly against the fabric. Knot the thread on the fabric wrong side.

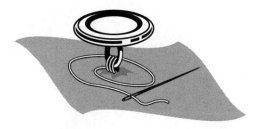

Stitch shank buttons securely, knotting the thread ends on the fabric's wrong side.

SNIP IT

Add interest by stacking various-size buttons together. Simply align the buttonholes and sew in place. Use thicker novelty thread or pearl cotton to tie buttons in place, knotting the thread on top of the button and leaving a ¼-inch tail.

Attaching Buttons by Machine

Two- and four-hole buttons can be sewn in place using a machine zigzag stitch. To machine stitch a button in place, follow the instructions in your owner's manual for your machine's accessory foot and button-attaching stitch. Alternatively, use a zigzag foot and stitch, setting the stitch width to align with the button's holes. (You don't want the needle to hit the button while stitching.) Set the stitch length to 0, and position the button on the fabric right side, making sure the holes are perpendicular to the feed dogs. If necessary, temporarily tape the button in place.

Turn the handwheel through one complete stitch to be sure the needle won't hit the button, and stitch slowly, zigzagging the button in place. Sew through the button four to six times. To tie off, reset the machine for a straight stitch, and sew three or four times in one hole. Cut the thread, leaving a long thread end. Using a hand needle, wrap both the top and bobbin threads around the thread shank, and secure beneath the button with several hand stitches.

A drop of seam sealant on the bobbin threads helps hold the stitches securely through wear and washing.

Buttonholes

Buttonholes are used on overlapping openings and may be worked by hand or machine. Use horizontal buttonholes at stress points; there's less risk of buttons coming undone. Use vertical buttonholes for loose-fitting items or decorative features.

Buttonholes may have rounded, flat, or keyhole-shape ends. Flat-end (or straight) buttonholes are used on light- and medium-weight fabric. Rounded buttonholes have stitches fanning out around the curved ends, securing loosely woven lightweight fabrics. Use keyhole openings for heavy shanked buttons on thicker fabrics.

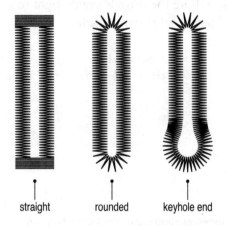

Choose a buttonhole type according to fabric weight.

straight   rounded   keyhole end

The size of the button determines the size of the buttonhole. For flat buttons, add ⅛ inch to the button diameter. Measure large, rounded buttons by pinching a thin strip of paper around the widest button part. Holding the pinched paper ends together, slip the paper off the button and fold it flat. Measure from pinch to fold, and add ⅛ inch to determine the buttonhole length. Always test the buttonhole length on fabric scraps before stitching on a garment.

Most buttonholes are placed near garment edges along a center front or center back line that determines edge overlap. Begin horizontal buttonholes ⅛ inch past the center front or back line, with the bulk of the buttonhole extending into the garment. Vertical buttonholes align along the center front or back line, with the buttonhole edge ⅛ inch above the button placement. On shirts and jackets, place a button at the fullest part of the bust and adjust spacing as needed to avoid gapping.

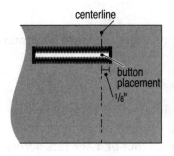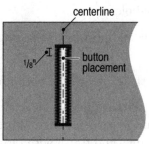

Align buttonholes with the centerline for proper fit.

PINPRICK

Always stitch and cut buttonholes before attaching buttons. It's far easier to adjust button placement than to "unsew" a buttonhole.

Check your machine manual for buttonhole capabilities. Most zigzag machines have a buttonhole foot, and some have automatic buttonhole settings.

Here's how to stitch a buttonhole by machine:

1. Use a temporary marking pen to mark the buttonhole size and position.

2. Select a buttonhole option or, if none is available, choose a zigzag stitch, setting a short stitch length. (Depending on the fabric weight, a satin stitch setting or slightly longer will work well.)

3. Following the marked lines, zigzag stitch around the buttonhole, leaving a thin, unstitched area between the two long buttonhole edges. Stitch again to reinforce the stitching.

Reinforce the buttonhole by adding bar tacks or a wider zigzag at each end.

4. End stitching, leaving long thread tails to bury between the fabric layers.

5. Carefully cut the buttonhole open, using the tips of small scissors to snip the fabric at the center of the buttonhole and leaving the stitches intact.

SNIP IT

Interfacing placed between the outer fabric and facing layer strengthens stitching and prevents buttonholes from stretching. Fusible interfacing helps prevent fraying.

Here's how to make hand-worked buttonholes:

1. Thread-mark the buttonhole size and position by basting together the fabric and interfacing layers.

2. Using sharp scissors, snip open the center of the buttonhole.

3. For horizontal buttonholes, use a buttonhole stitch around the upper buttonhole edge, starting at the end farthest from the garment edge. Work several stitches in a semicircle around the end near the fabric edge, and finish with satin stitches or a bar tack across the buttonhole end.

   Work vertical buttonholes the same way, substituting satin stitching or bar tacks on both buttonhole ends.

4. Knot and bury the thread ends on the garment's wrong side.

Elastic

Elastic is a stretchy fabric made from polyester- or cotton-wrapped rubber or synthetic cores. The wrapped cores are braided, woven, or knit together to make different types of elastic. More rubber equals more stretch, and quality elastic will stretch to twice its length and quickly revert to its original shape and size.

Many elastics are made for specific applications, so read the package descriptions for intended use. Choose elastic according to size and use, with the same care requirements as the fabric used.

Elastic Types and Widths

Most elastics look bland and flat, but there are subtle differences.

Braided elastic has lengthwise ribs. It narrows when stretched and loses its stretch if stitched through. Use braided elastic inside casings and for sleeve and leg bands.

Knitted elastic is lightweight, with a smooth, uniform surface. Soft and strong, knitted elastic doesn't narrow when stretched, and keeps its shape when sewn through. Use knitted elastic in casings, or sew it directly to fabric.

Woven elastic has a striped or windowpane appearance. It's very strong and can be thick, making it the best choice for heavyweight fabrics. Woven elastic doesn't narrow when stretched; use it in casings or sew it directly to fabric.

Braided, woven, and knitted elastics are available in a variety of widths, from $\frac{1}{8}$ to $2\frac{1}{2}$ inches. Thin elastic cord and thread are used for beading, gathering, and shirring. (See Chapter 10 for more on shirring.)

Attaching Elastic

Sewing elastic to fabric is called a *direct application*. If placing elastic around an opening, such as an armhole edge, finish the fabric edge first.

Here's how to attach the elastic:

1. Determine the needed length of elastic, adding 1 inch for seam allowances if needed. Some elastic may stretch—up to 8 percent!—while stitching. Test stitch a short length first. To sew around an opening, overlap and stitch the ends of the elastic together, pivoting the stitches to create a box shape and making sure the elastic isn't twisted.

2. Pin-mark the quarter points on both the elastic and the fabric opening, and pin the elastic to the fabric wrong side, matching pin marks.

3. Using a ball point needle and thread to match the fabric, sew the elastic to the fabric with a long straight or zigzag stitch; stretch stitches are ideal. Stretch the elastic to fit the fabric, holding the elastic and fabric at the pinned quarter points as they pass beneath the presser foot.

4. If necessary, fold the fabric to encase the elastic and stitch in place to finish the edge.

SNIP IT

Hide elastic in a casing if you don't want it to show. You'll avoid the risk of the elastic losing its stretch when stitched and have the added benefit of easily replacing it later, if necessary. See Chapter 19 for more information on casings.

Drawstrings and Ties

Some of the easiest and most often overlooked fasteners are drawstrings and ties. *Drawstrings* are enclosed in a casing or a channel between layers of fabric, surrounding an opening. When pulled, the drawstrings gather the fabric, tightening or pulling the opening closed. *Ties* are attached to either side of an opening. Knotting the ties together holds the opening closed.

Almost any type of flat trim, ribbon, or cord can be used as a drawstring or tie. Make self-fabric ties by folding and stitching fabric lengths into narrow strips. Whatever material you use, it must be strong enough to withstand repeated wear.

To make a turned-under side-seam drawstring casing, leave a section of the side seam un-stitched near the top edge. Press ¼ inch to the wrong side along the top edge. Press an additional 1 inch to the wrong side along the same edge. Edgestitch along both folds to create a channel. Using a bodkin or safety pin, thread the drawstring through the channel. Tie the drawstring ends together so they don't disappear into the channel, and pull the drawstring tight to close.

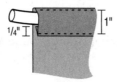

Make a drawstring casing from a turned and stitched edge.

Use a buttonhole as a drawstring opening when an inseam opening isn't an option. Reinforce the buttonhole with interfacing, and double-stitch it for extra strength.

Zippers

Zippers may seem daunting, but don't let "zipper foot fear" set in. A little zipper knowledge and a few simple steps will have you sewing zippers like a pro.

Your zipper foot is your best friend when it comes to sewing zippers. This presser foot has needle notches in the sides, not the center like most presser feet. This allows you to sew quite close to the zipper teeth—one secret to zipper success!

SEW SURPRISING

Your zipper foot probably comes with instructions about the correct needle position to use. Surprise! If you can change your needle position, it's probably possible to move the needle 0.5 to 1mm to the right or left and still use the zipper foot. This versatility is a big help when sewing piping or basting before permanently attaching zippers and trim. Always double-check by turning the hand wheel through a complete stitch pattern before proceeding to be sure the needle won't hit the foot, and use only straight stitches with your zipper foot.

Zipper Parts and Types

Zippers are made of two flexible tapes with interlocking teeth or coils along their facing edges. The slider moves along this edge, unlocking or locking the teeth or coils together. A pull tab attached to the slider makes it easier to grasp, and stops at the tape top and bottom keep the slider from slipping off the tape.

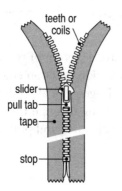

All zippers have the same basic parts.

There are three basic zipper types: all-purpose, invisible, and separating. *All-purpose zippers* are used on most garment and home décor items. *Invisible zippers* are concealed inside a seam and barely show in a finished project. *Separating zippers* are used when sections must separate completely, such as on jackets or travel bags. Some separating zippers have dual pull tabs so they can be opened or closed from either end. All three zipper types are available in different weights, lengths, and colors.

An unorthodox option is to choose a zipper that's a little longer than the zipper opening: you can move the slider out of the way when sewing and trim the excess tape after the zipper is in place.

Attaching Zippers

There are many ways to attach zippers. Two of the most common methods, a centered application and a lapped application, are outlined here.

A *centered* application places the zipper in the center of the seam with an equal amount of fabric on each side. To begin, baste the zipper opening together, and clip the stitches every 2 to 3 inches to make it easier to remove the basting later. Press the basted seam open, and finish the seam edges to prevent raveling.

Position the zipper, right side up, under the basted seam allowances, centering the zipper teeth or coils under the basting. Flip up the zipper pull tab, away from the body of the zipper, to reduce bulk at the top of the zipper. Pin the zipper tapes to the seam allowances, and machine- or hand-baste through all layers a little more than ¼ inch from the seam on both sides.

On the garment right side, beginning at the seam, topstitch across the zipper base, pivoting at the corner and continuing to the top edge of the zipper. Move the needle position, and stitch from the seamline at the zipper base to the upper edge along the opposite side. To finish, tie off the thread ends on the garment's wrong side and remove the original clipped basting.

SEW SURPRISING

Use a length of ordinary ½-inch-wide tape as a guide for topstitching by centering the tape over the basted seam. Stitch along the edge, but not through, the ½-inch tape guide, and remove the tape when the topstitching is complete.

A *lapped* application creates a narrow fabric flap over the zipper tape. Side zippers are sewn so the lap is on the garment front. Center back zippers place the lap on the garment left side. Preplan for the zipper upper edge. If there's a facing at the upper edge, the top zipper stop must be ½ inch below the seamline. If there's a waistband at the upper edge, the zipper stop should be placed just below the seamline. For example, to make the skirt in Chapter 8, the top zipper stop is placed 1 inch below the raw waistline edge.

Always stitch from the zipper base to the top on both sides.

To begin, baste the zipper opening together, and clip the stitches every 2 to 3 inches to make it easier to remove the basting later. Press the basted seam open, and finish the seam edges to prevent raveling.

Working on the garment wrong side, fold the fabric away from the right seam allowance. This will be the lapped edge. Unzip the zipper, and place it face down on the seam allowance, aligning the zipper teeth with the basted seam. Using a zipper foot and with the needle in the left position, baste the zipper tape to the seam allowance, sewing from the base of the zipper to the upper edge.

Close the zipper, and turn it right side up, folding back the basted seam allowance. Move the needle position to the right side of the zipper foot, and edgestitch the folded seam allowance to the zipper tape near the zipper teeth.

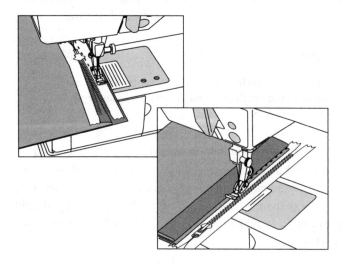

Baste the zipper tape to the seam allowance, and turn the zipper right side up. Edgestitch the folded seam allowance to the zipper tape.

To create the flap, place the garment wrong side up in a single layer with the seam allowances open, making sure the zipper teeth lie along the seam. A small pleat will form at the zipper bottom where the zipper tape has been sewn. Beginning at the seamline just below the bottom zipper stop, sew across the zipper tapes and seam allowances to a point ⅛ inch beyond the zipper teeth on the unattached zipper tape. Place the needle down, pivot, and continue sewing to the upper edge. This seam will be visible on the garment's right side.

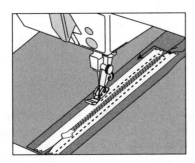

Topstitch across the zipper bottom and along the unattached tape edge.

To finish, tie off the thread ends on the garment's wrong side and remove the original clipped basting.

SNIP IT

To shorten a zipper, work several stitches over the zipper teeth just below the required length, securing the teeth together and creating a stop that will keep the slider from zipping off the teeth. Trim the excess zipper tape just below the stitches.

Project: Backpack Bag

This little backpack slips easily over the shoulders for a quick run to the store or an impromptu sleepover. As your skills increase, use it as a canvas for decorative stitching or appliqué.

Grosgrain ribbon does double duty as a drawstring and backpack straps.

Finished size:

11×15×3 inches

Tools and materials:

> 1/2 yard cotton print (home décor weight)*
>
> 1/2 yard coordinating cotton*
>
> 3 1/2 yards 7/8-inch grosgrain ribbon
>
> Basic sewing equipment
>
> Large safety pin

Suitable woven fabrics include quilting-weight cottons or lightweight home décor fabrics. Stretchy fabrics are not suitable for this project. Yardage is based on 45- or 54-inch-wide fabric with at least 40 (50) inches of useable width. Please note: these yardages require cutting the bag exterior on the crosswise grain. For directional or large-scale prints, purchase 1 1/8 yards of home décor fabric and cut the exterior lengthwise.

Cutting:

1. From the heavier cotton print, cut one 36×14 1/2-inch rectangle for the exterior.

2. From the coordinating fabric, cut two 16 1/2×14 1/2-inch rectangles for the lining.

SEW SURPRISING

Line this—or any—bag with a white or light-color fabric, and the bag's contents will be more visible.

Construction:

The seam allowance for this project is 1/2 inch. Be sure to backstitch at the beginning and end of each seam.

3. Fold the bag exterior in half, right sides together, so it measures 14 1/2×18 inches. Measure and mark two 1×1 1/2-inch rectangles at each end of the fold, and cut along the marked lines. This will be the bag bottom.

4. Stack the two lining rectangles with right sides together. Measure, mark, and cut a 1 1/2-inch square at each end of one 14 1/2-inch side. This will be the lining bottom.

5. With right sides still together, sew the lining bottom seam between the two cutouts. Leave a 6-inch gap near the center of the seam. Press the seam open.

6. Sew the lining side seams, and press them open.

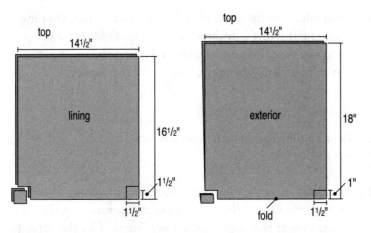

Measure, mark, cut, and remove two rect-angles or squares on the exterior and lining pieces.

7. Fold the lining, right sides together, aligning the bottom seam with one side seam. The cutout's edges will form a straight line perpendicular to the seams. Pin the cutout edges and sew the seam. Refold the lining so the other side seam aligns with the bottom, and repeat.

The cutout rectangle's edges align to create a straight seamline.

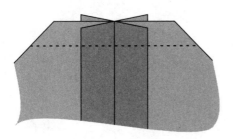

8. Measure and mark the backpack exterior 1½ and 2½ inches from the upper edges along both side seams.

Measure and mark the bag exterior.

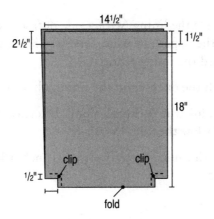

9. Staystitch ½ inch from the cutout edges on the exterior. Clip into the corner, clipping all the way to the stitches without cutting through the staystitching. Fold the seam allowance to the wrong side along the staystitching, and press, rolling the stitches to the wrong side slightly so they won't be visible from the outside of the backpack.

> **SNIP IT**
>
> To prevent fraying, apply a drop of liquid seam sealant to each corner and allow it to dry before clipping the seam allowances.

10. Fold the exterior in half along the bottom edge, right sides together, matching the marks along the side edges. Temporarily unfold the pressed seam allowances at the cutout. Stitch each side seam from the cutout rectangle to the lower mark. Cut the threads, and begin sewing again at the upper mark, continuing the side seam to the upper raw edge and leaving a gap in the seam. Note: don't box the bag exterior yet.

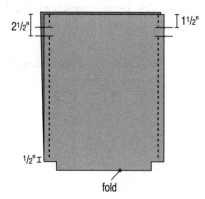

Leave the side seams open between the marks.

11. Press the seams open, pressing the seam allowances to the wrong side along the gap and refolding the cutout edges. Fold 1½ inches of the upper raw edge to the wrong side, press firmly to crease, and unfold.

12. Place the bag exterior, right side out, inside the lining (wrong side out) so the right sides are together. Align the side seams with the upper raw edges, and pin. Sew the upper edges together, and press the seam toward the lining fabric.

13. Turn the backpack right side out through the opening in the lining's bottom seam.

14. Tuck the lining inside the backpack, and fold the backpack along the crease made in step 11. The lining seam will lie 1 inch below the fold. Press again.

15. Edgestitch along the foldline through both thicknesses. Topstitch 1 inch below the fold, creating a casing for the drawstring.

16. Cut the ribbon in half. Attach the large safety pin to one end of the first ribbon strap. Insert the pin into the opening in the right side seam of the bag, and work it through the casing, drawing the ribbon into and through the casing. Work the safety pin and ribbon all the way around the bag's upper edge to emerge back at the right side seam.

17. Tuck the ribbon ends into the opening formed by the cutout on the right side. Be sure the ribbons are not twisted. Position one at each end of the seamline created by the gap, and be sure ¾ inch of ribbon is tucked inside the open seam. Pin the ribbons in place, pinning the pressed cutout edges at the same time.

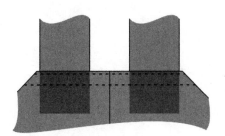

Tuck ¾ inch of the ribbon ends into the pressed, but open, boxing seam.

18. Edgestitch along the pressed folds to create the boxing seam, and attach the ribbon strap ends. Stitch again ⅛ inch from the edgestitching to reinforce the seam.

19. Repeat steps 16 through 18 to insert and attach the second strap, beginning and ending at the opening in the left side seam and tucking the ribbon ends into the left side's boxing seam.

20. Slipstitch the lining seam gap closed, and smooth the lining into place inside the backpack.

Add a handy patch pocket to your backpack bag—inside or out —for extra storage! See Chapter 19 to learn how.

The Least You Need to Know

- Fasteners are more than just the "finishing touch" on a project. Buttons, zippers, and snaps can provide pretty—and practical—closures.
- Frogs aren't always amphibious. In sewing, frogging is an ornamental braid or fastener made from looped and knotted cord.
- Buttons are either sew-through or shank. They can be attached by hand or machine.
- Don't be daunted by attaching zippers. Most machines have a zipper foot, which allows you to stitch along the zipper teeth without messing up your stitching.

Getting into Garments

Part 5 is where you put those sewing skills you've been practicing to wardrobe-related use! In these chapters, learn to take key measurements (a must for correctly fitting garments) and how to make simple alterations to patterns and ready-to-wear garments. We also take the mystery out of pattern markings, symbols, layouts, and guide sheets and offer alternatives to purchased patterns. You discover how to prepare patterns; how to plan ahead for laying out patterns and cutting fabric; and different methods for pinning, marking, and cutting projects from patterns.

We've packed this part with garment construction basics—from collars and cuffs to hemline finishes—every sewist needs to know. You'll make a fun flannel hat from our pattern, and you learn to create your own patterns for a boxy jacket and comfy pants. Follow our instructions to make a first version, then improvise to make each item truly your own. Replace an elastic waist with a drawstring casing, reposition pockets, and substitute ribbons for button closures—after all, you know how to sew now!

Measuring Up

In This Chapter

- How and where to take measurements
- Making sense of pattern sizing
- Adjusting patterns for custom fit
- Ready-to-wear alterations

It may be both the most basic and the most dreaded part of sewing: taking accurate body measurements. Every body is unique, and it's rare to fit into an unaltered pattern. As you measure and choose a pattern size, don't be bound by the ready-to-wear sizes you *always* wear; custom garment sizes are often different.

If possible, have a friend help you take measurements. A second pair of hands and eyes increases accuracy. Wear a leotard or close-fitting garments over the undergarments you usually wear so the measurements will be as close as possible to the real you. Wrap the measuring tape snugly around your body without pulling it too tight or pinching, and record the measurements as you go.

Key Measurements

Form-fitting garments and fashions of the past that were heavily darted and designed to fit over girdles and restrictive foundations required as many as 50 body measurements for fitting! Fortunately, today's relaxed styles require only a handful of fitting points.

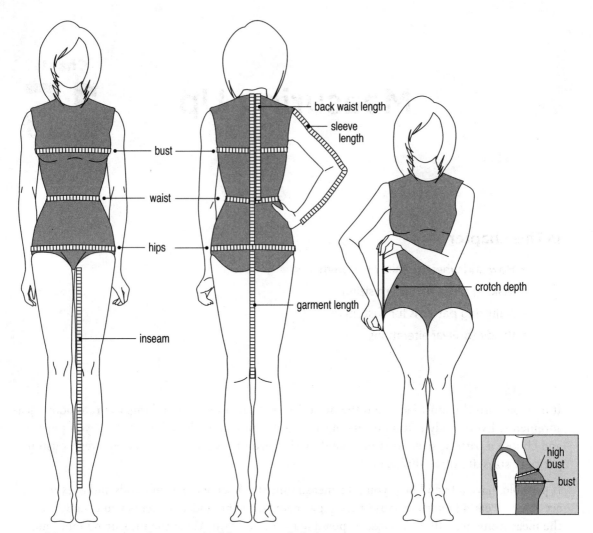

Measurements are taken at standard locations on the body.

Understanding Ease

Body measurements and pattern measurements are not the same. Your individual measurements and the standard body measurements on the pattern envelope will always be smaller than the pattern pieces measured at the same points. The difference is called *ease*, and it's essential for wearability.

Stretchy, form-fitting garments have very little ease because the fabric allows the body to move. Other garments must have a minimum amount of extra fabric (wearing ease) to allow for movement. Greater amounts, called *style* or *fashion ease*, may be added for full garments, gathers, etc.

It's important to keep ease in mind as you customize patterns. A pattern that measures 36 inches at the bust won't fit a 36-inch body! Be sure you leave that extra ease intact when altering patterns.

For Women

You'll need several measurements for women's wear. Compare the following descriptions with the key measurements illustration (earlier in this chapter) to take accurate measurements. Record your measurements as you take them in this handy pocket-size "What's My Size?" chart:

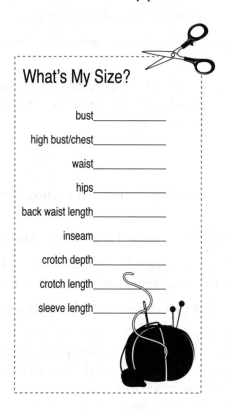

What's My Size?

bust_____

high bust/chest_____

waist_____

hips_____

back waist length_____

inseam_____

crotch depth_____

crotch length_____

sleeve length_____

Bust: Measure around the fullest part of the bust and across the back, keeping the tape parallel to the waist.

High bust: Measure directly under the arms, across the back, and above the fullest part of the bust.

Waist: Measure around the natural waist, usually the narrowest part of the body.

SNIP IT

Tie a ribbon or tape around your true waist—the place where you bend at the side—to use as a starting point for taking other measurements.

Hips: Measure around the fullest part of the hips, with the tape parallel to the waist. This is 9 inches below the waistline for most women. On petite and junior figures, the hips are about 7 inches below the waist.

Back waist length: This vertical measurement helps match the garment waist to the body length. Measure from the prominent bone at the base of the neck, down the center back, to the waistline.

In addition, you may need these garment-specific measurements:

Garment length: For a dress, measure from the prominent bone at the base of the neck to the desired hem length. For a skirt, measure from the waist, over the fullest part of the hips, to the desired hem length.

Inseam: Measure from the crotch to the desired length of pants.

Crotch depth: Sit in a chair, and use a ruler to measure from the waistline straight down to the chair seat.

Crotch length: Measure from the center back waist through the legs to the center front waist. Divide this measurement at the midpoint between the legs for front and back crotch lengths. The divided measurements may not be equal.

For Men

Men's fashions rely on chest, waist, hip, neck circumference, sleeve length, inseam, and crotch measurements:

Chest: Measure the chest under the arms and over the shoulder blades.

Waist: Many men wear belts and waistbands considerably below their natural waists. It's the natural waist measurement that determines pant size, so be sure to measure there.

Hip: Measure around the fullest part of the hips, holding the tape parallel to the waistline.

Neck circumference and sleeve length: Men's shirts require neck and sleeve measurements. The sizing of a purchased shirt can be used to determine pattern size, or you can take your own measurements. Hold the measuring tape around the base of the neck, where the collar will be worn, and add ½ inch to find the neck measurement. For sleeve length, begin at the center back neck base (the prominent bone) and measure across the shoulder, to the elbow, and to the wrist. For the most accurate measurement, hold the arm away from the body with the elbow bent.

Hold the arm at a slight angle when measuring sleeve length.

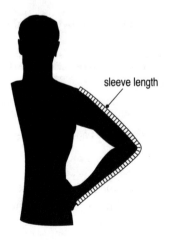

sleeve length

Crotch depth and inseam: See the "For Women" section to determine how to take these measurements. If you prefer, measure a pair of pants that fit well to determine the crotch depth and inseam.

SEW SURPRISING

Men's patterns are generally sized for average builds and a height of 5 foot, 10 inches without shoes.

For Children

Babies', toddlers', children's, girls', and boys' patterns are designed to fit a range of sizes as children grow and develop. The ranges overlap; for example, babies' patterns may include a 24-month size while toddlers' offers a size 2. Pick the appropriate size range by the child's stature and development rather than relying solely on age.

For babies' patterns, size is determined by size and weight. For larger children's sizes, take chest, waist, hip, and back waist length measurements as for women's sizes. If the natural waist is hard to find, have the subject bend sideways.

Made to Measure

Commercial patterns for women are divided into several categories. Each is geared toward a specific body type, which may also correspond to an age group:

Misses' patterns are for well-proportioned, fully developed women with a B-cup bust. Misses' figures are about 5 foot, 6 inches tall.

Miss petite patterns are proportioned like misses' patterns but are designed for bodies 5 foot, 2 inches to 5 foot, 4 inches tall and are correspondingly shorter in the back waist length.

Women's and *women's petite* patterns are for figures fuller overall than misses and miss petite.

Junior sizes are for developing figures 5 foot, 2 inches to 5 foot, 5 inches tall. Aimed at a younger crowd, the styling is more youthful than misses' patterns.

At the fabric store, flip to the back of a pattern book to find the size and measurement charts for all the different body types. Choose the size grouping that best fits your height and measurements (refer to the "What's My Size?" chart measurements you recorded earlier), and examine the measurements under individual sizes to pick the one best for you.

If you will be making a shirt or top, use your bust measurement to choose the pattern size. For pants, shorts, or skirts, use your hip measurement to determine the best size. It's easier to alter the garment waist, so choosing by bust or hip is most satisfactory. However, if your waist measurement is much larger than the one corresponding to the hip measurement you match, consider buying according to the waist size and altering the hip instead.

Most patterns are sized to fit B-cup bodies. If you wear a larger cup size, the difference will be revealed in your bust and high bust measurements. If there is more than 2 inches of difference between the two measurements, purchase the pattern according to the high bust measurement.

PINPRICK

Buying a much larger pattern to accommodate the full bust measurement often results in shoulders and necklines that are too wide for the body, and using the high bust measurement provides a good compromise.

If your project is a dress, robe, long jacket, or coat, both bust and hip measurements must be considered. It may be necessary to buy two patterns—one that fits the lower body and a second to fit the upper body. Before cutting the fabric, look at both patterns and determine the best way to merge the top and bottom at the waist; usually this involves widening the smaller waistline a bit and narrowing the wider waistline a similar amount so the two match in the final pattern.

Simple Pattern Adjustments

Entire books have been written on the subject of fitting patterns to an individual body, and many good resources are available in print and online. Pattern alterations can become very complex, but a few basics are easy to learn and carry out.

The Long and Short of It

Lengthening or shortening a pattern is as straightforward as it sounds. If you need a 26-inch skirt length and the pattern is only 24 inches, you'll need to add length before cutting the fabric. Begin by looking at the pattern pieces; many will have one or more pairs of horizontal lines and a label that says "Lengthen or shorten here." If your pattern includes these symbols, make your alteration there. If there are no lengthen/shorten lines, you can probably add or subtract length at the bottom edge of the pattern piece.

To lengthen a pattern, cut the tissue apart along one of the marked lines. Slip tissue or *pattern paper* under the cut edges. Use a ruler to measure the distance between the edges, and adjust it to equal the amount of extra length you need. Tape the pattern edges to the pattern paper. Use a ruler or French curve to blend the intersecting seam and cutting lines together across the added length.

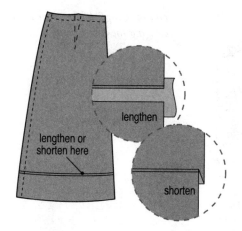

It's easy to lengthen or shorten a pattern piece.

SEWING SENSE

Pattern paper, or sewable Swedish tracing paper, is a strong, translucent material used to make durable master patterns. Use it to trace, sew, test-fit, and alter patterns before cutting final fabric.

To shorten a pattern, draw a line the required distance from the lengthen/shorten lines. Fold the pattern, wrong sides together, along one lengthen/shorten line. Bring the fold to meet the new line, and tape the tuck in place. Use a ruler or French curve to blend the intersecting seam and cutting lines together across the shortened length.

When changing the length of a pattern piece, remember to make the same change on all affected pattern pieces. For example, if the front is lengthened 1 inch, the back must be lengthened 1 inch as well.

Taking In and Letting Out

One of the biggest advantages in multisize patterns is the ease of customizing them to fit a multisize body. If your bust is a size 10 and your hips are a size 12, simply use a pencil to blend the seamlines together across the pattern waist.

Similar alterations can be made by cutting missized areas a little bigger or smaller than the pattern. Keep in mind that any alteration that crosses a seamline will affect other pieces, too. For example, if you widen a blouse by moving the side seam outward ¼ inch, you'll need to alter the sleeve as well.

Sometimes the alteration needs to be made in one area only, not across an entire pattern piece. In those cases, slash and spread or overlap pattern pieces to make the pattern fit. For example, consider a shoulder seam that's too wide or too narrow.

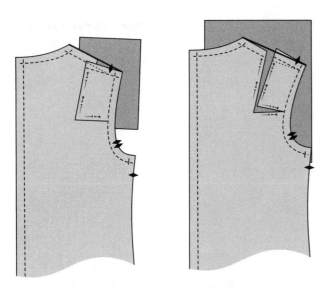

You can change the fit of one area without changing the entire piece.

Begin by drawing a line across the pattern where the alteration needs to be. The line can extend all the way across the pattern piece, or it may angle toward a nearby seamline/edge. Cut the pattern along the line, and spread it apart to add fabric or overlap the cut edges to tighten the fit. Remember that the alteration should be measured at the seamline, not the cutting line. Sometimes a corresponding overlap or spread must be made in the seam allowance at the end of the line to keep the pattern flat.

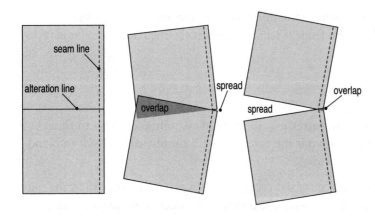

Overlap or spread seam allowances as necessary without changing the seam length to accommodate pattern alterations.

Alterations to fit the bust are very common. Many patterns accomplish bust fitting with darts, those interesting triangles of stitches that point straight to the body part, as you learned in Chapter 9. Understanding darts makes alterations easier.

A dart really should point directly to the fullest part of the body: the bust, a hip, etc. Also, the wider the dart's base, the fuller the body part it's made to fit. If the pattern has a dart 1 inch wide at the base to fit a B-cup body, the base may need to be 2 inches or more to fit larger cup sizes.

If the alteration is needed to move the dart point up or down without changing its size, simply redraw the dart, angling it to meet the corrected point.

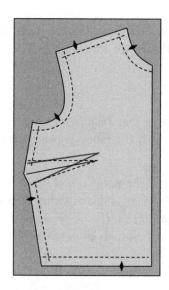

Sometimes all that's needed is an adjustment to the dart point.

On the other hand, a fuller bust may also need more fabric added to the pattern to encompass the larger body. How do you add more fabric to the bodice front without making the back, shoulders, and waist larger, too? The answer lies in the darts.

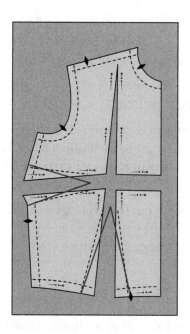

The adjustment for a large bust looks complex, but it's really very logical.

Begin by slashing and spreading the front pattern piece through the corrected dart so its width matches the body measurements plus ease. The front will lengthen, too, so there's more fabric between the shoulder and waist to pass over the bust. Then, to return the side and waist seams to their correct lengths so they match the corresponding pattern pieces, redraw the darts using the original end points and dart length as a guide. The new darts will be wider than the originals.

When sewn, the bodice will have plenty of fabric across the bust, but the darts will pull the fabric neatly down to size where the bodice back and skirt are attached.

Pin-Fitting and Muslins

When pattern adjustments are minor, a quick pin-fitting may be all you need before taking the scissors to your fabric. For more complex alterations, or if the fabric is pricey or one of a kind, it's wise to make and fit a muslin first.

To pin-fit a pattern, tape or pin all the darts closed. Pin the pattern pieces together: front to back, sleeve to armhole. Pin along the seamlines with wrong sides together rather than overlapping the seamlines; the seam allowances will stand away from the body as you fit. Obviously, you'll have only one half of the garment to fit, but that's enough to judge how the pattern will fit your body.

SNIP IT

It's usually not necessary to pin-fit smaller pattern pieces such as collars, facings, and pockets.

Carefully slip on the pinned pattern. Match the center front and center back to your body—it helps to have a friend assist. If the pattern is too small, note how much extra fabric is needed. If the pattern is too large, pin tucks into the pattern pieces to create a better fit.

Remove the pattern, and carefully unpin the pieces. Make any adjustments noted during the fitting; if necessary, do a second pin fitting. Now your pattern is ready to cut.

To make a muslin for fitting, purchase yardage of muslin or an inexpensive fabric as indicated on the pattern. Choose a fabric similar in weight and drape to the fashion fabric you'll be using for the garment; for example, use a knit to make the muslin for a knit garment, and don't choose heavy denim for fitting drapable challis.

Lay the pattern pieces on the inexpensive fabric and cut out the major garment pieces. Facings, collars, pockets, etc., are not needed. If desired, widen the seam allowances to 1 inch to provide more fabric for alterations. Pattern markings and even seamlines can be drawn directly on the fabric with a pen.

Sew the pieces together as directed in the pattern, using a lengthened stitch that will be easy to remove for changing the fit. Do not add zippers or other fastenings, and there's no need to finish raw edges. Try on the muslin, wrong side out, and alter it as necessary. Mark new seamlines, tucks, or other alterations directly on the inexpensive fabric with a pen or tailor's chalk.

Remove the muslin, and take it apart. Compare the left and right halves of the garment, and reconcile any differences between the two. Smooth curves and straighten straight edges. Measure and add seam allowances where needed.

Simply use the altered muslin as the pattern when you cut the fashion fabric to produce a garment custom-fit to your figure.

Altering Ready-to-Wear

Most bodies don't fit perfectly into ready-to-wear garments. Because they're already put together—and usually with tiny seam allowances—it may seem impossible to improve the fit, but with a few tricks from your sewing box, you'll be adapting purchased garments to your individual form in no time!

Taking It All In

Ready-to-wear rarely includes enough fabric to make a garment bigger, but it's certainly possible to downsize a purchase. If you're a "between" size, try on a larger garment and give it a discerning look in the mirror to determine its alteration potential.

Do the shoulders and neckline fit? Generally, it's harder to adjust the fit across the upper body. However, if the armhole seam falls off your shoulder but the fit is good elsewhere, consider making a tuck across the shoulder seam just above the sleeve to bring the fit into line.

A tuck can shorten the shoulder seam while adding a bit of style above the sleeve cap.

Is there extra fabric on the front, the back, or both? If the waist is too full on both front and back, taking in the side seams may be the answer. If the front fits well but the back is too blousy, consider adding darts across the back waist to rein in the excess fabric.

Add vertical darts at the waistline to elimi-nate excess fabric.

Tricks Up Your Sleeve

If a sleeve is too blousy, try adjusting the fit along the underarm seam. Be sure to taper the seamline gradually to avoid odd puckers at the armhole or cuff.

Cuffed sleeves that are too long can be taken apart and shortened. Remove the cuff as carefully as possible. Measure, mark, and cut the sleeve as desired, and reattach the cuff to the shortened sleeve.

When a sleeve is too short, a little addition may be in order. Stitch a bit of lace trim to the hem or cuff to add an inch or two. Ribbon or decorative trim can be added for a more tailored addition. Or take the alteration in the opposite direction by cutting off several inches of sleeve to make a cute ¾-length style.

Mind the Gap!

If the gap, or garment opening, is large, it may be time to go to a larger size. But some quick fixes for small gaps may keep you in a garment longer.

Buttoned shirts and blouses sometimes pull apart at the fullest part of the bust. The best solution is to respace the buttonholes, placing one exactly at the fullest point, but that's not an option in ready-made garments. Instead, hand sew a snap between the existing buttonholes, with one half on the right side of the button placket and the other half on the inside of the but-tonhole placket. Be sure the stitches don't show on the garment right side.

If a waistband has become too loose or too tight, it's often possible to move the button or the hook-and-eye closure. Adjustments up to ½ inch shouldn't affect the zipper closure too much.

"Take in" pants that fit in the hips but are a tad too large at the waist by darting in excess fabric or slimming along a seam. Examine the waistband, pockets, side, and center back seams for alteration options.

PINPRICK

Rivets at pocket edges can make side seam changes impossible; darts may distort back yokes.

To slim along a center back seam, try on the pants and pinch the excess fabric together at the center back seam. Pin the pinched fabric together, tapering to nothing along the seam. Remove the pants, and mark the pinned edge just below the waistband. "Unsew" the waistband from the center back seam, and open the center back seam to just beyond the tapered point. With right sides together, resew the center back seam along the tapered, marked line. Test the altered fit, and trim the tapered seam allowance. Make a center back seam in the waistband to fit the slimmer waist, and reattach the waistband to the pants.

Handling Hems

Hem adjustments may be the most frequent of garment alterations. If you need to make a garment shorter, try it on and have a friend mark the desired hemline with chalk or a removable marking pen. Add a hem allowance—from 3 inches for a straight garment to just ½ inch for a flared style—and cut, removing the original hem stitches if the hem won't be cut off completely. Press the new hem into place, and stitch by hand or machine.

To make a hem longer, you'll need to add a facing, and the amount of length that can be added is limited by the original hem allowance. Take out the existing hem, and press thoroughly. Stitch wide bias hem facing tape or another kind of facing to the cut edge. Press the new hem into place; the new hemline may lie along the facing seam or within the original garment, as long as the facing is hidden inside the garment. Stitch the hem as desired.

SNIP IT

It can be difficult to remove the original hemline crease when a garment is lengthened. Try moistening the crease thoroughly with plain water or a mixture of white vinegar and water. Cover with a press cloth, and press thoroughly to relax the fabric and remove the crease. If removal proves impossible, or if the fabric has become discolored along the original hemline, consider attaching a narrow trim or working a line of decorative stitches along the original crease to conceal it.

When making children's garments, many sewists incorporate one or more horizontal tucks above the hemline. As the child grows, the tucks can be removed, releasing fabric to add length to the garment. Other tried-and-true methods for lengthening include adding ruffles, trims, or contrasting bands to the original hemline.

The Least You Need to Know

- A few simple measurements are the doorway to pattern selection.
- Patterns are categorized by body types, measurements, and ages.
- Flat paper patterns can be reshaped to fit any body.
- Sewing techniques can be applied to ready-to-wear, too!

Pattern Play!

In This Chapter

- Pattern purchasing parameters
- Notes on notches and marking
- Touring the pattern envelope and guide sheet

Patterns are the flat paper equivalent of the wonderful fabric creations around us. They carry all the information a sewist needs to re-create a style in the fabrics and colors of her choice.

A pattern can be as simple as a rectangle drawn to size or as complex as a detailed multipiece pattern for a dress. One characteristic common to all patterns is the markings and symbols that make up the language of patterns. Commercial patterns include written instructions to take you step by step through the construction process, and decoding pattern symbols streamlines the process and prevents misunderstandings that lead to everyone's least favorite sewing task: undoing what you've done!

Unpuzzling Patterns

One little pattern envelope carries a lot of information! Fortunately, large commercial pattern companies produce fairly standard envelopes that contain all you need to know when selecting fabrics and notions to create your own finished garments. Even small, independent pattern producers include yardage and fit information on their packaging. Inside the envelope are two more pieces of the pattern puzzle: the tissue pattern pieces themselves and a step-by-step guide sheet to walk you through the construction process.

Pattern Books and Envelopes

When shopping for a pattern, your first stop is likely to be the fabric store's pattern counter. There, thick books containing hundreds of fashion, home décor, and craft patterns beckon. Choosing just one may be the hardest part of all!

Pattern books are organized by garment or project and figure type. Each section is marked by a tab along the book's right edge. Dresses, separates, plus sizes, and children's are some of the categories most pattern books contain. Flip to the section that interests you, and browse through the pages. Typically, one pattern is featured per page. A combination of photographs and drawings depicts the project and multiple illustrations showcase different views or pattern options. Views may differ by garment length, sleeve type, collar shape, etc. Many patterns are also labeled with an indication of difficulty.

The page also provides the pattern number, which you can use to locate the pattern in the nearby drawers, and descriptive information, including the figure type and size range for which the pattern is available. Some yardage information is usually included, too, although complete details are often left for the pattern envelope to save space in the book. Small thumbnail sketches show back views and the options available with different pattern views.

Make a note of the pattern number and size you need and head to the pattern drawers. Locate your pattern by the company name and number and check the envelope to be sure your size is included. Many pattern envelopes contain multiple sizes, which can be very helpful when customizing the pattern for your perfect fit.

The envelope front often looks like a smaller version of the catalog page with each garment view labeled with a letter. Look for these features on the envelope back:

SNIP IT

Once you've purchased the pattern, go ahead and mark on your pattern envelope and guide sheet! Circling the pertinent sizes or yardages can make the maze of numbers less confusing.

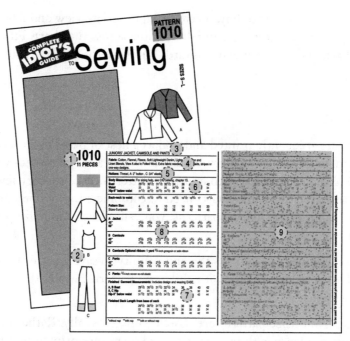

Pattern envelopes are a wealth of information!

1   *Pattern number and number of pieces:* Fewer pieces mean a simpler construction process.

2   *Back views:* These simplified line drawings reveal features not shown in photographs and fashion drawings.

3   *Garment description:* Look here for descriptors such as "loose-fitting" that can help when choosing a size.

4   *Fabric suggestions:* The textiles listed here have the weight, drape, and texture needed to create the style as the designer intended. Also look for cautionary notes about unsuitable fabrics or those that may require extra fabric, such as plaids and one-way designs.

5   *Notions:* Thread, zippers, buttons, etc., are listed here, with variations noted by view.

6   *Body measurements:* These are the standard body measurements. Compare them to your own measurements you took in Chapter 15 to determine pattern size.

7   *Garment measurements:* The measurements listed here vary by style and may include finished lengths, hemline width, and other dimensions. Garment measurements always include ease for wearing comfort, so they differ from corresponding body measurements.

8   *Yardage charts:* The length of fabric needed for each size is listed here, organized by view and fabric width. With and without nap notations may be marked by asterisks. Yardages for support fabrics (linings and interfacings) and trims are also listed.

9   *Multilingual and metric information:* These frequently appear on the envelope back, but sometimes a note directs readers to the guide sheet when space on the envelope is short.

To determine how much fabric to buy, locate the appropriate view and fabric width (including with/without nap) along the left edge and draw a line across the chart. Find the correct size at the top of the chart, and draw a line downward. Purchase the yardage listed where the two lines intersect.

Multisize Options

Modern patterns are frequently printed and sold as a nest of patterns in several sizes. Rather than finding a single size on the pattern envelope, we see a range of sizes within a single figure type. There are plenty of advantages to multisize patterns. Because very few bodies match the standard measurements, many sewists need to combine a top of one size with a bottom of another. Rather than purchasing two patterns, you can select a multisize pattern and combine the sizes as you cut.

Another plus to these mega-patterns is the opportunity to save a pattern and make it in more than one size. This is especially nice with children's patterns, where the size that fits today may be too small in a month.

On the other hand, multisize patterns are more complex visually. Rather than displaying one clearly marked pattern piece with both cutting and seamlines printed on the pattern, they present a stack of several sizes. Study the pattern carefully and note which line style—solid, dashed, dotted, etc.—or color indicates the size to be cut. In some cases, the cutting lines may be the same line style, with each marked at intervals with the corresponding size.

To use a multisize pattern only once, simply cut along the line for the desired size, or shift from one size to another to accommodate variations in personal measurements. To preserve the pattern so a different size can be cut later, trace the appropriate pattern outline onto pattern paper or lightweight nonwoven interfacing, shifting between size lines as necessary to create a custom pattern. Fold the original tissue back into the pattern envelope, and save it for the next garment.

Demystifying Pattern Markings

Patterns aren't just mysterious shapes; they're emblazoned with markings that carry a lot of useful information for putting the pieces together. Let's take a look at the basic marks you'll find on pattern tissue:

Pattern labels: Each piece is labeled with the pattern number, the size(s), the views for which the piece is needed, the number of pieces to cut, and a short description of the piece.

Grainline: This marking is not transferred to the fabric, but it's essential for placing the pattern piece correctly on the fabric. The grainline will be either a straight arrow that should be placed parallel to the lengthwise grain or a bent arrow indicating that one side of the pattern should be placed on a fabric fold. Occasionally, the grainline will be marked to indicate that you should place it on the crosswise or bias grain instead.

Cutting lines: On single-size patterns, this is a solid line; on multisize patterns, the cutting line for each size may be marked by a different type or color of line.

Seamlines: On single-size patterns, the seamline is indicated by a dashed line. On multisize patterns, seamlines are not shown or, in some cases, only the seamline for the smallest size is marked.

Double straight lines: These indicate the best location on the pattern piece for adding or subtracting length from the garment.

Dots: These small solid circles are used to mark locations or points to match. Patterns may include both small and large dots and sometimes squares. Drill holes, shown as a circle enclosing a +, are like dots and may be used to mark locations within a pattern piece (for example, a patch pocket location).

Notches: Whether single or in groups of two or three, these diamonds or triangles both indicate matching points and help differentiate between seamlines. For example, a skirt back often has a triple notch along the center back seamline and a double notch at the side seams, eliminating confusion that might result in sewing the center back seamline to the side of a skirt front.

 SEW SURPRISING

Originally, notches were meant to be cut into the seam allowance, but more modern guides recommend cutting the notches outward, away from the garment body. An intact seam allowance is stronger and keeps alteration options open.

Darts: These fitting features are shown as long, narrow triangles extending into the garment body. The dart center is sometimes indicated by a solid line; the dart "legs" are dashed. The dart point and seamline intersections are often marked with dots.

Pleats and tucks: Whether functional or decorative, these are marked with solid and dashed lines on the pattern pieces, sometimes in conjunction with arrows that show the folding direction. Consult the guide sheet for specific instructions on how to form the pleat or tuck.

Get to know these common pattern markings.

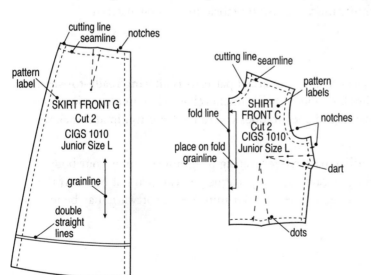

Patterning a Favorite Garment

You have the perfect shirt, but the cuffs are worn and the color is so last season. What to do? Perhaps you'll find a pattern that's similar, but making your own pattern may be an even better option.

If you're certain you'll never wear the garment again, carefully take it apart, noting how the pieces are sewn together and marking foldlines for darts, areas of gathers, etc., with a removable fabric marker. Press the garment pieces carefully, and use them as patterns to cut a new garment. On the other hand, if you want to re-create a favorite garment without destroying the original, you may be able to trace the garment and create a pattern.

> **SNIP IT**
>
> Commercially sewn garments are usually serged, leaving only ¼-inch seam allowances. Add ⅜ inch to each edge to bring your new pattern up to the usual ⅝-inch seam allowance before cutting the new pieces.

Work with one garment piece at a time, as it will probably be impossible to flatten more than one. Lay pattern paper, lightweight interfacing, or tissue on top of the garment section, and trace the seamlines with a pencil. Mark the locations of darts, gathers, and other design elements on the pattern.

Remove the tracing from the garment and true the traced lines—that is, smooth out any irregularities, and straighten the lines that should be straight. Add seam and hem allowances to the pattern. If necessary, split the pattern and insert more paper to fill darts and areas of gathers or pleats. Measure the seamlines to be sure the two pieces will fit together accurately and make any corrections as needed. Repeat the process to trace the other pieces of the garment.

Sew a quick mock-up in muslin or other inexpensive fabric—seam finishes aren't important here—and check the fit before committing your fashion fabric to the new pattern.

Another Pattern Option

Another alternative to making projects from commercial patterns is altering ready-to-wear. Pull techniques from the pages of this book to add embellishments that bring an older piece into present-day fashion, or use the constructions techniques you're learning to nip and tuck the garment to fit your unique form.

If you're computer savvy, you can utilize pattern-generating programs to enter your body measurements and style choices and generate custom patterns you can print at home. If the pattern books simply don't have the styles you see in your mind's eye, software may be just the way to go!

A Guide to Guide Sheets

The guide sheet is a comprehensive guide to construction and may contain all the information you need to successfully complete your pattern-based garment. Line drawings of the pattern projects, with front and back views, are shown. A sketch showing the pattern pieces is also given, as is a numbered guide listing the name of each pattern piece.

PINPRICK

Even if you're an experienced sewist, take time to read through the entire guide sheet before beginning a project. Sometimes the steps appear in an unusual order for reasons that aren't obvious until later in the process. Reading ahead is good preparation.

Guide sheets also include some general sewing information. This may be as simple as a guide to pattern markings, or it may go into specific detail about a special cutting or construction technique utilized in the pattern.

Cutting layouts are the meat of the guide sheet's first page. Layouts are given for each view in all pertinent fabric widths and for every size in which the pattern is available. There are also layouts for support fabrics such as interfacing and lining, if applicable.

After the layouts come the step-by-step sewing directions for constructing the garment. Pattern instructions are often organized into units for simplified construction; all the construction, including interfacing, for one unit is completed before moving on to another. This system makes it easy to devote small amounts of time to a sewing project—a real plus for busy stitchers.

Pattern Prep

When you first pull the pattern out of its envelope, it can look like a bewildering stack of large tissue rectangles. Begin by smoothing out the pattern sheets on a cutting table or large surface—after corralling all "helpful" pets in another room!

Take a look at the labels on each pattern piece. Check for your size and the view (usually designated by a letter or number) you want to make. Any pieces that don't display your size and view are unnecessary for your project and can go right back into the pattern envelope.

With paper-cutting scissors, roughly cut around the pattern pieces you need for your garment. Stack them separately. When you've worked through all the pattern sheets, count the number of pattern pieces in the project stack and check the total against the guide sheet to ensure you haven't missed any pieces. Fold the pieces you don't need and put them back in the pattern envelope.

SEW SURPRISING

To trim or not to trim? The experts' opinions differ. Trimming the pattern tissue exactly on the cutting line may prevent confusion, especially if you're customizing the pattern by switching between sizes for different garment areas. However, leaving the extra paper intact and cutting through both paper and fabric—cutting through the line rather than along it—is more accurate. Choose the method that works best for you.

Set your iron for a low temperature without steam. Press each paper pattern piece to remove the wrinkles and creases. This little step leads to more accurate cutting.

Pattern Layouts and Cutting

If your pattern has several views, there will be many cutting layouts on the guide sheet. Select the one you need by looking for the view letter or number, the appropriate size, and the width of your fabric. Circle the layout to avoid confusion. If your project also includes contrasting fabric, lining, or interfacing, find and circle those cutting layouts as well.

Fold your fabric as indicated on the guide sheet. Most often, the fabric is folded parallel to the selvages, along the lengthwise grain. Working on doubled fabric means you can cut two pieces at a time, with one reversed to form the other side of the garment. Fabric is usually folded with right sides together so it's easier to transfer pattern markings to the wrong side of the fabric.

Consult the layout for other ways to fold the fabric. Some pattern pieces are cut singly. Lay those pattern pieces right side up on right-side-up fabric. Other layouts may require a crosswise fold or some combination of folds to accommodate all the pieces.

PINPRICK

Don't allow the fabric to fall over the edge of a table as you pin and cut it. This is especially true with knit fabrics, which will stretch and then recover after the pieces are cut, adversely affecting fit.

Arrange the pattern pieces on the fabric as shown in the layout. Take note of any pieces that should be laid on the fabric fold, and position them accordingly. When cutting a pattern piece laid on the fold, leave the fold intact. When the piece is unfolded, you'll have one complete, symmetric piece.

Lay out all the pattern pieces before pinning, if possible, so you can easily make adjustments to the layout. Never begin cutting until all the pieces are pinned to the fabric so you can be sure there will be enough fabric for all.

The Least You Need to Know

- Pattern envelopes tell you all you need to know to plan a garment and buy the necessary fabric and notions.
- Whether single- or multisize, pattern pieces contain grainlines and construction markings to simplify construction and to ensure that your garment looks like the pattern illustration.
- The pattern guide sheet has step-by-step instructions for putting a project together.
- Pattern layouts are a road map for successful cutting.

Pin, Mark, and Cut

In This Chapter

- Preparing the fabric for cutting
- Pointers for perfect pinning
- Cutting edges and corners
- Marks: from pattern to fabric

You've purchased the pattern, the fabric is fabulous, and you're ready to take your shears and make that first cut! Some sewists find that to be the hardest part of all, but by the end of this chapter, you'll have all the skills you need to think twice and cut once on the path to making great garments.

Plan Ahead

After reading the pattern envelope to find the best fabric types for your project, chances are you found many suitable bolts at your local fabric store. Perhaps you fell in love with the color, or maybe it's the texture that caught your eye. Whatever the reason for your choice, be sure to check the end of the bolt before any fabric is cut.

That's where you'll find the nuts-and-bolts description of the fabric: width, manufacturer, fiber content, and color. The bolt end also reveals the care instructions, a very important factor in choosing fabric for a garment. If the project will be subject to heavy wear and tear, a dry-clean-only fabric could be impractical. Some silks are easily washed, while others are fabricated in a way that makes dry cleaning preferable. Take a moment to jot down the care instructions while you're waiting in line at the cutting table, and keep them with the fabric for future reference.

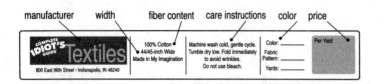

manufacturer   width   fiber content   care instructions   color   price

Always check the bolt end for vital information.

Most fabric should be prewashed or preshrunk before cutting. This also removes excess dye that might discolor other fabrics in later wash cycles. By shrinking the fabric before cutting, you eliminate the heartache of having a beautifully sewn project become too small the first time it hits the water. Dry cleaning is less likely to cause shrinkage, but it's still a good idea to pretreat dry-clean-only fabrics, too, removing finishes that could interfere with construction processes.

> **SNIP IT**
>
> Here's a good rule of thumb: pretreat fabric before cutting and sewing with whatever care processes will be used on the finished garment.

Interfacing should also be preshrunk. Simply fill a basin with warm water, soak the interfacing for a few minutes, and hang the interfacing up to dry. This gentle preshrinking won't disturb any fusing agents on the fabric.

For trims, preshrink according to the manufacturer's instructions to reduce later shrinkage and prevent dye transfer.

After pretreating the fabric, press it thoroughly to remove wrinkles and creases. If desired, use spray starch to give the fabric body for easier layout and cutting.

Following the appropriate cutting layout on the pattern guide sheet, fold the fabric as directed. Be sure to align the selvages neatly, even if the cut edges don't match, and arrange the pattern pieces as directed. Check the grainline on each pattern piece to be sure the piece is properly oriented; for pieces placed on a fabric fold, it's as simple as laying the fold edge on the fabric fold. For pieces that have a straight grain arrow, use a ruler or measuring tape to check that the distance from each end of the arrow to the selvage is the same.

Don't include the selvages in any pattern pieces when you cut. Even when preshrunk, the selvage tends to pucker more than the body of the fabric and may distort the finished garment.

Position all the pattern pieces on the fabric before cutting, beginning with the largest pieces and those placed on the fold. It's heartbreaking to be short on fabric when you position the last piece for cutting because you left a little too much space between pieces early on. If possible, lay the entire length of fabric on the cutting table or other flat surface and arrange all the pattern pieces before pinning.

SNIP IT

Don't despair if you don't have a large cutting table. Simply use a bed or the floor. To protect those surfaces, purchase an inexpensive, foldable, cardboard cutting mat to lie under the fabric being cut.

When the cutting surface is shorter than the fabric, fold the extra yardage out of the way on one side rather than allowing the fabric to spill off the table, which may cause stretching and fabric distortion. Pin the first few pattern pieces to the fabric using just one or two pins for each. Carefully roll the patterns and fabric together while unrolling the extra fabric and continuing to position the remaining pattern pieces. When you're sure the fabric is sufficient for all the pieces, pin them securely to prepare for cutting.

Some layouts will require pinning a single pattern piece to the fabric more than once. Four shirt cuff pieces, for example, are usually required for a single shirt. Position the pattern piece on the fabric at the first location, but instead of pinning the pattern to the fabric there, use pins or tailor's chalk to roughly mark the pattern location. Move the pattern piece to its second location in the layout, and pin it there. After cutting the pattern piece once, unpin it from the fabric and pin it in the original location to cut the remaining pieces.

Occasionally a pattern piece extends beyond the fold in the layout sketch. In that case, pin and cut the other pattern pieces before unfolding the remaining fabric and pinning the extended piece to a single fabric layer. Layouts may also be split into two parts folded in different ways. Refer to the pattern guide sheet for details, and follow the pattern-specific instructions.

Pinning Patterns

Just as there are different types of pins (see Chapter 1), there's a correct way to pin patterns to fabric. The tried-and-true procedure ensures that the pattern won't shift as you cut, resulting in the most accurate transfer of the pattern shape to your fabric.

How to Pin

Begin by pinning the grainlines to the fabric. Place one pin at each end of the straight grain arrow after making sure the arrow is parallel to the grain. For pieces placed on the fold, use a pin every 6 to 8 inches along the fabric fold to hold the pattern piece on the grain.

Next, smooth the pattern from the pinned points to the outer edges and pin the corners of each piece. With the point of the pin toward the edge of the pattern piece, position the pin diagonally, dividing the corner in half. Pin into the pattern and fabric, and rock the pin to bring the point out of the fabric and pattern a short distance away, with the pin point toward the pattern edge. The pattern and fabric should lie flat after pinning. Be sure the pin point lies within the cutting line to avoid damaging your scissors when cutting.

Finish pinning the pattern to the fabric, spacing the pins every 3 to 4 inches. Use more pins to secure curved pattern edges and fewer on long, straight cutting lines. Always pin perpendicular to the cutting line, with the pin head toward the center of the pattern piece.

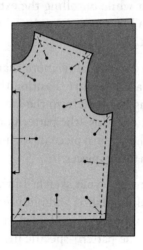

Pin perpendicular to the pattern cutting lines so the paper won't shift as the fabric is cut.

Working with Weights

Sometimes pattern weights are a great alternative to pinning. They don't make holes in the fabric, so weights are perfect for fabrics that will be marred by pins. If the pattern shape is simple, weights may also be faster than pinning.

You can find pattern weights in the notions section of your fabric store. Purchased weights may be small cylinders, button shapes, or longer bars angled to hug pattern curves. Look for easy alternatives around the house such as metal washers, extra scissors, thread cones, or tiny beanbags.

Make your own quick pattern weights with fabric scraps and rice or dried beans. Cut the scraps into 5-inch squares. Drop a tablespoon or two of dried beans or rice into the center of each square. Gather the fabric edges around the filling, and secure with a yarn, thread, or ribbon tie.

To use pattern weights, position the pattern pieces on the fabric as directed earlier. Place a pattern weight at each corner of the pattern piece and along the sides; use enough weights to keep the paper pattern securely against the fabric as you cut. If necessary, move the weights from one area of a piece to another as you cut.

Cutting Options

Now it's time to take shears to fabric and cut out the pieces. It's always a good idea—no matter how experienced you become—to take a moment and double-check the layout before cutting. Are you cutting the correct number of each pattern piece? Have you reversed the pattern piece if required? When cutting a single layer, have you oriented the pattern piece correctly, usually right side up on the fabric's right side?

> **SEW SURPRISING**
>
> Like people, shears come in right- and left-handed models. Be sure you have the correct version for you.

Now pick up your shears and cut. Begin at a fabric edge or with a cut perpendicular to the fold. Right-handed cutters should hold the shears to the right of the pattern piece, using your left hand to hold the pattern and fabric against the cutting surface; for lefties, the position is the opposite. Use long, steady strokes, never quite closing the tip of the shears; at the end of one stroke, open the blades, slide the shears forward, and begin cutting again. Strive to keep the blade that's underneath the fabric against the cutting table rather than lifting the fabric as you cut. Bent-handle shears are best for this cutting job.

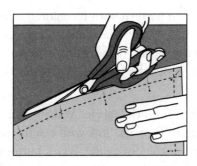

Position your off hand on the pattern and fabric while the main hand cuts with long, smooth strokes.

Do use the scissors' tip to snip accurately into corners. Shorten the stroke as you maneuver around curves. Cut notches outward, into the scrap fabric, and group two or three notches into one for easier and more accurate cutting. If you left part of the excess pattern tissue around the pattern pieces, cut precisely through the cutting line; if the pieces are already trimmed, carefully cut along the solid line.

Cut groups of notches as one.

Leave the patterns pinned to the fabric, and set the cut pieces aside, ready for transferring the pattern markings to the fabric pieces.

Make Your Mark

Transfer pattern markings to the fabric so the marks won't be visible in the finished garment. Usually, this means marking on the fabric's wrong side. If you're using interfacing or lining in your project, you may need to transfer some markings to those pieces instead. Note that cutting lines and seamlines are not usually transferred to the fabric.

> **SNIP IT**
>
> When a marking must be visible on the fabric's right side, such as a buttonhole or patch pocket location, mark it first on the wrong side and then use tailor's tacks, a removable marking tool, or pins to transfer the marks to the fabric's right side.

Transfer markings with tailor's chalk, dressmaker's tracing paper and wheel, removable fabric marking pens, straight pins, basting stitches, or tailor's tacks. When selecting chalk or tracing paper, pick a color that has enough contrast to be visible on the fabric without being bold enough to shadow through to the right side. Yellow tracing paper and chalk are often chosen for white fabrics as well as many light and dark colors.

Working with Dressmaker's Tracing Paper

Slip dressmaker's tracing paper between the fabric and pattern with its colored side against the fabric, and use a tracing wheel to draw directly on the pattern markings. The tracing paper transfers the marks made by the serrated wheel to the fabric. If the fabric is folded wrong side out for cutting, slip a second piece of tracing paper under the fabric and transfer the marks to both pieces at once.

For darts and pleat/tuck lines, transfer the entire line onto the fabric. Make a short, perpendicular line across the point or end of the line for clarity. To mark dots with tracing paper, draw perpendicular lines about ¾ inch long that intersect at the dot center. Mark buttonholes with straight lines, plus short lines crossing each end to better define the correct buttonhole length.

Working with Chalk and Markers

You can also transfer marks with tailor's chalk. Test the chalk on a fabric scrap to determine its removability; some chalks brush or wipe away easily, while others are removed with an iron or by washing the project. Chalk is available in pencil form, as a powder used in a wheeled applicator, and in flat rectangular pieces. Chalk is also sold in a clever tool designed to punch through the tissue at a dot and make chalk dots simultaneously on both fabric layers.

Removable marking pens are used like tailor's chalk. They come in two formulas: air-removable and water-soluble. The former usually disappears unaided within two days, sometimes as quickly as a few minutes after marking. The latter is removed with plain water. Always test markers on fabric scraps, and determine whether their marks are still removable after ironing. In general, the best way to remove either type of pen marks is by rinsing in plenty of plain water, making these tools best suited for washable projects.

To use chalk or markers: with the pattern still pinned to the fabric, release a few pins, fold the pattern tissue along the marking, and trace the marking onto the fabric. To transfer dots and small marks, stick a pin straight through the pattern and fabric perpendicular to the fabric surface. Carefully pull the pattern off the pin head, and use chalk to mark the fabric where the pin enters.

Working with Quick Clips and Tailor's Tack

More experienced sewists may use only tiny clips (⅛ inch or less) along the cut edges to mark construction details. Always be sure the clips won't interfere with the seamlines or weaken the fabric. For darts, it's also necessary to mark the point with a tailor's tack or chalk.

Tailor's tacks are another option for transferring pattern marks. Work a tailor's tack at each dot, or use several tailor's tacks to indicate a line.

To make a tailor's tack, thread a hand-sewing needle with a doubled thread. Take a small stitch into and out of the fabric at the dot, sewing through all fabric layers. Leave a 3-inch or longer tail of thread. Take a second stitch on top of the first, leaving a 1- to 2-inch loop of thread. Cut the thread 3 inches or more from the tailor's tack. Gently pull the fabric layers apart and clip the threads between the layers, leaving a tailor's tack in each layer.

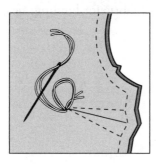

Use a tailor's tack to temporarily mark dart ends.

Project: The Fudd Cap

Warm up your winter with this fuzzy fleece cap that takes its name from the well-known cartoon character who wears a similar hat.

Fabricate a fabulous cap—for hunting wabbits or any other activity—using your new sewing skills!
(Photo by Matthew H. Caddell)

Finished size:

One size fits most adults

Tools and materials:

⅜ yard light- to medium-weight fleece* for main fabric

⅜ yard light- to medium-weight cotton** accent fabric for binding, ties, and hatband

6×9-inch piece of ultra-firm fusible stabilizer

⅛ yard nonwoven fusible interfacing

¾-inch half-ball covered button form

Thread

Basic hand- and machine-sewing tools

Yardage is based on 60-inch-wide fabric with at least 55 inches of useable width. For 44- or 45-inch-wide fabric, buy ½ yard.

**Yardage is based on 45-inch-wide fabric with at least 40 inches of useable width. You will have excess fabric.*

Pattern prep and cutting:

1. Prior to cutting, trace or photocopy pattern pieces A, B, and C (at the end of the chapter) onto pattern paper, transferring the grainline and other markings.

2. From the main fabric, cut the following:

   6 cap crown pieces (pattern piece A)

   2 cap brims (pattern piece B)

   2 earflaps (pattern piece C)

   (Note: The earflap is not quite symmetric. Mark the front edge.)

   From the accent fabric, cut the following:

   Two 1½×15-inch bias strips for earflap bindings

   Two 1×15-inch strips for back ties

   One 2×28-inch strip for hatband

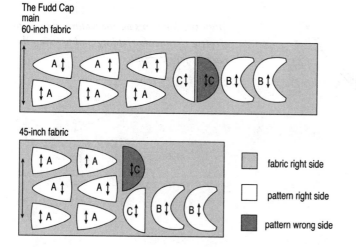

The Fudd Cap
main
60-inch fabric

45-inch fabric

fabric right side

pattern right side

pattern wrong side

accent
45-inch fabric

Use this cutting layout to place and cut pattern pieces.

3. Cut one 1×27-inch strip from the nonwoven interfacing, piecing as necessary.

4. Trim the seam allowance from pattern piece B, and cut one brim support from the 6×9-inch piece of ultra-firm stabilizer.

Construction:

Use a ½-inch seam allowance unless otherwise noted.

5. Press ¼ inch to the wrong side on one long edge of each earflap binding strip. Pin the right side of the long unpressed edge of one strip to the wrong side of one flap's curved edge. Stitch the strip to the flap, using a ¼-inch seam. Fold the pressed strip edge over the flap edge, encasing the raw edges. Edgestitch the pressed strip edge to the flap. Trim the excess strip even with the flap upper edge.

> **PINPRICK**
>
> Don't press fleece! The synthetic fabric will melt. Instead, finger press seams open, and topstitch where indicated.

6. Press ¼ inch to the wrong side on one short end of each back tie. Next, press ¼ inch to the wrong side along each long edge of each tie. Finally, fold the strip in half lengthwise, and press. Using a zigzag stitch 1.5mm long and 2.5mm wide, edgestitch along the folded edges, forming two narrow ¼-inch ties.

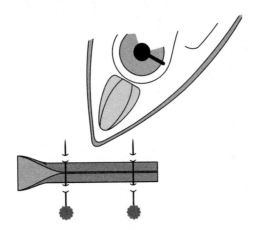

Align two long pins on the ironing surface to create a channel for folding and pressing the narrow fabric strips.

7. Center the brim support, fusible side down, on the wrong side of the outer brim. Using parchment paper and low dry heat, lightly fuse the support to the brim, being careful not to melt the fleece fabric.

8. Place the inner brim against the outer brim, right sides together. Stitch the brims together around the outer curve of the stabilizer. Grade the inner brim seam allowance, and turn the brim right side out, making sure the seam allowances lie flat.

9. Pin the brims together along the inside curve, matching the raw edges. Using a ¼-inch seam allowance, stitch the inside curve, securing brim edges together.

10. Topstitch ¼ inch from the outer curve of the cap brim.

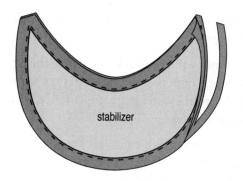

Stitch next to, but not through, the stabilizer, and trim the seam allowance that's farthest from the stabilizer.

11. Select one crown piece as the center back. Referring to the two lower dots on pattern piece A, position and pin the short end of one back tie at each lower dot, aligning the raw edges, with the bulk of the tie toward the center of the crown.

12. With right sides together, pin the center back to a second crown piece, matching the side edges. Using a ½-inch seam, stitch the crown pieces together from the top dot to the lower side edge, catching the pinned tie in the seam. Sew a third crown piece to the opposite side of the center back so there are three panels sewn together, with one tie end in each seam.

13. On the crown wrong side, finger press the seams open. Topstitch ¼ inch on both sides of each seam to anchor the seam allowances, folding the tie ends away from the center back.

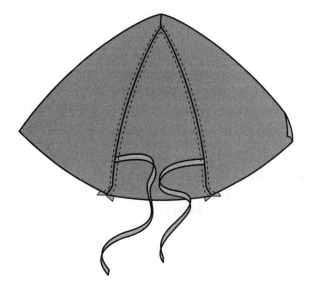

The topstitching anchors the back ties toward the center of the center back panel.

14. Repeat steps 11 through 13 with the remaining crown pieces to form the cap front without ties.

15. Pin-mark the center lower edge of the crown front. With the nongraded brim edge against the right side of the crown front, align the crown front with the brim center.

Pin the crown and brim together, being careful not to stretch either edge. Stitch the brim to the crown front using a ¼-inch seam.

16. With right sides together, pin the cap front to the cap back, matching the top dots and raw edges. Using a ½-inch seam allowance, stitch the sections together. Finger press the seam open. Working from the top dot to the outer edge, topstitch ¼ inch on both sides of the seam, anchoring the seam allowances.

17. Pin-mark the lower edge of the cap center back. With right sides together and aligning raw edges, pin the flaps to the cap lower edge, abutting the bound edges of the flaps at the center back and overlapping the brim. Stitch the flaps to the cap with a ¼-inch seam.

18. Position the 1-inch strip of nonwoven fusible interfacing on the wrong side of the hatband, ¼ inch below the long top edge and ¼ inch from the right end. Fuse the interfacing, following manufacturer's instructions. Press the ¼-inch unfused fabric allowance to the wrong side at the right end and along the long hatband edge. Edgestitch the long pressed edge.

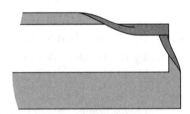

Fuse the interfacing to the hatband, leaving ¼ inch of fabric unfused along the top and right side edges, and press the unfused fabric edges to the wrong side.

19. With the right side of the band against the underside of the earflaps and brim, pin the band to the bottom cap edge, placing the short pressed band end to one side of center back and aligning the raw hatband edge with the cap raw edges. Overlap the pressed end by 2 inches, and trim the excess band. Stitch the band to the cap using a ½-inch seam allowance.

SNIP IT

Cutting the interfacing so it falls short of the seamline allows a little bit of stretch along the brim. For a tighter fit, cut interfacing 1¾×27 inches before fusing it to the band.

20. Fold the band to the inside of the cap, hiding the seam allowances. Hand-tack the hatband in place at the crown seams. Slipstitch the overlapped ends together.

21. Following manufacturer instructions, create a covered button using a scrap of accent fabric. Sew the button to the crown center.

Make a fair-weather version of the Fudd Cap using light- to medium-weight home décor canvas and eliminating the earflaps.

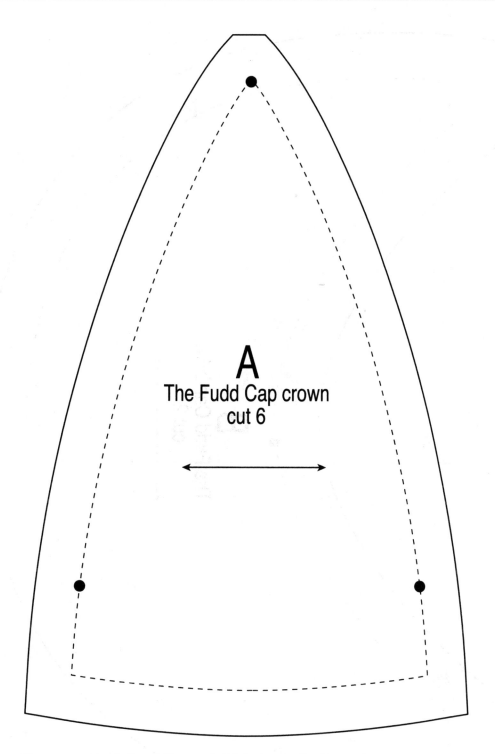

A
The Fudd Cap crown
cut 6

Use pattern pieces A, B, and C to cut the fabric pieces outlined in step 2.

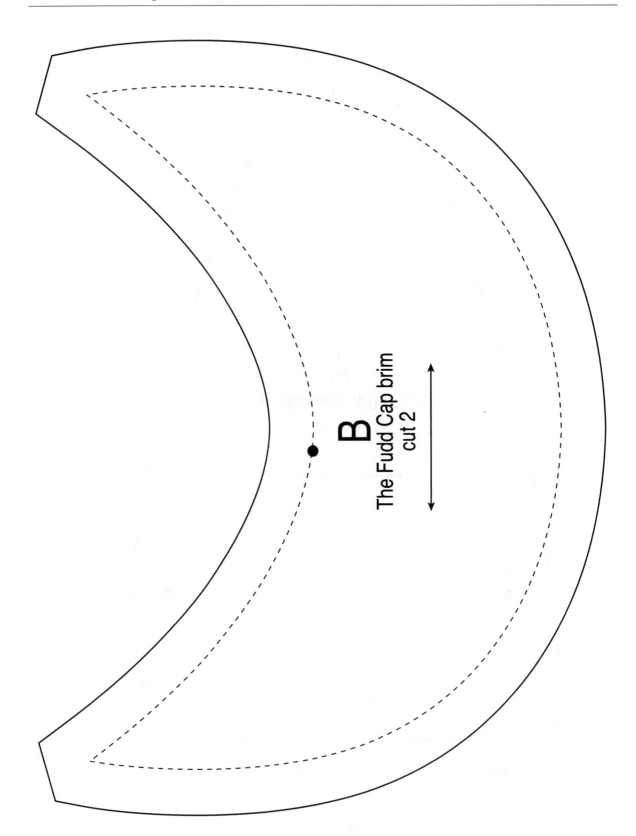

B

The Fudd Cap brim
cut 2

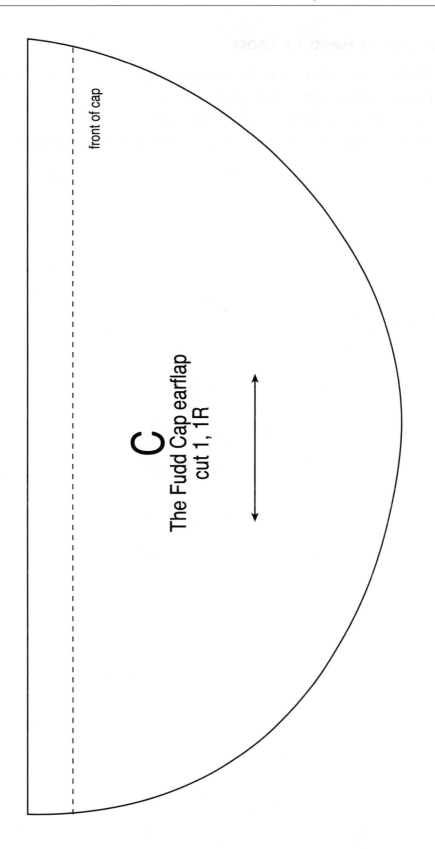

C

The Fudd Cap earflap
cut 1, 1R

front of cap

The Least You Need to Know

- Fabric preparation should include washing or dry cleaning (preshrinking) and ironing.
- Pins or weights are essential for accurate cutting.
- Practice smooth scissor technique for best results.
- Pattern marks can be transferred from paper to fabric in a variety of ways.

Top Details

In This Chapter

- Tips and techniques for tops
- Sewing sleeves
- Creating collars and cuffs
- Figuring out facings, linings, and underlinings

Whether you want a special top with fancy frills and designer details or you need a neatly finished shirt to wear to work, being able to make your own blouses and jackets is, well, the tops!

Sleeves

Although some tops, like sleeveless shells and tanks, are finished without sleeves, arm coverings are a part of most shirts and dresses. A sleeve may be as simple as an extended shoulder seam, or it can be a fantasy of gathers and tucks. Fitted sleeves even include elbow darts, although in this age of flexible fabrics and easy-to-wear styles, that technique is usually reserved for tailored jackets.

The simplest sleeve styles to sew are cut in one piece with the garment front or back. The shoulder seam extends beyond the shoulder point to form the top of the sleeve, and the side seam curves away from the body to become the underarm seam. No special sewing techniques are needed for these sleeves, but be aware that all-in-one styles, with their large pattern pieces, typically use more fabric.

Set-In Sleeves

The trick to setting in sleeves lies in knowing how to join a convex curve (the sleeve cap) to a concave one (the armhole). Just remember that it's the seamline that needs to match, not the cut edges!

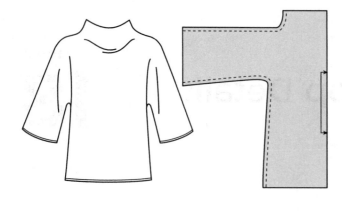

Dolman sleeves are cut in one piece with the garment front and back.

Set-in sleeve styles fit smoothly around the armhole and shoulder.

To prepare the sleeve, lengthen the stitch to 3 to 4mm, and sew two lines of ease stitches on the sleeve cap, one along the seamline and another ⅛ inch inside the seam allowance. The ease stitches usually run from one dot to another or between the sleeve notches; check the pattern guide sheet for specific instructions. Sew with the sleeve fabric right side up. Return the machine to the normal stitch length, and sew the underarm seam if directed by the pattern; some styles set the sleeve cap into the armhole first before sewing the side and underarm seams.

Place the sleeve and corresponding armhole right sides together and pin at the notches, dots, and underarm/side seamline. This is a good opportunity to be sure you're putting the left sleeve in the left armhole! Carefully pull the bobbin threads of the ease stitches as if to gather, but pull only enough to bring the sleeve seamline to match the armhole seamline. Pin the entire seam securely.

Sew the sleeve into the armhole. It can be helpful to place the sleeve on the bottom as you sew, where the feed dog action will help ease extra fullness into place. Check the seam from both sides to ensure there are no tucks or pleats, and stitch again ⅛ inch inside the seam allowance. Remove any ease stitches visible from the right side, and trim the seam if directed on the guide sheet.

The armhole/sleeve seam is often pressed toward the sleeve, where its bulk extends the shoulder slightly for an attractive fit over the shoulder joint. The seam allowances can also help support fullness in a gathered sleeve. However, the seam allowances can also be pressed toward the body of the garment. This is often the case in tailored shirts, where the seam allowances are held in place by topstitching around the armhole.

Flat Cap

Sleeves with a flat cap, whether it's a shallow curve or a straight line, are used in garments with a relaxed upper body fit. T-shirts are a good example. To accomplish fitting, the shoulder seam is extended and the armhole is moved outward so the underarm curve is correspondingly shallow.

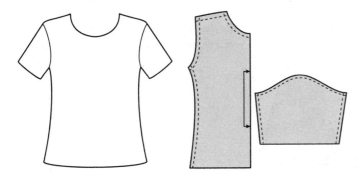

The relaxed fit of a T-shirt relies on a flat sleeve cap and an extended shoulder line.

Flat sleeve caps can usually be inserted without ease stitching. Simply pin the sleeve to the armhole, right sides together, matching the raw edges and the pattern markings. Sew or serge with the sleeve on the bottom, against the feed dogs, to ease the sleeve slightly for a smooth fit.

Rounded Cap

Almost all sleeve caps are rounded. The highest sleeve caps are correspondingly narrow and are designed to fit the upper arm closely. Ease stitching is crucial when setting in these sleeves. When fitting a high sleeve cap, be sure to fit the armhole as well so the sleeve doesn't restrict movement, especially if the garment is cut from a stable woven fabric.

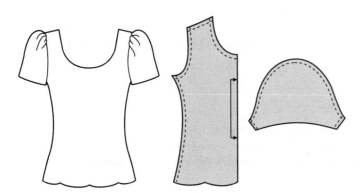

Rounded sleeve caps can be high and smooth or low and spread apart for gathers.

To attach a gathered sleeve cap, begin with ease stitches, as you would for any set-in sleeve. The difference is that there's much more fabric in a gathered sleeve cap, so the ease stitches will be used to form gathers at the seamline. In some styles, the gathers may lie between the sleeve cap notches, with the remaining stitches used to ease the fabric between each notch and the nearest dot.

Raglan Sleeves

Raglan sleeves, often seen in athletic wear and starship uniforms, provide superior range of movement by eliminating the armhole seam. Instead, the patternmaker grafts part of the shoulder area onto the sleeve cap, resulting in seams that angle from the neckline to the armhole. The exact shape of the seam varies and provides an opportunity for unique styling. Raglan seams can easily be accented with piping or decorative stitches.

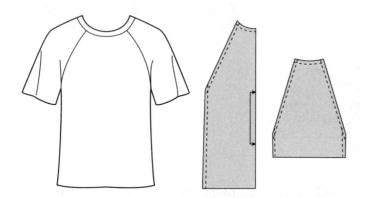

Raglan sleeves are constructed for comfort and ease of movement.

Some raglan sleeves are cut in two pieces, with a seam running from the neck/shoulder intersection down the center of the sleeve to the cuff. These sleeves fit more closely than single-piece raglans because the seam provides an opportunity for shaping the sleeve to curve over the shoulder point.

Attaching a raglan sleeve is as simple as matching the notches and stitching the seams. Be sure to match the sleeve front and back to the correct garment pieces so the neckline is correctly shaped.

Collars and Cuffs

A beautiful collar can be the focal point of an entire garment. Learning to tease out those sharp points and keeping collars and cuffs looking crisp are techniques you'll use time and again.

SEW SURPRISING

Truly tailored collars come in two pieces, the stand and the fall. Sometimes a patternmaker will combine the two into one pattern piece. The stand can also be used alone to create a mandarin collar. Collars with no stand have been drafted to lie flat on top of the garment rather than first rising up around the neck.

The Inside Story

One secret to successful collars and cuffs is the support staff: the interfacing that hides inside the finished garment. For most light- to medium-weight shirts and blouses, a light- to medium-weight nonwoven or woven interfacing is the best choice. Select one that's crisp, not a fluid knit, unless you're constructing a tailored jacket with interfaced front panel and lapels. Both fusible and sew-in interfacings are appropriate, although most sewists prefer the convenience of fusible.

Cut the interfacing pieces as directed by the pattern. In most cases, the same pattern pieces are used for the garment pieces and for the interfacing. Where that's the case, carefully trim all but ⅛ inch of the seam allowance from the fusible interfacing pieces before fusing to reduce bulk, but leave the seam allowances intact on sew-in interfacing. If separate pattern pieces are provided for cutting interfacing, check the pattern to see whether the seam allowances have already been trimmed.

Where the interfacing extends to a point (for example, on a collar or cuff), reduce bulk in the finished project by snipping off the interfacing corners. Cut across the corner about ⅛ inch inside the seamline intersection before applying the interfacing as usual.

Snip the points from the interfacing to reduce bulk in pointed garment areas.

Lay the garment sections to be interfaced wrong side up on the ironing board and preheat the iron according to the fabric type and the interfacing manufacturer's fusing instructions. Press the fabric to remove any wrinkles before placing the interfacing, fusible side down, on the fabric's wrong side.

Cover the interfacing with a press cloth, and press to fuse. Many manufacturers recommend steam pressing, either with the iron's steam setting or by moistening the press cloth. Use a firm up-and-down motion to fuse the interfacing rather than gliding the iron along, which could distort or misalign the cut pieces. Allow the iron to remain in place for 10 seconds or as directed before lifting it and moving to a new area.

When all the interfacing has been fused, leave the fabric on the ironing board until cool. Check the bond by attempting to lift a corner or side of the interfacing, and press again if necessary. When the bond is complete, turn over the interfaced fabric and press again from the fabric's right side.

To work with sew-in interfacing, baste the interfacing to the corresponding fabric pieces by stitching ⅛ inch inside the seam allowance. Carefully trim the interfacing very close to the basting, leaving only ⅛ inch of interfacing to be caught in the seams.

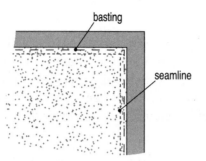

basting

seamline

Trim sew-in interfacing close to the basting stitches to remove seam allowance bulk.

Getting the Point

Perfectly formed points on collars and cuffs elevate your project from homemade to handmade, and it's not hard to learn how. Check Chapter 8 for pointers, and read on for project-specific know-how to use when constructing custom tops.

Typically, the point on a collar is an acute angle; that is, it's less than 90 degrees. When the point is stitched and turned right side out, the seam allowances, interfacing, and thread are crowded within that tight angle, which is why some collar points become rounded, lumpy, and stiff.

Plan ahead by trimming the interfacing out of the points as directed earlier. When stitching the seam, stop one stitch length before the point, and pivot halfway around the corner. Take two or three stitches (the heavier the fabric, the more stitches are needed) across the point, pivot again, and continue stitching along the adjacent side. The extra stitches provide a little space for all the material that must fit inside.

Another area to perfect for the best points is trimming and grading the seam allowances. In addition to trimming along all the collar seams, snip off the seam allowances just a few threads beyond the point, cutting across the point. Then trim away a little extra from the seam allowances on both sides of the point, as directed in the earlier "The Inside Story" section.

When stitching and trimming are complete, it's time to turn. Not surprisingly, the closely trimmed corner is structurally weak, so be very careful not to push through the fabric as you turn the point. For best results, use a rounded blunt tool; bamboo point turners from the notions department are ideal, but knitting needles and dry ball point pens can also work.

Gently work the point into position, using the tool tip to stroke along the seamlines. When everything is in place, take the collar or cuff to the ironing board and press. Use a press cloth to help avoid shine from the iron's heat and pressure on the accumulated layers.

SEW SURPRISING

If you find you really, really don't enjoy turning points, or if your personal style is curvier, why not convert collar and cuff points to curves? Use a large coin or a thread spool to draw a new seamline that rounds off the point, and trim the cutting line to match.

Learning Curves

In addition to armhole curves, garments worn above the waist must have curves to skim across the bust and hips. Shapely seams, such as princess styles, and cleverly curved darts help bring fabric closer to the body's contours.

Princess seams run from shoulder to waist or lower or begin at the armhole before curving over the bust and heading down. In reality, these seams incorporate darts to shape the fabric for a lovely fit.

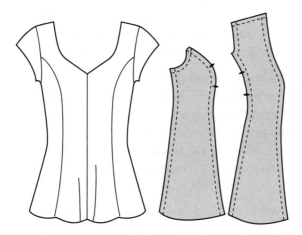

Princess seams create a long, slimming look that closely follows your curves.

SNIP IT

The first time you sew a princess-seamed garment, make a muslin (see Chapter 15) to check and refine the fitting. By altering the seamline curves, you can move the bust and waist up or down, in or out.

The front and back of princess-seamed garments are each divided into sections. As you pin and cut the fabric, make careful note of each notch and dot, the guideposts for seaming the pieces together. One side of each seam is a convex curve while the other is concave. The curve may be slight, as on a garment back where the only bulge is the shoulder blade, or very pronounced, as around the bust.

Before sewing the princess seam, staystitch each garment piece along the curves. Use a regular stitch length, and sew just a thread width or two inside the seam allowance, keeping the actual seamline free. Clip the concave surface to, but not through, the staystitching so it can open up when pinned to the corresponding convex piece. If necessary, ease stitch the convex piece to control the fullness.

Pin the two pieces right sides together, distributing the fullness evenly along the curved section. Stitch the seam and clip or trim as directed on the guide sheet. Press the seam open or to one side on a pressing ham to help shape the garment.

Some tops and blouses incorporate vertical darts that cross the natural waistline, controlling fullness. The result is a smoother fit when tucked inside pants or a shapelier silhouette when worn over pants or skirts.

These waistline darts are typically long and have two pointed ends. Begin stitching at the center of the dart (the widest part) and stitch toward one end. Finish the point as directed in Chapter 9. Turn the project around, and begin sewing at the center again, overlapping the stitches slightly. Sew toward the second point and finish it as before.

It's also easy to add waistline darts to ready-to-wear items. Put on the blouse, wrong side out, and pin out the extra fullness at the waist. Take off the blouse and refine the dart placement, making two darts equidistant from the center front or back. Each dart should be the same depth and length. When the darts are correctly shaped, stitch them as directed earlier.

Another curve found in upper-body garments is the curved shirttail hem. Because the hem winds its way around both convex and concave surfaces, the hem allowance is usually no more than ⅝ inch. Stitch along the hemline with a regular stitch length, and press the shirt to the wrong side along the line of stitches. Fold the raw edge to the wrong side to meet the stitches, and press. Fold again along the line of stitches, allowing the stitches to roll very slightly to the wrong side so they won't be visible on the outside of the garment. Press carefully to create a double-fold hem, and topstitch the hem near the upper fold to secure.

A serger can make even quicker work of curved hems. Serge the raw edge, leaving only a ¼-inch hem allowance (about the width of the serger stitches). Press the hem to the wrong side, making sure the stitches aren't visible from the right side. Topstitch the hem to secure.

Facings and Linings

At first glance, facings and linings—those extra, sometimes duplicate pattern pieces hidden inside a finished garment or bag—may seem like a lot of unnecessary work. After all, no one will see those efforts but you! In fact, facings and linings provide structure and shape and can make garments more comfortable to wear.

Facings

Facings provide a tidy finish for edges that aren't sewn into other pieces at a seam, such as the neckline and armhole edges on a sleeveless, collarless shirt. At their simplest, facings are duplicates of the first 2 or 3 inches of the garment along the edge. It's easy to add a facing to a garment that doesn't have one by tracing the main garment pattern.

Facings are often interfaced to help the garment edge maintain its shape. Choose an interfacing that matches the fabric weight and drape; crispness isn't desirable. Prepare and attach the interfacing as directed earlier in this chapter.

If the facing is cut in pieces, sew the pieces together as directed on the guide sheet. Usually neckline facings are sewn together at the shoulders; if there's a center back seam, the facing is left open there to be finished later around the closure.

Next, hem the facing's outer edge. The hem allowance is usually just ¼ inch. Press the hem to the wrong side, and stitch it in place. If a serger is available, it's acceptable to serge the facing outer edges, finishing the raw edges while eliminating bulk by keeping the fabric flat. The facing outer edge can also be completed by stitching ¼ inch from the raw edge and finishing the edge with pinking shears.

Pin the facing to the garment edge, right sides together, matching the raw edges, intersecting seams, and pattern markings. Stitch, and trim, grade, and clip the seam allowances as necessary. Press the facing and seam allowances away from the garment.

SNIP IT

If the garment's seams are pressed to one side rather than open, as typically occurs with serged seams, minimize bulk by turning the facing seams in the opposite direction.

The next step, called understitching, works to keep the facing in place so it doesn't roll toward the outside. With the seam allowances and facing pressed away from the garment, edgestitch the facing and seam allowances together a scant ⅛ inch from the garment seam.

Press the understitched facing to the garment inside along the seamline. Whipstitch the facing to the intersecting seamlines to hold it in place. Alternatively, pin the facing to the garment alongside the seams, and stitch in the ditch through the garment and the facing along the garment seam. The stitches will sink into the garment seam and be invisible from the right side.

Linings

Linings are sometimes used in conjunction with facings. They add opacity to transparent fabrics, cover the raw edges of seam allowances, improve garment structure and drape, and make it easier to slide garments on and off. Lining fabrics are usually lightweight and drapable and often smooth or even slippery to the touch.

Constructing a lining is usually much like making the garment, and many of the same pieces are used. The lining front may connect to the front facing rather than being seamed directly to the garment front. The pattern envelope and guide sheet will specify when a lining is used and will include the yardage for lining fabric alongside the other fabric information.

Underlinings are always cut from the main garment pattern pieces. The underlining is attached to its corresponding garment piece before construction begins, and the two fabrics are then treated as one. An underlining is used to hide seam allowances in sheer fabric (also taking the place of a lining there), to support loosely woven materials, or to add structure to major garment seams. A pattern may call for underlining, but the decision to add this extra layer is often up to you.

Project: Simple Shapes Jacket

Practice pattern-making skills with easy-to-draft trapezoids. Three pattern pieces are all you need to make this quick cover-up. Use coordinating fabrics for a versatile, reversible look.

Sew a simple jacket and practice those top details!

Finished size:

Variable

Tools and materials:

2 coordinating 45-inch-wide fabrics (amount determined by measurements)* **

Two 1½-inch and two ½-inch buttons

6 inches of ribbon or cord for button loop***

Pattern drafting paper, wrapping paper, or other wide paper

Thread

Basic sewing equipment

Suitable woven fabrics include quilting-weight cottons or lightweight home décor fabrics. Very stretchy fabrics are not suitable for this project. Extra ease may be needed for fleece or heavier fabrics.

**To make the reversible jacket shown here, choose equal yardages of two coordinating fabrics.*

***Test-fit button loop length before attaching to garment.*

Make the pattern:

1. You'll need to draw just two trapezoids—the back and sleeve—for this project; the jacket front is based on the back. Plug your measurements into the following pattern formula to find values for A through F. Then draft the back and sleeve shapes on pattern paper, following the drafting guide.

Pattern formula:

back measurement, from shoulder point to shoulder point + 2 inches ease + 1 inch seam allowance = A

(hips at hemline ÷ 2) + 2 inches ease + 1 inch seam allowance = B

length from shoulder point to hemline + 1 inch seam allowance = C

arm from shoulder point to wrist + 1 inch seam allowance = D

(shoulder point to underarm × 2) + 1 inch ease + 1 inch seam allowance = E

wrist circumference + 1 inch ease + 1 inch seam allowance = F

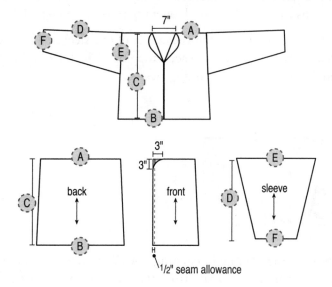

2. To make the jacket front pattern, fold the back pattern piece in half vertically, with the center fold perpendicular to the hemline. Trace the folded pattern piece onto pattern paper, adding ½ inch along the folded edge; this will be the jacket center front. Measure and mark 3 inches from the upper corner along both edges. Sketch a curve connecting the marks, using a small round plate or French curve as a guide.

SNIP IT

Draw symmetrical trapezoids by marking a center line to base measurements on. For example, to draft the sleeve, draw a vertical line the length of D. Place the center point of F at one end of the line, and draw F perpendicular to the line. Repeat to draw E at the opposite end of the center line, and connect the endpoints of E and F to complete the trapezoid.

Cutting:

3. Refer to the pattern pieces and the "Yardage Conversion Chart" in Appendix C to determine needed yardage. Take note of the grainline arrows; they indicate how to position the pattern on the fabric. Buy equal amounts of both fabrics.

4. Cut one back, two fronts, and two sleeve pieces from each fabric.

Construction:

Use a ½-inch seam allowance unless otherwise noted. Backstitch at the beginning and end of each seam except where indicated.

5. Working with the pieces cut from one fabric, pin-mark the center back at the upper edge. Measure and mark points 3½ inches on each side of the pin to define the back neck opening.

6. Place the fronts and back right sides together, with the curved edges of the front pieces overlapping slightly at the center front. Aligning the upper and side edges, stitch the shoulder seams from the back neck opening to the side edge. Press the seams open.

7. With right sides together, match the center of one sleeve edge E with one shoulder seam. Pin and sew the sleeve in place, stopping ½ inch from the raw edges. Press the seam open. Repeat for the remaining sleeve.

Leave ½ inch unsewn at each end of the seam.

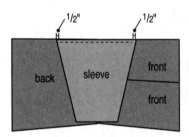

8. With right sides together and matching raw edges, pin the underarm seam of one sleeve. Stitch the underarm seam from the underarm to the wrist. Press the seam open.

9. Fold the armhole and underarm seam allowances out of the way, and pin the side seam together. Stitch the side seam from underarm to hemline, making sure the seam ends align so there's no gap at the underarm. Press the seam open.

10. Repeat steps 8 and 9 to finish the remaining underarm and side seams.

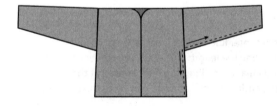

Stitch the underarm and side seams, sewing from the underarm to the raw edges.

11. Try on the jacket, and mark the button loop placement on one center front edge. Remove the jacket. Fold the button loop in half, and pin it in place on the jacket right side, aligning raw edges. Stitch the loop to the jacket edge, using a ⅜-inch seam.

12. Repeat steps 5 through 9 to sew the remaining pieces together.

13. Place the two jackets right sides together, aligning the center back neckline. Pin and stitch the jackets together along the back neck opening. Pin and stitch the front and hemline edges together, pivoting at the corners and curves. Leave a 6-inch opening along the back hemline edge for turning, and catch the button loop in the front edge seam.

14. Press to set the seam, clip the curved front edges, and trim the front bottom corners to reduce bulk.

15. Turn the jacket right side out through the opening and tuck the sleeves in place. Press the neckline, front, and hemline edges. Slipstitch the back opening closed, and topstitch ¼ inch from the pressed edges.

16. Press ½ inch to the wrong side along each wrist edge (both fabrics), and slipstitch the wrist openings together. Topstitch ¼ inch from the pressed edge to finish the wrist edges.

17. Using the button loop as a placement guide, align one button on the lining and one on the outer jacket. Stitch through the jacket to sew both buttons in place.

Alter the basic pattern to make a fun fall jacket from flannel or fleece. Add extra ease to A, B, E, and F in the pattern formula to accommodate bulkier garment layers.

The Least You Need to Know

- Sleeves come in several basic forms: set-in, raglan, flat cap, and rounded cap, for example.
- Crisp collars and cuffs are a mark of well-made tops. Techniques for sewing, interfacing, and trimming are key to excellent results.
- Princess seams and waistline darts are used to shape tops and dresses.
- Facings and linings may be unseen, but they are crucial to achieving the best results in some garments.

Bottom Lines

In This Chapter

- Working with waistlines
- Planning and stitching pockets
- Measuring and making hems
- Fun hem finishes

Stitching up a skirt or pair of pants is the perfect complement to a custom-made blouse or top. The sewing techniques are the same, but the focus shifts to waistlines and hems.

Around the Waist

Although you couldn't tell from recent grunge fashions, every bottom garment needs something to hold it in place around the waist. Garments may be styled to fit the natural waist, usually 7 to 9 inches above the widest part of the hips and often the narrowest part of the body, or they may be tailored to cling lower on the hips.

The type of waistline finish is often a style decision, but it's also an area of flexibility as you experiment with pattern alterations.

Casings

A casing is a fabric tunnel designed to hold elastic or a drawstring that can be tightened around the body. Casings can be made from garment fabric or contrasting material and can range from all-but-invisible to stand-out style feature.

To be a candidate for waistline casings, a bottom should have little or no shaping above the hips. There will be no zipper or button placket to open the garment as it's pulled over the full hips, so there must be enough fabric at the waist to fit over the hipline.

To construct a simple self-fabric casing, sew the pants together at the center front, center back, and sides. Finish the upper edge by pressing ¼ inch to the wrong side or overcast, pink, or serge the raw edge.

Press the finished upper edge to the wrong side as directed in the pattern. The casing should be at least ⅛ inch, but no more than ¼ inch, wider than the elastic that will be used. Edgestitch the inner fold to secure the folded edge and form the casing, leaving a 2-inch gap in the seamline at the center back.

Cut a length of elastic equal to your waistline measurement plus 1 inch for overlap. Use a bodkin or safety pin to thread the elastic through the casing, beginning and ending at the gap in the seam. Be sure the elastic doesn't twist. Overlap the elastic ends 1 inch, and sew back and forth through both elastic layers to secure. You could also sew an X inside a square to provide an especially secure join.

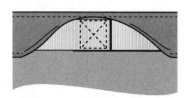

Leave a gap for inserting the elastic, and stitch the overlapped elastic ends securely.

SNIP IT

Fitting elastic can be tricky, as different widths and brands of elastic have different degrees of stretch. After cutting the elastic for a project, pin it around your waistline and wear it for a few minutes. The elastic should be stretched slightly without binding. Adjust the length as necessary before threading the elastic through the casing. It's also a good idea to try on the garment before closing the gap in the casing, while it's still a simple matter to shorten the elastic if necessary.

Slip the overlapped elastic into the casing, and distribute the elastic evenly around the garment. Sew the gap closed, matching the previous stitches.

Waistband elastic has a tendency to roll, fold, and twist when worn. These strategies help keep the elastic straight and steady:

- Use nonroll elastic.

- Before inserting the elastic, edgestitch the upper fold of the casing as well as the inner fold. There's no need to leave a gap in the upper fold edgestitching.

- After the casing is complete, distribute the elastic evenly around the garment. Stitch in the ditch at each seamline (front, back, and sides), sewing across the casing and through the elastic. The stitches will slip into the seam and be hidden but keep the elastic from rolling.

Casings can also be used for drawstring closures. (See the "Drawstrings and Ties" section in Chapter 14.) The construction is similar to elastic casings, but before stitching the casing, a drawstring opening must be made. One option is to leave a gap in a seamline, usually the center front.

Another is to work one or two buttonholes within the casing area through which the drawstring is inserted. Buttonholes or a seam gap can be on the inside or outside garment surface.

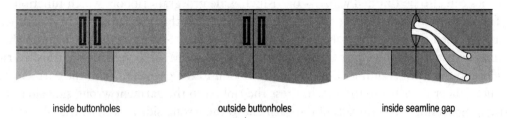

inside buttonholes   outside buttonholes   inside seamline gap

Options for drawstring openings include buttonholes inside or outside a garment or a seamline gap.

Casings aren't always constructed from garment fabric. Instead, sew a length of bias tape wide enough to accommodate the elastic to the garment to make a casing, or topstitch ribbon to a garment after hemming the upper edge to make a decorative casing on the garment right side. Contrasting fabric on a garment exterior creates an interesting "paper bag" waistline.

SEW SURPRISING

When the elastic is narrow and won't be under much stress, sometimes there's no casing at all. An example is a gathered pocket opening; the elastic there can be attached by sewing directly through the stretched elastic and garment fabric.

Facings

Finishing a waistband with a facing is just like facing a neckline or armhole (see Chapter 18). Because a bottom often weighs more than a top due to fabric weight or volume, there are some additional factors to consider.

Like the garment itself, the facing's waistline edge should be staystitched to prevent stretching. Apply the interfacing first, and staystitch on the seamline or very slightly within the seam allowance. Join the facing sections as directed, leaving one seam open to accommodate the zipper or other closure. Finish the facing's outer edge, and apply the facing to the garment.

If the bottom-weight fabric is thick or heavy, consider cutting the facing from a medium-weight woven fabric such as broadcloth or poplin. Be sure to interface the facing to preserve its shape, using a medium-weight nonwoven or woven interfacing.

Garments that are gathered or pleated at the waistline require a separate waistline facing pattern. The facing lies flat inside the garment, without pleats or gathers. Pull the gathering stitches as the garment is pinned to the facing, using the facing as a guide for the finished seamline length, or fold, press, and baste the pleats before attaching the facing.

For the most secure, nonstretch waistline, add a stay tape to the facing seam. Twill tape ¼ inch wide is most often used, but a straight-grain strip of lightweight fabric with pinked edges can be substituted; the vital characteristic is that the stay does not stretch. Before sewing the facing to the garment, center the stay tape along the seamline on the facing wrong side and baste.

The stay will be caught in the seam and hidden between the garment and facing in the finished project. Do not clip or trim the stay tape.

Waistlines can also be finished with ⅝- or ¾-inch-wide grosgrain ribbon, which functions as both facing and stay tape. Cut the ribbon 1 inch longer than the finished garment waistline, and press ½ inch to the wrong side at each end of the ribbon. Staystitch the garment on the seamline, and lay the ribbon over the garment raw edges, right sides up, with the finished ribbon edge close to the waist seamline. Edgestitch the ribbon to the garment. Trim the garment seam allowance (under the ribbon) to ¼ inch. Press the ribbon to the garment wrong side along the staystitching, rolling a few threads of the garment to the wrong side as well so the ribbon isn't visible from the outside. Topstitch ⅛ inch from the seamline to hold the ribbon facing in place.

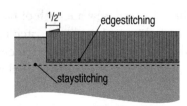

Edgestitch a ribbon facing to a garment waistline to cover raw edges and prevent the fabric from stretching.

Waistbands

A waistband is the strip of fabric that holds a skirt or pants in place around the waist. The waistband height and its position on the body may change with current fashions, but the method for attaching a waistband is the same.

Waistbands should always be interfaced to discourage rolling and prevent stretching. Choose a firm interfacing, and cut it the same length as the waistband but only half as wide. Prepare and attach the interfacing as you would a collar or cuff (see Chapter 18), removing excess interfacing in the seam allowances. If the interfacing is not fusible, secure the long edge along the waistband fold with basting stitches that will be removed when the garment is complete. Topstitching the finished waistband will catch and secure the interfacing there, or the pattern may call for invisibly slipstitching the interfacing to the waistband instead.

SEW SURPRISING

A waistband is pressed in half lengthwise and with wrong sides together at the beginning of its construction, and unfolded. The resulting crease provides a useful guideline for positioning the interfacing.

Press the seam allowance to the wrong side along one long waistband edge. Trim the pressed seam allowance to ¼ inch. This side of the waistband will lie inside the garment and is sometimes called the waistband facing, especially if the waistband has been cut in two parts. Pin the remaining long waistband edge to the garment, right sides together, matching notches and other construction symbols.

The waistband will extend beyond the garment at each end. Depending on the pattern styling, the extra length may be as little as one seam allowance or long enough to provide an underlap at the waist closure. Follow the construction symbols to be sure.

Stitch the waistband to the garment, and trim and grade the seam allowances. Fold the waistband in half lengthwise, with right sides together, and sew the ends as directed on the pattern. Clip across the corners to reduce bulk, trim the seam allowances, and turn the waistband right side out. Use a point turner to create crisp corner angles into place. Press the ends thoroughly, using a press cloth to prevent shine.

> **SNIP IT**
>
> Review the construction tips for crisp corners on collars and cuffs in Chapter 18, and use the same techniques on waistband ends.

Match the pressed waistband edge to the waist seam, and press. Slipstitch the folded edge to the waist seam, concealing the seam allowances.

Finish the waistband with a hook-and-eye closure or a button and buttonhole. If the waistband is wide (high), the pattern may call for two or even three closures to secure the entire width.

Pocket Pleasers

Pockets are certainly one of mankind's most useful innovations. They can take on many shapes and be attached in several ways, both decorative and utilitarian.

Patch Pockets

Patch pockets may be the easiest to apply. They're hemmed and stitched in place on the garment, just as a patch would be. They are easy to add to a pattern and can be created in almost any size or shape.

> **SEW SURPRISING**
>
> How big should a pocket be? The answer varies with the pocket's purpose and location. A handy rule of thumb for functional pockets is based on hand size: make the pocket opening at least 6 inches wide for a man, 5 inches for a woman, and 4 inches for a child.

Begin constructing the patch pocket by pressing ¼ inch to the wrong side on the upper edge and edgestitching. Turn the edge to the right side along the foldline. Beginning at the folded edge, stitch on the seamline around the sides and bottom, backstitching at both ends.

Trim the upper corners on the diagonal to reduce bulk, and trim the side seam allowances of the folded hem only to ¼ inch. Turn the pocket right side out, flipping the hem to the wrong side. Use a point turner or other tool to shape the corners.

Press the pocket seam allowance to the wrong side, rolling the stitches slightly to the wrong side so they won't be visible in the finished project. If the pocket has a rounded shape, notch the seam allowance along the curves to reduce bulk.

Position the patch pocket on the garment right side as directed by the pattern, and pin in place. Edgestitch the pocket sides and lower edge to the garment. Reinforce the upper edge by backstitching or by stitching a small triangle at the pocket upper edges.

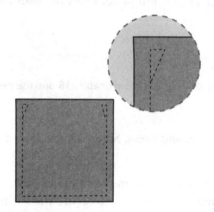

Reinforce a patch pocket opening with stitched triangles.

In-Seam Pockets

As the name implies, in-seam pockets are concealed within a garment seam. The pocket pattern piece is usually a broad curve with one straight edge. Transfer all construction symbols from the pattern pieces to the fabric so you can accurately insert the pocket.

With right sides together and symbols matched, stitch each pocket piece to one garment seam allowance. Some patterns include extended seam allowances for this step; others attach the pocket with a ¼-inch seam allowance included within the garment's regular ⅝-inch seams. Press the seam allowances as directed in the pattern.

Pin the garment/pocket pieces right sides together along the seam. Stitch the seam, pivoting at the pocket's seamline and sewing around the pocket's curved edge. Shorten the stitch length for ½ inch on each side of the corners to strengthen the pocket opening. The seam remains open along the pocket straight edge.

Some patterns call for extending the seamline for 1 to 3 inches above the bottom pocket pivot. These extra stitches deepen the pocket to make functional pockets more secure for carrying keys or other objects.

Clip the seam allowance of the garment back only above and below the pocket extension, clipping to but not through the seam. Press the garment seam open above and below the pocket while pressing the pocket itself toward the garment front. Turn the project to the right side, and press a tidy crease in the garment front across the pocket opening, visually extending the seamline across the pocket.

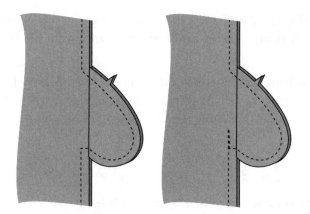

Extend the seamlines above the bottom pocket edge, as shown at right, to make pockets more secure.

SNIP IT

If the garment fabric is heavy, cut the front portion of the pocket from a lightweight fabric. The pocket front won't be seen in the garment even if the pocket falls open.

Hemlines

It's the finish to most garments, the real bottom line: a nearly invisible hem that finishes the raw edge while enhancing the garment's drape. Choosing which hem to use is partly a matter of style, but some hems work better on a particular fashion silhouette than others.

Marking Hems

Before the hem is stitched, the hemline must be determined. For some garments, when precise length isn't critical and the stable fabric is unlikely to shift or droop, using the hem foldline printed on the pattern yields good results. Other projects need more attention to achieve the perfect length.

SNIP IT

Hem marking is one sewing task impossible to do alone. Recruit a friend to help with measuring and marking, or invest in a dress form that duplicates your shape so you can become the friend with the ruler!

Unlike other measurements that can be determined on the pattern, a skirt hemline needs to be marked while the garment is worn to lie parallel to the floor. A special notion is available to simultaneously measure and mark the hemline with chalk, but a yardstick and removable marking tool work as well.

Try on the skirt, preferably with the shoes you'll wear with the garment. Determine where the hemline should fall—at the knee, mid-calf, and above the knee are three potential options. Measure from the floor to the desired location, make note of the measurement, and mark the skirt with a short line of chalk or removable ink. Move a few inches to the right or left, measure, and mark again. Continue around the skirt, marking a consistent distance from the floor without regard to the skirt raw edge.

When marking is complete, decide on the hem depth and mark it by measuring downward from the hemline. For a straight skirt, the hem can be 2 to 3 inches deep; for flared styles, 1 to 1½ inches; and for full skirts, just ½ to ⅝ inches. Cut away the excess fabric along this mark, not the marked hemline.

> **SEW SURPRISING**
>
> For a smooth hem, the hem allowance should lie flat against the garment. A little extra fullness can be eased into place, but a deep hem on a full skirt would be impossible to ease.

Press the hem allowance (the fabric between the raw edge and the hemline) to the wrong side along the marked hemline. If there's fullness to ease into place, sew ease stitches ¼ inch from the raw edge before pressing the hem, and draw them up to fit the hem to the garment. Be careful not to ease too much, causing puckers to form in the garment. Steam pressing helps shape the eased hem; with some fabrics, the extra fabric seems to disappear as the eased hem flattens under the steam.

To hem a pair of pants to a specific inseam measurement, measure from the crotch and mark the hemline at the inseam. Add the hem depth to determine how much fabric should be trimmed before hemming. Trim the same amount of fabric from the entire pant leg and press the hem into place. It's a good idea to try on the pants with the hem pinned in place before cutting away the excess fabric, especially if the pants will be worn with heels.

Hem-Edge Finishes

After you've pressed and eased a hem deeper than 1 inch, finish its raw edge appropriately for the fabric type and weight:

Clean finishing is appropriate for garments with little or no flare and fabrics that aren't heavy or bulky. Press ¼ inch to the wrong side along the hem's raw edge, and stitch. Clean finishing can be done before ease-stitching the hem, with the finishing stitches doing double duty as ease stitches.

Hem tape is a good choice for fabrics that ravel easily or where a doubled fabric thickness would be too bulky. It's available as a satiny solid tape or in a lacy design that's both functional and decorative. Lap the hem tape over the right side of the prepared hem edge by ¼ inch and edgestitch the tape to the hem allowance.

> **SNIP IT**
>
> Look for hem tape near precut packages of bias binding and rickrack in your local fabric store.

Stitching and pinking the raw edge is fine for nonraveling fabrics and garments in which the hem will be concealed and protected by a lining. Sew a straight stitch or narrow zigzag ¼ inch from the hem edge, and pink the raw edges.

Serging the raw edge of a hem is acceptable for most fabrics. Save time by using the serger to trim away the excess fabric as you sew, and set the serger's differential feed to ease in hem fullness.

When the hem has been measured, marked, pressed, and edge finished, use a slipstitch or machine blind hem stitch to sew the hem edge to the garment. Avoid tight thread tension, which can create dimples that are visible on the garment's right side, whether you're hemming by hand or machine.

Narrow Hems

When the hem allowance is less than 1 inch, the hem is finished differently. Double-fold, shirttail, and rolled hems all fall into this category. Methods differ slightly from one pattern to another, but all are narrow, clean-finished hems.

To construct a basic double-fold hem, press half of the hem allowance to the wrong side. Fold the fabric to the wrong side a second time, using the remaining hem allowance, and press firmly. Topstitch close to the inner fold to secure the hem.

For a very narrow rolled hem, often used on featherweight and sheer fabrics, leave just a ⅜ inch hem allowance on the garment. Stitch ¼ inch from the raw edge, and press the hem to the wrong side along the stitching. Edgestitch a scant ⅛ inch from the fold. Trim the hem allowance close to the second line of stitches, being very careful not to cut the outer garment. Roll the tiny remaining hem allowance to the wrong side and stitch close to the inner fold, just ⅛ inch from the hemline fold.

You can make a simple and very flat narrow hem by serging the raw edge, leaving a ¼-inch hem allowance (about the width of the serger stitches). Press the hem allowance to the wrong side, and topstitch to complete the hem.

Specialty Hems

Sometimes a hem can be fused rather than stitched. Iron-on hem tape is a notion resembling satin ribbon, with two narrow bands of adhesive along its length. To use, press the hem into place and lay the iron-on hem tape along its length, with one long edge overlapping the hem and the other lying on the garment's wrong side above the hem. Press to fuse the tape, following the manufacturer's instructions, securing the hem in place.

Another method for fusing a hem uses ¼-inch-wide strips of fusible web. To begin, press the hem into place, and unfold it. Apply the fusible web tape to the wrong side of the fabric at the raw edge, following the manufacturer's instructions. Remove the paper backing from the fusible tape, refold the hem, and press once more to fuse the hem to the garment.

For variety, turn a hem in fabric with no discernable wrong side to the garment's right side, and cover the raw edge with decorative trim, ribbon, or bias tape. This novel hem can also be used when the right and wrong sides of the fabric are equally attractive but contrast in color or texture.

Fringing is another fun hemming technique in which the hemline isn't folded and the hem allowance extends away from the garment. If the edge to be hemmed lies on the straight grain, sew a zigzag stitch along the hemline, and remove fabric yarns from the cut edge to the zigzag stitches to create the fringe.

To add self-fabric fringe to a garment edge that isn't on grain, first cut straight-grain strips of the fabric ½ inch wider than the desired finished fringe. Trim the garment hem allowance to ½ inch. Sew the fringe strips to the garment, right sides together, with a ½-inch seam allowance. Press the fringe strip away from the garment, and finish the seam allowances as desired. Remove fabric yarns from the strip raw edge to the seamline to create the fringe.

Project: Fun Flannel Pants

These quick-to-stitch flannel pants are perfect for a slumber party or a lazy, lounge-around night. Add a colorful cuff and pocket, as shown here, or go for a simpler, single-fabric look.

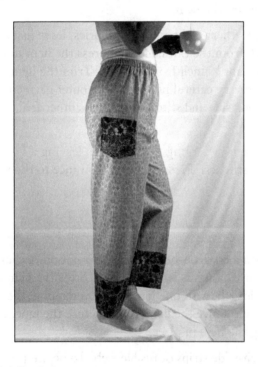

Cozy flannel stitches up easily for soft, lounging-around pants.

Finished size:

Variable

Tools and materials:

> 45-inch-wide fabric for pants (amount determined by measurements)*
>
> 45-inch-wide fabric for cuffs and pocket (amount determined by measurements)*
>
> ¼-inch woven, nonroll elastic
>
> Pattern drafting paper, wrapping paper, or other wide paper
>
> Thread
>
> Basic sewing equipment

Suitable woven fabrics include mid-weight cotton or flannel fabrics. Very stretchy fabrics are not suitable for this project.

Make the pattern:

1. You'll need four measurements to draft this pattern: waist, hip, crotch length, and inseam. Plug your measurements into the pattern formula to find values for A through D. Draft the front and back pants, pocket, and cuff shapes on pattern paper, following the drafting guide.

   Pattern formula:

   (hip measurement + 1 inch seam allowance + 6 inches ease) ÷ 4 = A

   (crotch length ÷ 2) + 1¼ inches for casing = B

   inseam + ½ inch seam allowance = C

   waist measurement + 1 inch = D

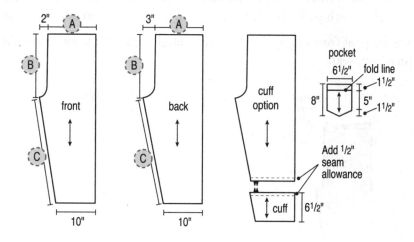

If adding a coordinating cuff, draft the pants pattern, and add a line 6½ inches above the pants hem on both the pants front and back. Draw a single notch across the line on the pants front and a double notch on the pants back, and transfer the notches to both the pant and cuff pieces as a guide for matching while sewing. Cut the patterns on the lines to make the front and back cuff patterns. Add ½ inch to the shortened pants front and back lower edges and to the upper cuff edges for seam allowances.

> **SNIP IT**
>
> Mark the project name, piece, and grainline on each pattern piece as it is drawn. Keep patterns pinned to cut pieces to avoid confusion.

Cutting:

2. Refer to the pattern pieces and the "Yardage Conversion Chart" in Appendix C to determine needed yardage. Take note of the grainline arrows; they indicate how to position the pattern on the fabric.

3. From the main fabric, cut two pants fronts and two pants backs. Place a safety pin in front pants pieces to avoid confusing them with the backs. From the coordinating fabric, cut two front and two back cuffs and one pocket.

Construction:

Use a ½-inch seam allowance and press seams open unless otherwise noted. Backstitch at the beginning and end of each seam except where indicated. Finish seam edges as desired with a flat, unobtrusive edge.

4. With right sides together, align the front cuff to the pants front lower edge. Using a ½-inch seam allowance, stitch the cuff and pant leg together. Press the seam open. Topstitch ¼ inch on both sides of the seam to anchor seam allowances in place.

5. Place the pant fronts right sides together, aligning center front edges. Pin and stitch the center front seam.

center front seam

Be careful not to distort the curved crotch seam.

6. Repeat steps 4 and 5 to construct the pants back.

7. Place the pants front and back right sides together, aligning side edges and cuff seams. Pin and stitch the side seam. Repeat for remaining side seam.

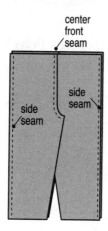

Stitch the pants front and back together at side seams.

8. Fold ½ inch to the wrong side along the top pocket edge. Press and topstitch ¼ inch from the folded edge. Fold an additional 1 inch to the right side at the top pocket edge. Stitch along the pocket sides and bottom edges, a scant ½ inch from the raw edge. Clip points and corners to reduce bulk and turn the top pocket edge right side out. Roll the stitching along the pocket sides and bottom to the wrong side and press the rolled edges.

Anchor the top pocket hem and stitch along pocket sides and bottom.

9. Pin-mark the center of the top pocket edge. With the pants right side out, center the pocket on the right pants side seam, 10½ inches below the raw waistline edge. Stitch the pocket sides and bottom edges in place.

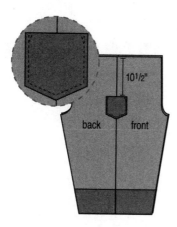

Stitch a small reinforcing triangle at top pocket edges.

10. Pin the inseam edges with right sides together, matching center front to center back seam and cuff seams on lower legs. Stitch the inseam.

11. Follow the instructions in the earlier "Around the Waist" section to make a waistline casing, using measurement D to determine the beginning elastic length and altering the elastic to fit.

12. Straight stitch ¼ inch from the raw edges of the pants hem. Press ½ inch to the wrong side. Topstitch ⅜ inch from the folded edge to finish.

For warm weather wear, substitute a light- to medium-weight woven cotton fabric for flannel. For capri pants or shorts, simply shorten the leg length.

The Least You Need to Know

- Waistlines can be finished with casings for elastic or drawstrings. Facings are another waistline option.
- Attaching a separate waistband to a skirt or pants waist is a classic technique. Interface the waistband for crisp results.
- Patch pockets can be applied to almost any garment. In-seam pockets hide inside the garment, with an opening concealed within a seam.
- Hem depth is determined by garment fullness. There are many techniques for finishing a garment with a hem.

appliqué   Fabric cutouts sewn or fused on top of other fabric. Also, the process of attaching them.

backstitch   Sewing in reverse at the start and end of a seam to secure the seam ends. Backstitch is also the name of a hand-sewing stitch. Also called backtack.

backtack   *See* backstitch.

basting   Long stitches worked by hand or machine to temporarily join fabric layers. Basting stitches may be removed once the permanent seam is sewn.

bias   Any off-grain direction on woven fabric; true bias runs at a 45-degree angle to the lengthwise and crosswise grains. Woven fabric stretches along the bias grain.

binding   A narrow strip of fabric used as a trim or seam finish. Fabric binding may be cut on the straight or bias grain. Single-fold binding is prefolded along two long edges. Double-fold binding has a single lengthwise fold and is often used by quilters to finish quilt edges.

bobbin   A form onto which thread is wound. In machine sewing, the bobbin is a metal or plastic flattened spool shape positioned under the stitch plate.

bodkin   A needlelike sewing tool shaped with a ball point or blunt tip at one end and an over-sized eye at the other. Thread elastic, cording, or ribbon through the eye and pull the bodkin through a casing to create a waistline or drawstring closure.

bolt   A roll of fabric, usually 15 to 100 yards long. Fashion fabrics are folded onto flat card-board blanks, while home décor and upholstery fabrics are rolled onto cardboard tubes.

boxing   Boxing is a technique used to create depth at the bottom of bags and corners of cushions. Folding and stitching the corners of a flat fabric bag creates a bag with a flat bottom and distinct sides. Achieve the same effect by sewing a boxing strip—a narrow length of fabric—between front and back panels.

burr   A rough spot usually caused by one piece of metal striking another. A burr on the point of a needle causes irregular holes or pulled threads in the fabric as it sews. A burr in the needle eye shreds sewing thread.

charm pack   A collection of coordinating precut 5-inch fabric squares. Quilters collect charm packs to add different designs to their fabric stash at a minimal cost.

clapper   A wooden block used to pressure-set folds and creases, often in combination with steam.

clip   To cut into a seam allowance to mark a placement, reduce bulk, or prevent distortion along curved seams. The clips are positioned at right angles to the seamline or diagonally across a point.

crosswise grain   The fabric threads running from selvage to selvage.

dart   A stitched, tapered fabric tuck used to shape fabric around body contours.

ease   The amount of extra fabric built into a garment pattern for freedom of movement. Also, to fit extra fabric into a seam without creating puckers or tucks.

ease stitch   One or two rows of longer-than-normal straight stitches sewn on either side of a seam. When pulled, these stitches gather the fabric very slightly to ease a longer seam smoothly into a shorter seamline.

edgestitching   A variation of topstitching, edgestitching is a line of stitching sewn close to the fabric edge to hold a facing or fold in place, to prevent an edge from rolling, to prevent raveling, or as a decorative element. Use a blind stitch or edge stitch foot on your sewing machine to guide your stitching.

elastic thread   Elastic thread, or shirring elastic, is a thin, polyester-wrapped rubber thread commonly used in the bobbin to make stretchable shirred fabric. Available in a limited number of colors, elastic thread can be found in the notions section of fabric stores.

emery   A hard, abrasive mineral that resembles fine metal shavings when ground. In sewing, emery is used in small, specialty cushions (called emeries) to clean and sharpen the tips of pins and needles.

eye   The hole in one end of a needle that carries thread through the fabric. The eye of a needle may be large or small and round or elongated in shape, depending on the needle type. Self-threading needles have a slot instead of a hole at the top or side of the needle for easier threading.

fat quarter   A precut fabric length created by cutting a $\frac{1}{2}$ yard of fabric in half lengthwise. Fat quarters measure approximately 18×22 inches.

felt   A nonwoven cloth produced by matting and condensing wool fibers together or by needle-punching synthetic fibers.

finger press   Using your fingers or a wooden iron to press a seam or coax seam allowances into place. Finger press a seam to quickly smooth it into place, or when it isn't practical to use an iron to press a seam.

fray   To unravel or become worn at the edge. If their edges aren't finished, woven fabrics fray at cut edges.

fusible tape or web   A manmade fiber web that melts when heated. In sewing, fusible web is placed between fabrics to hold them together without stitching. When heated with an iron, the fusible web melts and fuses the fabrics together. Narrow strips of fusible material, called fusible tape, are used to hem edges.

grade   Trimming seam allowances to different widths. In patternmaking, *grade* means to make a pattern in a new size.

grain   The direction of threads or yarns in woven fabric. *Straight of grain* means parallel to the lengthwise or, sometimes, crosswise threads.

hem gauge   A small specialty ruler, usually 6 inches long, with a slider to mark measurements. Set the slider at the desired measurement, and you can use the gauge as a quick visual reference when pressing, pinning, or sewing hems or seams. Also called a seam gauge.

interfacing   Fabric used to reinforce or add body and structure to a garment or project. Interfacing is available in a variety of weights; in fusible or sewn-in versions; and in woven, nonwoven, and knit constructions.

interlining   A second fabric layer added for body, strength, or opacity and treated as one with the main fabric.

invisible thread   A clear or smoke-colored nylon or polyester monofilament thread that blends into many fabric colors for an almost invisible stitch. Use clear for light-colored fabrics and smoke with darks.

lengthwise grain   The fabric threads running parallel to the selvages.

lining   An extra fabric layer that conceals seams for a neat interior and improves garment drape.

lockstitch   The type of stitch a home sewing machine makes. Top and bobbin threads are looped together, with the loop lying between the fabric layers.

miter   A diagonal seam formed at the corner of a hem or applied trim. Also, the process of forming a miter.

monofilament   Monofilament refers to threads made from a single fiber, not spun or twisted. The word is sometimes used as a synonym for invisible thread.

nap   The fuzzy or furry surface of velvet and similar fabrics. Napped fabrics must be cut with the nap running in the same direction on all pattern pieces to avoid color variations, and extra fabric may be required. Also called pile.

notch   Pattern markings used to match seamlines and differentiate similar edges. Can also mean to reduce bulk by making a series of V-shape cuts in the seam allowance, evenly spaced along a curved edge.

notion   Any item other than fabric used in sewing such as thread, zippers, snaps, needles, pins, etc.

one-way design   A fabric design that has a definite top and bottom.

pattern paper   Also called sewable Swedish tracing paper, this strong, translucent paper is durable yet drapably soft. Use pattern paper to trace, sew, and test-fit garments before cutting your final fabric. Alternatives include plain paper, blank newsprint, wrapping paper, and physician's examining table cover paper.

pile   *See* nap.

pin-mark   To place a pin in fabric as a temporary marker, often to indicate a center point or the right side of a fabric.

pinking shears   Specialty sewing scissors with a saw-toothed blade designed to cut a zigzag or pinked edge. Pinked fabric edges are less likely to fray than smooth-cut edges.

ply   The number of individual yarns that make up a strand of thread. Two-ply means a thread is composed of two yarns twisted together to create a single thread; three-ply indicates three yarns were used.

point turner   A small, handheld sewing tool, usually made of wood or plastic, with a blunt point at one end. The point is used to shape corners and points of collars, pockets, and other items.

pressing cloth   A piece of fabric placed between the iron and the item to be pressed. Pressing cloths are commonly made of cotton and protect the fabric from scorching and damage when heavy pressing and high heat are needed to set a shape or seam.

pressing ham   A firmly stuffed, curved, pillowlike pressing tool covered in cotton on one side and wool on the other. Pressing hams are used when pressing curved seams to steam in shape and prevent puckers and tucks.

remnant   The fabric remaining when the bulk of the yardage has been used or sold. Remnant size varies; some pieces may be large, while others are $\frac{1}{8}$ yard or less. Bags of fabric scraps, or cuttings, are sometimes sold as remnants.

rickrack   A flat, zigzag-shape trim of polyester or cotton. Available packaged or by the yard in a number of colors and widths, rickrack is sometimes called waved or snake braid.

right side   The surface of a garment, project, or fabric that's meant to be seen on the project exterior.

rotary cutter   This time-saving tool resembles a pizza cutter with a round, razor-sharp blade. Specialty blades for pinked or wavy edges are also available. Quilters use rotary cutters to slice through multiple fabric layers quickly and easily. Always use a special cutting mat under a rotary cutter to protect surfaces from damage. Cut freehand or use as a guide special acrylic rulers that the blade won't cut.

rough cut   To quickly cut pieces from fabric yardage, $\frac{1}{4}$ inch or more away from the actual cutting line, without careful shaping.

roving   Unspun fiber. Wool roving is good to use as pincushion stuffing because its natural lanolin lubricates and protects pins from moisture.

seam allowance   The fabric between the seamline and the edge of a piece.

seam gauge   *See* hem gauge.

seam ripper   A handheld sewing tool with a small curved blade at one end that's used to remove stitches or open seams.

seam roll   A firmly stuffed, tubular pressing tool used to press seams open without leaving seam imprints on the fabric right side, especially helpful for pressing seams in sleeves or pants legs. Like a pressing ham, a seam roll is covered in cotton on one side and heavy wool on the other.

selvage   A narrow, tightly woven border along the lengthwise edges of woven fabric or the finished lengthwise edges of knit fabric. The selvage on printed woven fabrics may contain manufacturer, designer, and printing information.

serger   A specialty sewing machine that trims and encases seam edges at the same time. Sergers use two or more threads to construct seams and are often used when sewing knit fabrics.

stabilizer   Stabilizers support and hold fabric flat while dense or heavy stitching is applied. Available in many types and weights, some stabilizers are meant to remain in the finished project, while others should be removed after stitching is complete.

staystitching   A line of straight stitching that stabilizes fabric edges. Sewn through a single fabric layer, $\frac{1}{8}$ inch inside the seamline, staystitching prevents fabric from stretching and distorting. Most staystitching is done in curved or angled seams at the neckline, armholes, sleeve caps, or waistlines. Staystitch fabric pieces immediately after cutting, before handling.

stitch in the ditch   Stitching very close to, or on top of, a flat seam. The name refers to sewing in the small indentation formed when two fabric pieces are stitched together.

tailor's chalk   A temporary marking chalk used to indicate cutting, hemming, and stitching lines on garments as they're constructed or altered. Tailor's chalk comes in powdered, pencil, or wedge forms and is easily brushed off or washed out of most fabrics.

thimble   A small leather, metal, or rubber covering worn on the thumb or finger to protect the fingertip while sewing. Thimbles can be used to help push the needle through the fabric.

topstitching   Worked from the right side of a garment or project, topstitching is most commonly a straight stitch that parallels a seamline. It strengthens seams and is usually decorative.

trim   To cut away excess fabric, often to reduce seam allowance after sewing. Also, braid, fringe, lace, or other relatively narrow decorative material applied to a project.

turning tool   A long, slim tool, usually with a hook at one end, designed to facilitate turning fabric tubes right side out after sewing.

understitching   A line of stitches about $\frac{1}{16}$ inch from a facing seamline that holds the facing and seam allowances together to prevent their rolling to the right side.

unsew   A colloquial, humorous word for removing stitches or undoing a seam to correct mistakes or remove basting. Sometimes called *frogging*, because you "rip it, rip it" out.

warp   Fabric threads that run parallel to the selvages; the lengthwise grain.

weft   Fabric threads that run from selvage to selvage; the crosswise grain.

wof   An abbreviation for "width of fabric," regardless of the exact fabric width, that indicates you should cut or sew from selvage to selvage.

wooden iron   A small, handheld sewing tool with an angled edge used for pressing or shaping seams by applying pressure without heat.

wrong side   The surface of a garment, project, or fabric that's meant to be hidden or worn inside a project or garment.

Resources

The best sewing resources may be those just beyond your own front door, but in the Internet age we know you may also be looking for fabrics, notions, ideas, and more online. In this appendix, we list some of our favorite go-to sites and blogs, plus resources such as books that we wouldn't want to be without.

We know how frustrating it can be to fall in love with a particular fabric seen in a book but have no information about it, so we're providing a list of most of the fabrics we used in our projects. A word of caution: fabric life spans tend to be very short, and these fabrics may no longer be available. If you can't find the exact print, peruse the manufacturer's website for similar styles and make something uniquely your own.

Suppliers

Westminster Fibers provided many of the fabrics used in the projects in this book. Visit the Westminster website for Free Spirit Fabrics at www.freespiritfabric.com to view current fabric offerings and find an online vendor or store near you.

The following fabrics were used in these projects:

- *Bare Necessities Needle Case:* reclaimed wool
- *Biscornu Pincushion:* PopGarden by Heather Bailey*
- *Handy Hip Bag:* Gypsy by Felicity Miller*
- *Easy-Peasy Apron:* Luna by Gail Fountain and Maywood Studio (www.MaywoodStudio.com)
- *Sweet Seamed Wrap:* Midwest Modern by Amy Butler*
- *Lettuce-Edge T-Shirt Scarf:* reclaimed T-shirts
- *Half-Circle Skirt:* Deer Valley by Joel Dewberry*
- *Hobo Bag:* Nest by Valori Wells*
- *Sweet Shirred Summer Dress:* Little Folks Voile by Anna Maria Horner*

- *Trendy Tank:* reclaimed T-shirts
- *Pop-Up Storage Cube:* McKenzie by Dena Designs*
- *Double-Bind Pillow:* April Showers Bring Sunflowers by Art of Possibility*
- *Backpack Bag:* Love by Amy Butler*
- *The Fudd Cap:* FTS (from the stash)
- *Simple Shapes Jacket:* California Dreamin' by Jenean Morrison*
- *Fun Flannel Pants:* Folksy Flannels by Anna Maria Horner*

*Free Spirit Fabric

Coats & Clark provided many of the threads and zippers used in these projects. Visit the Coats & Clark website at www.coatsandclark.com to see the complete product line and find a store near you.

Further Reading

To learn more about sewing, explore project possibilities, or simply find inspiration, browse these books and online offerings:

Betzina, Sandra. *More Fabric Savvy.* Newtown, CT: Taunton Press, 2004.

Brent, Rebecca Kemp. *Redwork from The WORKBASKET.* Cincinnati, OH: Krause Publications, 2010.

Griepentrog, Linda Turner, and Missy Shepler. *Print Your Own Fabric.* Cincinnati, OH: Krause Publications, 2007.

Horner, Anna Marie. *Seams to Me: 24 New Reasons to Love Sewing.* Indianapolis, IN: Wiley Publishing, 2008.

Talbert, Barbara Weiland. *The Sewing Answer Book.* North Adams, MA: Storey Publishing, 2010.

Yaker, Rebecca, and Patricia Hoskins. *One Yard Wonders.* North Adams, MA: Storey Publishing, 2009.

Stitch **magazine**
interweave.com (Interweave Press)

Sew News **magazine**
sewnews.com (Creative Crafts Group)

HELLOmynameisHeather
heatherbailey.typepad.com

Anna Maria Horner
annamariahorner.blogspot.com

Yahoo! Groups—Sewing
groups.yahoo.com (search for "sewing")

About.com: Sewing
sewing.about.com

Local Connections

Don't dismiss the world right outside your door when searching for sewing information and supplies. Check your phone book and other local listings for fabric stores, quilt shops, sewing machine dealers, and specialty suppliers. Library bulletin boards often list special interest group gatherings. Area fabric stores may host meetings or have contact information for sewing groups. Check national organizations for local chapters in your area.

The American Sewing Guild
asg.org

Machine Manufacturers and Information

Having worked with many sewing machine brands, we've concluded that the best one is one of each! When choosing your own machine, look to local dealers for information and service after the sale, including classes. These manufacturer websites will get you started, with basic machine information and dealer locaters.

Baby Lock
babylock.com

Bernina
berninausa.com

Brother
brother-usa.com/homesewing

Husqvarna Viking
husqvarnaviking.com

Pfaff
pfaffusa.com

SewUSA
SewUSA.com (for sewing machine manuals)

Fabric Companies

You can never have too much fabric! Browse these manufacturer's websites for an overview of available textiles; you'll find that each has a unique style and vision. Then, check local and online retailers for the prints and styles you love. Buy what you need for a special project, or purchase a few choice cuts for stash enhancement.

Benartex
benartex.com

Cranston Fabrics (VIP Fabrics)
cranstonvillage.com

Hoffman California Fabrics
hoffmanfabrics.com

Moda Fabrics
ModaFabrics.com

Westminster Fabric
westminsterfibers.com or freespiritfabric.com

Thread Companies

Thread may be basic and essential, but it isn't boring! Visit these manufacturer's websites to see what wonders await in the world of thread, then check your favorite fabric and sewing machine shops to see which lines they carry.

Aurifil Threads
www.aurifil.com

Coats & Clark
www.coatsandclark.com

Gütermann of America
gutermann.com

Sulky Thread
sulky.com

WonderFil
wonderfil.net

YLI
ylicorp.com

Quick References

Find quick answers to common sewing questions and machine maintenance tips here. We've also included information on standard pattern sizing plus resources for figuring and converting fabric yardage.

Troubleshooting Tips

The following sections cover some of the most common questions and concerns sewists have.

My Machine Hates Me!

Every sewist has said this at one time or another. The good news is that most common problems have simple solutions. Many difficulties can be solved by replacing the needle and rethreading the machine. It helps to keep the bobbin area clean, too, regularly brushing away lint and trapped threads.

Become acquainted with your machine's normal sound, and listen for variations that could mean a bobbin is nearing empty, a needle has dulled, or other trouble may be brewing. When in doubt, stop and check it out rather than forcing your way through a task.

Why Did My Needle Break?

Be sure the needle is properly inserted and that the needle clamp is tightened. Turn the hand wheel to be sure the needle is properly aligned; the needle should not touch the stitch plate or any other machine part as it moves up and down. If it does, take the machine in for service.

Always remove fabric from the machine by pulling it behind the presser foot. Pulling fabric out from the front puts undue stress on the needle and may cause it to bend or break.

Be sure you're using the proper needle size and type for the fabric; use a large, sharp needle on denim or heavyweight fabrics.

Don't move the fabric while the needle is down. The exception is pivoting on curves and corners; you may rotate the fabric around the needle, but don't pull it forward, back, or to the sides. Instead, guide the fabric gently with your fingers.

Why Does My Thread Keep Breaking?

First, determine which thread is breaking: the top or bobbin thread. Too-tight tension; poor-quality thread; a bent, blunt, or damaged needle; and a damaged stitch plate can all be culprits for top (needle) thread troubles. Start troubleshooting by replacing the needle even if it's new; it's not impossible to discover a burr, or rough spot, on a brand-new needle. Be sure the needle is properly inserted and try to stitch again.

A needle-nicked stitch plate can shred thread. Carefully polish away any rough spots you find with a bit of emery cloth, or ask your machine dealer to do so. In extreme cases, the stitch plate may need to be replaced.

Reduce the needle thread tension, or try a different thread. Poor-quality, old, knotted, or dried-out thread breaks easily, and even new thread can break under too much tension.

Breaking bobbin threads can also be caused by overly tight tension, a damaged stitch plate, or needles that are blunt or bent. A bent bobbin or bobbin case may also be the problem. Be sure the bobbin can rotate freely in the bobbin case and that the thread is properly wound on the bobbin.

I'm Having Tension Trouble

A little knowledge goes a long way when tension issues arise. Reread the "Tension Time" section in Chapter 2 for an explanation of balanced, tight, and loose tension; adjusting bobbin tension; and common tension trouble culprits.

There's a Tangle of Thread on the Back of My Stitching

If you've got bird's nests, or a thread mess, on the back of stitched pieces, you may not be lowering the presser foot before sewing, or the thread tails may be getting caught in the seam. Hold the thread tails to the back of the presser foot while taking the first few stitches to prevent them from being pulled into the bobbin area.

Thread that's slipped out of its guides can also cause thread nests because the thread travels to the needle without proper tension.

My Machine Is Skipping Stitches

A number of things can cause skipped stitches: faulty or wrong-size needles, incorrect threading, or lint or thread remnants in the machine. A small needle may skip stitches because it can't push the fabric threads apart efficiently to interlock the needle and bobbin threads, but a large needle may skip stitches because it's too big to pass between the fabric threads! Trial and error—and a multisize package of needles—are the best way to settle on needle size.

Pushing, pulling, or holding the fabric in place while sewing can also result in uneven stitches. Let the feed dog do the work; it moves fabric forward with each stitch. The stitch length setting determines the amount of fabric moved.

Basic Machine Maintenance

A sewing machine requires regular maintenance to keep it in top condition. ***Check your machine's manual!* Some machines must be serviced and oiled by a trained technician.**

Here are some DIY tips to keep your machine in great sewing shape:

If your machine can be oiled at home, follow the manufacturer's instructions to oil your machine. Oil can evaporate; if your machine has been unused for a length of time, oil it before stitching. Always stitch on scrap fabric after oiling to absorb excess oil.

Cover your machine when it's not in use to protect it from dust, dirt, and pet hair. Machine covers are available for purchase, or you can use a pillowcase in a pinch. Better yet, style and stitch a cover of your own!

Clean your machine. Don't let lint and thread accumulate beneath the stitch plate or in the bobbin area. Use a small, clean paint brush for those hard-to-reach spots and sweep the inside of the bobbin case as well. Wipe the outer case with a soft cloth or batting scrap.

Protect your machine against power surges and lightning strikes by using a surge protector. Unplug your machine when it's not in use. Why risk it?

Standard Pattern Sizes

Major pattern companies base sizing on a standard set of body measurements, provided in pattern catalogs and on pattern envelope backs. Just as ready-to-wear sizes vary among manufacturers, sizes vary from one pattern company to the next. Always check your personal body measurements against information on the pattern envelope back. Read Chapter 15 for tips on taking your measurements.

Fabric Yardage Chart

Figuring fabric yardage can be a bit like piecing together a puzzle. One of the easiest ways we've found to determine yardage is to roughly sketch a pattern layout, keeping fabric width, grain line, and pattern piece quantities in mind. Use the following chart and yardage equivalents to figure fabric yardage.

Yardage Chart

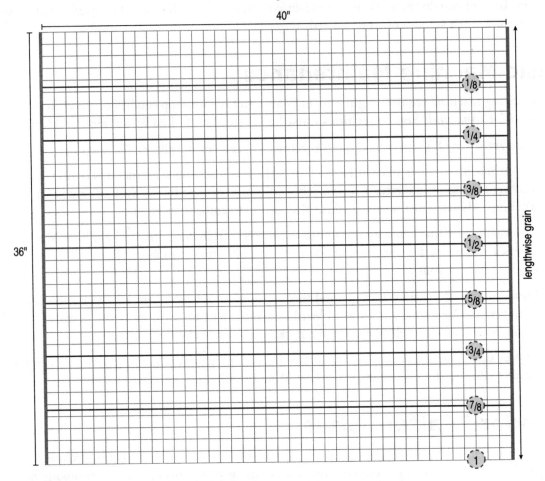

One square is equivalent to 1 inch. This chart depicts 1 yard of fabric with 40 inches of usable width.

Yardage Equivalents

1 yard = 36 inches	1/2 yard = 18 inches
7/8 yard = 31 1/2 inches	3/8 yard = 13 1/2 inches
3/4 yard = 27 inches	1/4 yard = 9 inches
5/8 yard = 22 1/2 inches	1/8 yard = 4 1/2 inches

Quick Yardage Conversions

One yard of fabric is equal to .9144 meters. To convert meters to yards, divide the metric measurement by .9144 and round up to the nearest eighth. For example:

3.25 meters ÷ .9144 = 3.554 or 3⅝ yards

The following yardage conversion chart can be a valuable tool if you want to cut a pattern from a different fabric width or if you've fallen in love with a handmade fabric or remnant in a nonstandard width. However, be aware that yardage conversions aren't an exact science. Some pattern pieces, such as full skirt sections or all-in-one dolman sleeves, cannot be cut from narrower fabric without piecing.

Yardage Conversion Chart

Fabric Width	32"	36"	40"	44/45"	50"	52/54"	58/60"
Yardage	$1\frac{7}{8}$	$1\frac{3}{4}$	$1\frac{1}{2}$	$1\frac{3}{8}$	$1\frac{1}{4}$	$1\frac{1}{8}$	1
	$2\frac{1}{4}$	2	$1\frac{3}{4}$	$1\frac{5}{8}$	$1\frac{1}{2}$	$1\frac{3}{8}$	$1\frac{1}{4}$
	$2\frac{1}{2}$	$2\frac{1}{4}$	2	$1\frac{3}{4}$	$1\frac{5}{8}$	$1\frac{1}{2}$	$1\frac{3}{8}$
	$2\frac{3}{4}$	$2\frac{1}{2}$	$2\frac{1}{4}$	$2\frac{1}{8}$	$1\frac{3}{4}$	$1\frac{3}{4}$	$1\frac{5}{8}$
	$3\frac{1}{8}$	$2\frac{7}{8}$	$2\frac{1}{2}$	$2\frac{1}{4}$	2	$1\frac{7}{8}$	$1\frac{3}{4}$
	$3\frac{3}{8}$	$3\frac{1}{8}$	$2\frac{3}{4}$	$2\frac{1}{2}$	$2\frac{1}{4}$	2	$1\frac{7}{8}$
	$3\frac{3}{4}$	$3\frac{3}{8}$	$2\frac{7}{8}$	$2\frac{3}{4}$	$2\frac{3}{8}$	$2\frac{1}{4}$	2
	4	$3\frac{3}{4}$	$3\frac{1}{8}$	$2\frac{7}{8}$	$2\frac{5}{8}$	$2\frac{3}{8}$	$2\frac{1}{4}$
	$4\frac{3}{8}$	$4\frac{1}{4}$	$3\frac{3}{8}$	$3\frac{1}{8}$	$2\frac{3}{4}$	$2\frac{5}{8}$	$2\frac{3}{8}$
	$4\frac{5}{8}$	$4\frac{1}{2}$	$3\frac{5}{8}$	$3\frac{3}{8}$	3	$2\frac{3}{4}$	$2\frac{5}{8}$
	5	$4\frac{3}{4}$	$3\frac{7}{8}$	$3\frac{5}{8}$	$3\frac{1}{4}$	$2\frac{7}{8}$	$2\frac{3}{4}$

Index